fit fürs abi

Oberstufenwissen
Englisch

Schroedel

Oberstufenwissen
Englisch

für Schülerinnen und Schüler zur Vorbereitung auf das Abitur

Lara Jost unterrichtet Englisch an einer Gesamtschule von der Unter- bis zur Oberstufe. Englisch ist neben Deutsch ihre zweite Muttersprache. Neben ihrer Unterrichtstätigkeit verfügt sie über langjährige Erfahrung als Nachhilfelehrerin. Sie ist Verfasserin von Lernhilfen und von Publikationen zum Thema Theaterspiel im Fremdsprachenunterricht.

Sarah Nowotny stammt aus London und verfügt über langjährige Erfahrung als Englisch-Lehrerin. Außerdem arbeitet sie als freie Autorin und Übersetzerin.

Es ist leider nicht in allen Fällen gelungen, die Rechteinhaber ausfindig zu machen und um Abdruckgenehmigung zu bitten. Ansprüche der Rechteinhaber werden selbstverständlich im Rahmen der üblichen Konditionen abgegolten.

© 2012 Bildungshaus Schulbuchverlage
Westermann Schroedel Diesterweg Schöningh Winklers GmbH, Braunschweig
www.schroedel.de

Das Werk und seine Teile sind urheberrechtlich geschützt. Jede Nutzung in anderen als den gesetzlich zugelassenen Fällen bedarf der vorherigen schriftlichen Einwilligung des Verlages. Hinweis zu § 52a UrhG: Weder das Werk noch seine Teile dürfen ohne eine solche Einwilligung gescannt und in ein Netzwerk eingestellt werden. Dies gilt auch für Intranets von Schulen und sonstigen Bildungseinrichtungen.
Auf verschiedenen Seiten dieses Buches befinden sich Verweise (Links) auf Internet-Adressen. Haftungshinweis: Trotz sorgfältiger inhaltlicher Kontrolle wird die Haftung für die Inhalte der externen Seiten ausgeschlossen. Für den Inhalt dieser externen Seiten sind ausschließlich deren Betreiber verantwortlich. Sollten Sie bei dem angegebenen Inhalt des Anbieters dieser Seite auf kostenpflichtige, illegale oder anstößige Inhalte treffen, so bedauern wir dies ausdrücklich und bitten Sie, uns umgehend per E-Mail davon in Kenntnis zu setzen, damit beim Nachdruck der Verweis gelöscht wird.

Druck [6] / Jahr 2016
aktualisierte Auflage

Redaktion und Satz: imprint, Zusmarshausen
Kontakt: lernhilfen@schroedel.de
Herstellung: Sandra Grünberg
Umschlaggestaltung und Innenlayout: Janssen Kahlert Design & Kommunikation, Hannover
Umschlagfoto: Getty Images / Martin Moos
Druck und Bindung: westermann druck GmbH, Braunschweig

ISBN 978-3-507-**23045**-3

Inhalt

Vorwort 5

1 Die Prüfungen 6
1.1 Wie sieht die Prüfung aus? 6
1.2 Die mündlichen Prüfungen 11
1.3 Vorbereitung und Methodenkompetenzen
    für die schriftliche Prüfung 12

2 Mitschriften und Notizen 19

3 Grammar 23
3.1 Use of the tenses 23
3.2 The passive voice 30
3.3 Conditional sentences 31
3.4 Use of the gerund 32
3.5 Phrasal verbs 34

4 Landeskunde „Great Britain" 38
4.1 Politics in Britain 38
4.2 Education 45
4.3 Working life in Britain 52
4.4 British society 55
4.5 Religion 64
4.6 Foreign affairs 60

5 Landeskunde „The USA" 76
5.1 Politics in the USA 76
5.2 Education 83
5.3 Working life in the USA 87
5.4 American society 90
5.5 Religion 105
5.6 Foreign affairs 109

6 Focus on world issues – Globalisation 113
6.1 What is globalisation? 113
6.2 Globalisation today 115
6.3 Globalisation and the economy 120
6.4 Migration 126
6.5 Globalisation and environmental issues 129
6.6 Globalisation and local character 138

7 Kurze Literaturgeschichte: Großbritannien und USA ... 139
7.1 Tabellarischer Überblick ... 140
7.2 Alt- und Mittelenglisch ... 143
7.3 Renaissance und 16. Jahrhundert ... 144
7.4 Das 17. Jahrhundert ... 145
7.5 Das 18. Jahrhundert ... 147
7.6 Das 19. Jahrhundert ... 149
7.7 Das 20. Jahrhundert ... 151

8 Die Interpretation literarischer Texte ... 153
8.1 Vorbemerkung ... 153
8.2 Lyrik ... 154
8.3 Dramatik ... 172
8.4 Prosa ... 184

9 Analyse und Interpretation von Sachtexten ... 195
9.1 Verschiedene Texttypen ... 195
9.2 Womit befasst sich der Text? ... 197
9.3 Was ist die Funktion des vorliegenden Textes? ... 198
9.4 Was bringt der Text zum Ausdruck? ... 200

10 Bildbeschreibung und Bildanalyse ... 201
10.1 Bildbeschreibung ... 201
10.2 Bildanalyse/Bildinterpretation ... 205
10.3 *Cartoons* beschreiben und analysieren ... 209

11 Idioms and sayings ... 214
11.1 Colour idioms ... 214
11.2 Idioms connected to time ... 215
11.3 Idioms with food ... 216
11.4 Idioms connected to parts of the body ... 217
11.5 Animal idioms ... 219
11.6 Idioms with clothes ... 220
11.7 Miscellaneous idioms ... 220

12 Eine „*composition*" schreiben ... 222
12.1 Welche Art von Text soll ich schreiben? ... 222
12.2 Wie sollte der Text strukturiert sein? ... 223

Glossar ... 226

Stichwortverzeichnis ... 247

Vorwort

Die Abitur-Vorbereitung

Wenn das Abitur näher rückt, wird die Zeit zur Behebung der einen oder anderen Wissenslücke knapper. Der Prüfungsstoff türmt sich zu einem Berg auf, der höher und höher wächst, und manchmal scheint es fast unmöglich, all das wirklich oder vermeintlich erforderliche Wissen auch nur ansatzweise zu speichern.

In dieser Situation hilft nur eins: kühlen Kopf bewahren und die noch verbleibenden Monate so arbeitsökonomisch wie möglich zu nutzen. Dabei möchte Ihnen **Fit fürs Abi Englisch ⊙ Wissen** helfen.

Natürlich ist klar, dass Versäumnisse aus den vergangenen Jahren Englischunterricht sich nicht in ein paar Wochen einholen lassen. Ein bisschen früher müssen Sie mit ihren Vorbereitungen also schon anfangen — idealerweise mindestens zu Beginn des zweiten Halbjahrs in der vorletzten Jahrgangsstufe. Aber gleichgültig, wie knapp die Zeit auch immer ist: zielgerichtetes, systematisches Lernen und sichere Unterscheidung von wichtigen und weniger wichtigen Dingen führt in jedem Fall zu größerer Effektivität.

Zur Arbeit mit diesem Buch

Die ersten beiden Kapitel dienen der Information über die anstehenden Prüfungen und zur Orientierung bezüglich Methoden und Techniken.

- Wir beginnen mit dem Aufbau der schriftlichen und mündlichen Prüfungen und den üblichen Bewertungskriterien und Operatoren.
- Darauf folgen wichtige Methoden und Techniken.
- Sie finden Kapitel zur Grammatik, zur Landeskunde und zum aktuellen Thema Globalisierung, bei denen die Einleitungen und Zusammenfassung (jeweils am Kapitelanfang und -ende) auf Deutsch gehalten sind. Sonst ist der Text dort in englischer Sprache gehalten, um Ihnen bereits beim ersten Durchlesen themenspezifische Formulierungen und Redewendungen als Vorbild oder Anregung zu präsentieren.
- Die abschließenden Kapitel befassen sich mit der Textproduktion. Dazu gehören das Vorwissen im Bereich der Literaturgeschichte – aber auch wesentliche Begriffe rund um Stilmittel und Aufbau. Klare Hilfestellungen, von Redemitteln bis hin zum Aufbau eines eigenen Textes, runden diese Kapitel jeweils ab. Beispieltexte sollen Ihnen als Anregung und Vorbild dienen.

Wir wünschen Ihnen viel Erfolg bei der Arbeit mit
Fit fürs Abi Englisch ⊙ Wissen.

1 Die Prüfungen

Prüfungsstress ist kaum vollständig vermeidbar. Reduzierbar ist er aber sehr wohl.

Die „Zauberwörter" hierzu lauten: Wissen, wie die Prüfung aussehen wird (beispielsweise sollte man die Unterschiede zwischen schriftlicher und mündlicher Prüfung kennen), die Möglichkeiten guter Vorbereitung ausschöpfen und wichtige Methoden beherrschen. Das macht zwar Arbeit, aber es lohnt sich. Und auch wer – wie wohl nicht wenige – etwas spät dran ist mit dem Start ins „Abenteuer Abitur" kann sich mithilfe dieses Kapitels und aller weiteren erfolgsversprechend vorbereiten.

1.1 Wie sieht die Prüfung aus?

Kommunikative Kompetenz/Interkulturelle Kompetenz/ Umgang mit Texten und Medien/Erwerb von Lernstrategien

Der gemeinsame europäische Referenzrahmen für Sprache gibt vor, dass die schriftliche Abiturprüfung in Englisch im Wesentlichen aus drei Anforderungsbereichen besteht, in denen sowohl Ihre sprachlichen – als auch Ihre Methodenkompetenzen überprüft werden.

> Der vorgelegte Text befasst sich mit Themen, die Sie im Unterricht ausführlich behandelt haben. Diese inhaltlichen Kenntnisse dienen Ihnen als Grundlage für die weitere Bearbeitung.

Im **Anforderungsbereich I** wird Ihr Textverständnis, also das Leseverstehen, geprüft. Dazu müssen Sie die Inhalte sowie die zentralen Aussagen oder Problemstellungen eines vorgelegten Textes entsprechend der konkreten Aufgabenstellung wiedergeben.

Beim Teilbereich Reproduktion, der hier ebenfalls geprüft wird, geht es darum, Inhalte oder Abbildungen mit eigenen Worten sprachlich angemessen wiedergeben oder beschreiben zu können. Möglicherweise ist eine dieser Aufgaben eine Mediation, d.h. Sie geben die erforderlichen Informationen auf Deutsch entsprechend der Situation wieder. (Für wen ist die Information? In welchem Rahmen oder Zusammenhang ist sie gefordert?)

Beispiel: Sum up the passage you have just seen.
Outline the situation in the given extract from "Ulysses".

Der **Anforderungsbereich II** betrifft Analyse sowie Reorganisation und umfasst die vertiefte Auseinandersetzung mit einem Thema auf der Grundlage eines vorgelegten Textes. Die Aufgabenstellungen gehen über die Textvorlage hinaus, sodass Sie hier Ihre im Rahmen des Unterrichts erlangten Kenntnisse entsprechend einbringen und auf neue Fragestellungen anwenden sollen.

Beispiel: Analyse the way the story is told and the way the language is used; relate your analysis to the historical background and refer to the structure of the text.

In der Regel haben Sie im **Anforderungsbereich III** die Möglichkeit, aus einer größeren Anzahl von Aufgabenstellungen eine auszuwählen und diese zu bearbeiten. Hier geht es um „Werten und Gestalten". In diesem Aufgabenbereich müssen Sie anhand ihrer Methodenkompetenz komplexe Sachverhalte und Materialien strukturiert verarbeiten. Dazu gehören eigene Stellungnahmen, Deutungen, Begründungen und persönliche Wertungen. Auch hier dienen Ihnen die im Unterricht erworbenen themenspezifischen Kenntnisse aber auch Methoden und Arbeitstechniken als Grundlage.

> Der Aufgabenbereich III kann sich mit dem literarischen Schwerpunktthema aber auch mit Themen der Landeskunde befassen. Denkbar ist auch eine Verknüpfung beider Gebiete.

Beispiel: Comment on the problem of "the brain drain", which developing and third world countries are experiencing.

Based on the interpretation of the following cartoon, outline the social challenges globalisation creates and the various ways in which developing and developed countries deal with them.

Im Folgenden finden Sie die Operatoren nach Anforderungsbereichen geordnet.

Anforderungsbereich I: Reproduktion und Textverstehen

Operator	Definition	Beispiel
complete	Complete the sentence with words from the text.	
describe	Give a detailed account of sth.	Describe the soldier's appearance.
fill in / fill the gaps	Fill in the gaps in the text with a letter (a – n).	
match	Match each paragraph of the text with a suitable heading.	
outline	Give the main features, structure or general principles.	Outline the author's views on love, marriage and divorce.
point out	Find and explain certain aspects.	Point out the author's main ideas on …
present	(Re-)structure and write down, quote from the text to justify your answer.	Present the situation of the characters.

Operator	Definition	Beispiel
state	Specify clearly.	State briefly the main developments in the family described in the text.
summarize, write a summary	Give a concise account of the main points.	Summarize the information given in the text about the hazards of cloning.
tick	Tick off the correct answers.	Which adjectives characterize the girl most appropriately?

Anforderungsbereich II: Reorganisation und Analyse

Operator	Definition	Beispiel
analyse	Break down a problem into separate factors, then draw a conclusion based on your break-down.	Analyse the narrative perspective in the given excerpt.
characterize	Describe somebody's character and provide suitable examples.	Characterize the protagonists in the given excerpt.
compare/contrast	Point out and analyse similarities and differences, use concrete examples.	Compare the protagonist's attitude with the idea of the "melting pot".
contrast/juxtapose	Describe and analyse the differences between two or more things.	Contrast the two forms of imperialism mentioned in the text.
delineate	Present the central elements of a line of action or line of argument	Delineate the concept of integration.
describe	Give an account in words, present a picture with words.	Describe the situation the protagonist finds himself in.
examine	Systematically describe and explain in detail certain aspects and/or features of the text.	Examine the author's use of language.
explain	Describe and define in detail, make clear and plain; give the reason or cause.	Explain the symbolic meaning of the black Madonna in the given excerpt.
illustrate/show	Use examples to explain or make clear.	Illustrate the character's narrow-mindedness.
outline	Present the main features, structure or general principles of a topic omitting minor details.	Outline the author's views on love, marriage and divorce.
point out	Identify and explain certain aspects.	Point out the author's main arguments in the article.
put into the context of …	An incident, statement or argument is linked to relevant historical or topical knowledge (on the basis of knowledge gained in class).	Put this speech into the context of the Hispanic experience in the U.S.
relate	Take an aspect/aspects of one text and establish a meaningful connection to an aspect/aspects of the text of reference. Show the relationship between concepts.	Relate the protagonist's principles to a text read in class Relate the photo to the overall situation in the USA.

Operator	Definition	Beispiel
summarize / sum up	Condense the main points, use relatively few and your own words.	Sum up the main points of the newspaper article.

Anforderungsbereich III: Werten und Gestalten

Operator	Definition	Beispiel
assess / evaluate	Form a carefully considered opinion after presenting advantages and disadvantages, include all the important aspects of a question.	Assess whether the statement applies to all migrants. Evaluate the chances of the protagonist's plan to succeed in life.
comment on / state	State clearly your opinions on the topic in question and support your views with evidence.	Comment on the future of multiculturalism in the USA.
contrast	Emphasize the differences between two or more things.	Contrast the author's idea of human aggression with the theories of aggression you know.
discuss	Consider and analyse all sides of an issue, give reasons for and against and come to a justified conclusion by providing relevant arguments and concrete examples.	Discuss advantages and disadvantages of globalization.
interpret	Analyse the text and establish its meaning in a wider context. Interpret the message the author wishes to convey. Explain the meaning or purpose of something.	Interpret the author's use of stylistic devices. Interpret the drawing.
justify	Show adequate grounds for decisions or conclusions.	Justify the position the protagonist holds on to.
write a + text type	Compose a text in line with the conventions of the required genre.	Write the protagonist's diary entry.

Zugelassene Hilfsmittel

Ihnen stehen ein einsprachiges Wörterbuch und ein Duden zu Verfügung. In einigen Bundesländern können Sie zusätzlich ein zweisprachiges Wörterbuch verwenden.

→ „Das Wörterbuch schnell und sinnvoll nutzen", Seite 14

Punkteverteilung

Bei der Bewertung Ihrer Texte werden die Punkte für Sprache und Inhalt gesondert voneinander gegeben. Es ist also wichtig, sowohl inhaltlich als auch methodisch gut vorbereitet zu sein. Die optische Gestaltung der Texte spielt ebenso eine Rolle, das heißt Aufbau und Gliederungen Ihrer Texte werden ebenfalls bewertet.

So muss beispielsweise eine sehr gute inhaltliche Leistung folgende Merkmale aufweisen:
- vollständige Erfassung aller Aspekte bezüglich des Textverständnisses,
- Sachkompetenz und vollständige Bearbeitung der analysierenden Teilaufgaben,
- differenzierte, methodische Kompetenzen im Umgang mit Texten,
- im besonderen Maße schlüssiger und reichhaltiger Gehalt des eigenständigen, kreativen Textes.

Eine sehr gute sprachliche Leistung zeichnet sich unter anderem durch folgende Merkmale aus:
- durchgängige Lesbarkeit des Textes,
- die Verwendung entsprechender komplexer syntaktischer Strukturen (und somit die Demonstration sprachlicher Sicherheit und Gewandtheit),
- angemessener, sicherer und eigenständiger Wortschatz,
- transparente Strukturierung des Textes durch den sinnvollen Einsatz sprachlicher Mittel (→ Kapitel 12),
- nahezu korrekte formale Darstellung.

Sie finden in diesem Buch an vielen Stellen Wortlisten und/oder phrases and idioms angeboten, die Ihnen helfen können, Ihre sprachlichen Ausdruck zu verbessern.

1.2 Die mündlichen Prüfungen

Die mündlichen Abiturprüfungen sind nicht bundesweit einheitlich geregelt. Daher müssen Sie sich über die konkreten Regelungen Ihres Bundeslandes informieren. In vielen Bundesländern gibt es zwei zu unterscheidende mündliche Prüfungen, die **Präsentationsprüfung** und die **mündliche Nachprüfung**. Die Präsentationsprüfung besteht aus einer von Ihnen vorbereiteten Präsentation sowie einem Fachgespräch mit den Mitgliedern des Prüfungsausschusses, in dem es sowohl um die Inhalte der Präsentation als auch um themenübergreifende Inhalte geht. Eine Dokumentation Ihrer Präsentation, welche Inhalt, Ablauf und die Angabe der verwendeten Quellen enthält und maximal zwei DIN A4 Seiten umfassen sollte, wird eine Woche vor dem Prüfungstermin eingereicht.

Die jeweils für Schulen zuständigen Landesministerien bieten auf ihren Internetseiten Informationen, die einen guten Ausgangspunkt für Recherchen darstellen.

Präsentation:
- Sach- und Adressatengerecht
- angemessener und kompetenter Medieneinsatz
- angemessene Präsenz (Auftreten, Blickkontakt)
- klare, deutlich modulierte Sprache
- klarer Abschluss
- sinnvolle Zeiteinteilung
- aktives Reflektieren und Reagieren auf Fragen

Inhalt:
- sicheres, strukturiertes Wissen
- Verwendung von Informationen aus verschiedenen Quellen
- Herstellen von Zusammenhängen
- klare Struktur
- eindeutige Schwerpunkte
- schlüssige und überzeugende Argumentationsweise

Für das Prüfungsgespräch, das sich der Präsentation anschließt, sollten Sie versuchen, aktiv am Gespräch teilzunehmen und dieses mitzugestalten. Sie sollten in der Lage sein, Ihre Ansichten und Argumente zu begründen und zu verteidigen und sich dabei entsprechender Formulierungen (Wort ergreifen, Äußerungen einleiten, Zustimmung, Ablehnung, etc.) bedienen.

Ein weiteres Modell der mündlichen Prüfung ist das sogenannte **Kolloquium**. Es wird Ihnen etwa 30 Minuten vor Prüfungsbeginn das Thema für ein Kurzreferat genannt (teils auch Material zur Verfügung gestellt). Darauf bereiten Sie sich dann unter Aufsicht vor. Die Prüfung selbst besteht aus dem Kurzreferat (ca. 10 Minuten) mit anschließendem Gespräch über das Thema des Referats und weiteren Themen.

1.3 Vorbereitung und Methodenkompetenzen für die schriftliche Prüfung

Die im Folgenden aufgeführten Methoden und Vorgehensweisen bei der Erschließung eines Textes werden Sie im Laufe Ihrer Schulzeit bereits kennengelernt haben. Denken Sie an die **Grundschritte**, bevor Sie beginnen, den Text lesend zu erschließen:

Sachtexte:
newspaper articles, scientific texts, essays, comments ...
Fiktionale Texte:
novel, short story, drama ...
Lyrische Texte:
ballads, sonnets

Schritt 1: Zuordnen zu einer Textgattung –
    Sachtext (*non-fictional text*),
    Fiktionaler Text (*fictional text*),
    Lyrischer Text (*poem*) (→ Glossar, S. 242)
Schritt 2: Autor/Autorin, Erscheinungsdatum, Titel
Schritt 3: Abbildungen auf zusätzliche Information prüfen

Lesetechniken

Ihnen stehen verschiedene **Lesetechniken** zur Verfügung und Sie müssen je nach Aufgabenstellung entscheiden, welche Technik angemessen ist.

- *Skimming:* Schnelles Überfliegen eines Textes, um die Kernthemen zu erkennen. Sie sollten auch auf Kursiv- oder Fettgedrucktes achten. Jetzt sollten Sie in der Lage sein, zu umreißen, worum es geht.
  Beispiel: What is the article about?
  Outline the main issues the texts deals with.
- *Scanning:* Ist sinnvoll, wenn Sie auf der Suche nach spezifischen Informationen sind. Suchen Sie nach Schlüsselwörtern, den *key words*, und lesen Sie den Abschnitt, in dem Sie fündig werden, sorgfältig durch. Diese Technik ist für eine Textanalyse sehr nützlich, in der Sie beispielsweise nach Belegen für Ihre Aussagen suchen werden.
  Beispiel: Compare the reactions and the behaviour of the two protagonists.
- *Intensive Reading:* Lesen Sie den Text gründlich und im Detail. So sind Sie in der Lage, Gesamtaufbau, Struktur, Stilmittel und Inhalt vollständig zu erkennen und zu verstehen. Es ist sinnvoll, wichtige Textstellen zu markieren und Randnotizen anzubringen.
  Beispiel: Illustrate how narrative technique and stylistic device influence the reader.

> Im letzten Abschnitt eines Textes finden Sie oft eine kurze Zusammenfassung des Textinhalts – es lohnt sich also, diesem Abschnitt besondere Beachtung zu schenken.

Tipp

Worterschließungstechniken

Um das **zweisprachige Wörterbuch** sinnvoll nutzen zu können, sollten Sie sich mit den dort verwendeten Abkürzungen vertraut gemacht haben. Lesen Sie immer die vollständige Angabe und treffen Sie, falls nötig, Ihre Auswahl dem Kontext entsprechend. Als Gegenprobe kann zur Sicherheit im einsprachigen Wörterbuch nachgeschlagen werden.

Bevor Sie ein einsprachiges Wörterbuch zur Hand nehmen, um ein unbekanntes Wort nachzuschlagen, sollten Sie verschiedene Techniken anwenden, um das Wort zu erschließen.

„Intelligent guessing" im Textzusammenhang

Oftmals hilft Ihnen der Textzusammenhang, den Sinn eines unbekannten Worts zu erraten. Lesen Sie also die Sätze vor und nach dem zu „enträtselnden" Wort.

„Intelligent guessing" mithilfe der Wortfamilie

Häufig können Sie sich zusammengesetzte Wörter anhand Ihrer Kenntnisse der Wortbildungslehre erklären. Achten Sie also auf Vor- und Nachsilben, z. B. -ly, und deren Bedeutung.

prefix	Beispiel	Bedeutung
bi-	bicycle, bifocals, biceps, billion, binary, bivalve, bimonthly, bigamy, bimetal, biathlete, bicarbonate	zwei
co, con-, com-	convene, compress, contemporary, converge, compact, confluence, concatenate, conjoin, combine, convert, compatible, consequence, contract	zusammen mit, begleitend
contra-, counter-	contradict, counteract, contravene, contrary, counterspy, contrapuntal, contraband, contraception, contrast, controversy, counterfeit, counterclaim, counterargument, counterclaim, counterpoint, counterrevolution	gegen, Gegenteil
de-, dis-, dif-	deescalate, dismiss, differ, disallow, disperse, dissuade, disconnect, dysfunction, disproportion, disrespect, distemper, distaste, disarray, dyslexia	loswerden, nicht, Gegenteil von, nicht, umgekehrte Aktion

> Suchen Sie in Ihrem einsprachigen Wörterbuch nach einer Liste mit einem Definitionsvokabular *(defining vocabulary)*. Gehen Sie diese Liste daraufhin durch, ob Ihnen alle Wörter bekannt sind.
> Falls nicht, lernen Sie sie. Dann verstehen Sie die meisten Definitionen dieses Wörterbuchs wesentlich schneller und besser.

Tipp

prefix	Beispiel	Bedeutung
in-, im-, il-, ir-	illegal, immortal, inviolate, innocuous, intractable, innocent, impregnable, impossible, irregular	nicht
mis-	misinform, misinterpret, mispronounce, misnomer, mistake, misogynist, mistrial, misadventure, misanthrope, misread	falsch, irregeleitet
out-	outcome, outnumber	besser, höher, schneller, darüber hinaus
over-	overdo, overcome	zu viel, über hinweg
post-	postpone, postwar, postdated	nach, später
pre-	preview, prepare	vorher, davor
re-	report, realign, retract, revise, regain, reflect, rename, restate, recombine, recalculate, redo	wieder, zurück
semi-	semifinal, semiconscious, semiannual, semimonthly, semicircle	halb
sub-	submerge, submarine, substandard, subnormal, subvert, subdivision, submersible	unter

„*Intelligent guessing*" mithilfe der Etymologie (Sprachgeschichte)

Die englische Sprache entstand aus germanischen sowie normannischen Sprachen, daher gibt es viele Wörter, die der deutschsprachigen oder französischsprachigen Entsprechung ähneln. Sie werden zwar anders geschrieben, sind aber trotzdem gut zu erkennen.

Andere Wörter sind lateinischen oder alt-griechischen Ursprungs und werden auch im Deutschen verwendet.

Sollten Sie trotz Anwendungen dieser Techniken ein unbekanntes Wort, welches zum Verständnis des Textes unbedingt notwendig ist, nicht entschlüsseln können, folgt der Griff zum Wörterbuch.
Denken Sie auch daran, das Wörterbuch beim Schreiben Ihrer Texte mit einzubeziehen, denn Sie können dadurch nicht nur Fehler vermeiden, sondern auch sprachlich abwechslungsreicher schreiben und idiomatische Ausdrücke verwenden.

Das Wörterbuch schnell und sinnvoll nutzen

Wörterbücher sind eine oftmals ungenutzte Datenbank. Es ist nachgewiesen worden, dass etwa 40 % der Fehler, die Schülerinnen und Schüler beim Verfassen englischer Texte machen, mithilfe eines Wörterbuchs vermieden werden könnten.

Um sinnvoll mit Wörterbüchern zu arbeiten, sind drei Dinge zu beachten:

Dass

Sie müssen erkennen, **dass** Sie etwas im Wörterbuch nachschlagen müssen! Viele schlagen nicht nach, weil sie nicht erkennen, dass sie etwas nicht wissen. Wenn eine Schülerin oder ein Schüler ein Wort wie ~~*pattern pupil*~~ verwendet, dann wahrscheinlich, weil sie oder er glaubt, dass es existiere. Sie sollten also ein Gespür für die Grenzen Ihrer eigenen Kompetenz in der Fremdsprache entwickeln, um überhaupt zu wissen, was Sie sicherheitshalber nachschlagen sollten.

Was

Sie müssen wissen, **was** im Wörterbuch steht. Viele verwenden Wörterbücher nur, wenn sie beim Verfassen englischer Texte ein bestimmtes Wort suchen oder wenn sie beim Lesen englischer Texte nicht wissen, was ein Wort „bedeutet". Wörterbücher bieten aber wesentlich mehr Information. Insbesondere die modernen englischen Lernerwörterbücher sind auch als Schreibwörterbücher konzipiert, d. h. als Hilfen bei der Produktion von Texten. Nutzen Sie diese Informationen.

Wie

Sie müssen wissen, **wie** etwas im Wörterbuch steht, in welcher Form also die gesuchte Information gegeben wird. Das heißt, Sie müssen mit den Konventionen der Wörterbücher, die Sie benutzen, vertraut sein. Wenn man nachschlagen will, ob *manage* mit einem *to*-Infinitiv oder mit einer *-ing*-Konstruktion verwendet wird, sollte man wissen, ob solche Informationen im eigenen Wörterbuch im Eintrag selbst oder in einer eigenen Spalte am Rand gegeben werden, ob sie durch Fettdruck hervorgehoben sind oder in eckigen Klammern stehen, ob Codes wie *to-INF* verwendet werden oder ob da einfach steht *manage to do sth*. Je besser Sie mit den Abkürzungen und der Struktur des Wörterbuchs vertraut sind, desto schneller werden Sie Informationen finden und desto mehr werden Sie es benutzen können, um Fehler zu vermeiden.

Beispiel für Wörterbucheinträge

thun·der [thən-dər]
noun
1: the sound that follows a flash of lightning is caused by sudden expansion of the air in the course of electrical discharge
2: a loud utterance or threat
3: bang, rumble <the *thunder* of big guns>
Examples
- There was a loud clap of *thunder*.
- It was a night of *thunder* and lightning.
- Lightning flashed and *thunder* boomed.

Origin: Middle English *thoner, thunder*, from Old English *thunor*; akin to Old High German *thonar* thunder, Latin *tonare* to thunder.
First Use: before 12th century

thunder
intransitive verb
1a: to produce thunder — used impersonally <it *thundered*>
1b: to produce a sound that resembles thunder <they *thundered* down the road>
2: roar, shout
transitive verb
1: to utter loudly: roar
2: to strike with a sound likened to thunder
Other forms: thun·dered; thun·der·ing [-də-rin]; thun·der·er [-də-ər]
Examples
- It thundered and the rain poured down.
- Pieces of artillery thundered in the distance.
- It was raining and thundering all night.

First use: before 12th century

Nutzen Sie das Wörterbuch nicht nur zum Verstehen englischer Texte, sondern auch zum Schreiben in der Fremdsprache.
Wörterbuchbenutzung = Fehlervermeidung!

Tipp

Welche Bedeutung wir einem Wort zuschreiben, hängt mitunter sehr stark davon ab, mit welchen anderen Wörtern es in einem Satz vorkommt (Kontext). Oftmals stellt sich auch die Frage, in welchen Situationen ein Wort verwendet werden kann. Aus diesem Grund ist es wichtig, alle Definitionen zu lesen, um das ganze Spektrum eines Wortes zu überblicken.

Nutzen Sie die Kollokationsangaben in Ihrem Wörterbuch. Suchen Sie gezielt danach, ob Informationen besonders hervorgehoben werden – durch Fettdruck, in Farbe unterlegt oder in eigenen Kästen –, die Ihnen beim Schreiben von Nutzen sein könnten. Ihr Englisch wird dadurch wesentlich natürlicher klingen!

Tipp

Was findet man wo?

Zusammenfassend lässt sich sagen, dass Wörterbücher eine unschätzbare Quelle für Informationen für das **Verstehen** und für das **Produzieren** von Texten bilden. Man wird immer, wenn man mit Fremdsprachen zu tun hat, auch mit Wörterbüchern umgehen müssen. Deshalb sollten gute und aktuelle Wörterbücher zur Verfügung stehen und Sie sollten wissen, wie man damit umgeht. Das heißt vor allem auch, dass Sie wissen sollten, was man von diesen Wörterbüchern erwarten kann und was nicht und in welchem Wörterbuch was nachzuschlagen ist.

Beachten Sie bei der Benutzung von Wörterbüchern, dass einzelne Wörter nur in wenigen Fällen weiterhelfen. Achten Sie immer auf die Angaben zur Verwendung der Wörter in größeren Einheiten: grammatische Konstruktionen, Gruppen von Wörtern etc.

Tipp

Bei der Lektüre englischer Texte oder beim Übersetzen ins Deutsche wollen Sie wissen …	
… welchen Gegenstand oder Sachverhalt ein englisches Wort wie *double glazing* oder *guillemot* bezeichnet:	→ zweisprachiges Wörterbuch (englisch-deutscher Teil) oder einsprachiges Wörterbuch
… welche Bedeutung ein englisches Wort in einer bestimmten Textstelle hat:	→ einsprachiges Wörterbuch (unter Umständen alle Bedeutungen) oder auch zweisprachiges Wörterbuch

Bei der Lektüre englischer Texte oder beim Übersetzen ins Deutsche wollen Sie wissen …	
… was kulturspezifische Wörter wie *pub* oder *public school* bezeichnen:	→ einsprachiges Wörterbuch oder zweisprachiges Wörterbuch (eventuell auf ausführliche Erläuterungen in Kästen etc. achten)

Beim Verfassen englischer Texte suchen Sie ein englisches Wort …	
… weil Sie eine bestimmte Bedeutung ausdrücken wollen:	→ zweisprachiges Wörterbuch (deutsch-englischer Teil) mit Überprüfung im einsprachigen Wörterbuch
… das in einem sachlichen Zusammenhang mit anderen Wörtern steht (also *Küchengeräte* oder einen Vogelnamen):	→ zweisprachiges Wörterbuch oder im einsprachigen Wörterbuch Illustrationen (zu Feldern wie *Kitchen*, *Birds* usw.)
… das Sie zusammen mit einem englischen Wort verwenden können, das Sie kennen (also: Wie drückt man „Bedenken erheben" aus, wenn man weiß, dass „Bedenken" „*objections*" heißt? Was heißt „schwacher Tee" oder „Tee mit Milch?"):	→ einsprachiges Wörterbuch: hervorgehobene Kollokationsangaben (bei *objection* oder *tea*) bei den entsprechenden Bedeutungen der Wörter oder in eigenen Kästen
… das einem anderen englischen Wort in der Bedeutung sehr ähnlich oder entgegengesetzt ist (Synonyme/Antonyme):	→ einsprachiges Wörterbuch: Querverweis
… das einem britischs Wort im amerikanischen Englisch entspricht oder umgekehrt:	→ einsprachiges Wörterbuch: Querverweis

Beim Verfassen englischer Texte wollen Sie ein englisches Wort verwenden und …	
… Sie suchen Konstruktionen zur Valenz (mit *to*-Infinitiv, mit *that-clause* oder bestimmten Präpositionen):	→ einsprachiges Wörterbuch: Codes + Beispielsatz oder fettgedruckte Konstruktionsangabe + Beispiele
… Sie suchen Phrasen oder Kollokationen:	→ einsprachiges Wörterbuch

Überblick

Die schriftliche Prüfung setzt sich zusammen aus drei Anforderungsbereichen, in denen jeweils verschiedene Kompetenzen abgeprüft werden. In diesem Kapitel konnten Sie sich damit vertraut machen.
Für jede schriftliche Prüfung ist es wichtig, die genaue Aufgabenstellung zu beachten, sich die Zeit gut einzuteilen. Hektik ist aber verboten, daher: Lassen Sie sich Zeit, um sich gedanklich mit den anzusprechenden Themen zu befassen. Und erstellen Sie sich unbedingt ein Konzept, bevor Sie mit dem eigentlichen Schreiben beginnen. Vergessen Sie nicht, auch einen Zeitpuffer für das Korrekturlesen zu berücksichtigen.
In der mündlichen Prüfung versuchen Sie, das Gespräch aktiv mitzugestalten, ihre Argumente zu begründen, nötigenfalls zu verteidigen und die sprachlichen Mittel angemessen zu verwenden.

Mitschriften und Notizen

2

Ach, ist es nicht schön, faul sein zu können? Mitschriften gleich richtig zu machen, Notizen konsequent und angemessen anzufertigen, ist das A und O, um effizient lernen zu können. Auch wenn das Thema zunächst etwas spröde klingt, es hat nicht nur mit Ordnung zu tun, Kreativität ist ebenso gefragt: Ideen müssen erst entwickelt werden, bevor man sie (optisch sinnvoll) festhalten kann.

Was Sie im Unterricht hören, sollten Sie nicht einfach an sich „vorbeirauschen" lassen, sondern verwerten, das heißt, mitschreiben. Von einer vernünftigen **Mitschreibe-Technik** können Sie ein Leben lang profitieren.

- Schreiben Sie in Stichworten,
- verwenden Sie Abkürzungen und Kürzel bzw. Symbole.
- Schreiben Sie in kleineren Absätzen,
- geben Sie diesen Absätzen zusammenfassende Überschriften.
- Führen Sie eine Kopfzeile mit einer allgemeinen Angabe ein,
- nummerieren Sie die Seiten.
- Lassen Sie Ränder für spätere Ergänzungen und lassen Sie, für den gleichen Zweck, die Rückseite frei.
- Lesen und ergänzen Sie die Notizen in kürzeren Abständen,
- bereiten Sie sie optisch mit Farben auf, um überfliegend lesen zu können.
- Legen Sie einige (aber nicht Dutzende) Ordner an.

Tim's played = Tim has played. Achtung: In einigen Bundesländern dürfen Sie die Shortforms schriftlich nicht verwenden.

> Ordnung des Wissens und Zugang dazu sind fast so wichtig wie das Wissen selbst – aber bedenken Sie: Ein Selbstzweck ist dieses Organisieren nicht. Wenn Sie nur noch am Schreiben und Umstecken von Karteikarten sind, sind Sie auf keinem guten Wege.

Tipp

Während der Oberstufe, aber auch sonst im richtigen Leben, ist es manchmal nötig, sich Spezialwissen anzueignen, oft in kurzer Zeit. Es kann sein, dass man solches Wissen für eine Besprechung im Unterricht braucht, für Kurzreferate, Essays, für die Facharbeit, für mündliche Prüfungen, für erwartete Fragen in der schriftlichen Prüfung.

Die Techniken für den Erwerb solchen Wissens haben sich in den letzten zehn, fünfzehn Jahren radikal verändert. Das Internet mit seinem meist über Suchmaschinen organisiertem Zugriff auf Information und zunehmend für verschiedene Zwecke angebotene Videotutorials oder sogenannte Apps für Computer und Smartphones bieten vielfältige Möglichkeiten des Wissenserwerbs. Lesetechniken und gekonnte Notizen bleiben dennoch unverzichtbar.

Um einen vorliegenden Text erarbeiten zu können, ist es notwendig, die Informationen aus dem Text herauszufiltern und anhand von **Notizen** entsprechend zu ordnen.

→ Seite 12
- **Skimmen** Sie den Text nach zentralen Punkten. Konzentrieren Sie sich auf die relevanten Informationen.
- **Scannen** Sie den Text nach Schlüsselbegriffen für gezielte, aufgabenrelevante Informationen.

Markieren Sie Informationen beim *intensive reading* durch Unterstreichen, Einkreisen oder farbige Kennzeichnungen. Verwenden Sie verschiedene Farben für unterschiedliche Informationen, z. B. Schlüsselwörter rot, Detailinformation grün.
Verwenden Sie Abkürzungen oder Symbole, um zum Beispiel unbekannte Wörter zu markieren, wesentliche Passagen zu kennzeichnen oder offene Fragen oder Interpretationsansätze am Rand zu vermerken. Stellen Sie jedoch sicher, dass Sie ihr eigenes *„Code System"* gut beherrschen und Ihre Schrift gut lesen können.

Es ist ratsam, vor dem Schreiben Ihrer Texte die benötigte **Information entsprechend zu ordnen oder zu gruppieren**.

Tabellen oder Raster (*tables or grids*) sind hilfreich, wenn sie anhand bestimmter Kriterien Vergleiche zwischen Situationen, Personen oder ganzen Texten erarbeiten sollen.
Beispiel: Compare the attitudes of the protagonists in story 1 and story 2 towards arranged marriage.

Protagonist Story 1	Protagonist Story 2
accepts arranged marriage as part of culture	accepts arranged marriage as part of her culture
hardly knows her future husband	knows her betrothed very well and liking is mutual
etc ...	etc ...

Ein **Flussdiagramm (*flow chart*)** hingegen hilft Ihnen einen Prozess schematisch klar darzustellen.
Beispiel: Break the play down into beginning, middle and end segments outlining the events of the story.(Romeo and Juliet)

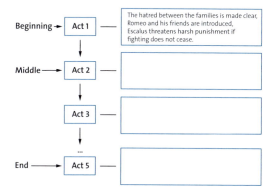

Ein **Baumdiagramm (*mind map*)** dient der Anordnung von Fakten, Begriffen etc. rund um einen zentralen Schlüsselbegriff. Durch das Verwenden einer Mindmap entsteht eine Struktur, welche die Begriffe sinnvoll miteinander vernetzt.
Beispiel: Characterize Will (About a boy, Nick Hornby) and his sense of identity.

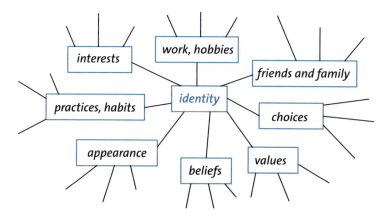

Beim **Brainstorming** notieren Sie in einem ersten Schritt alle Informationen, Ideen, Gedanken, Assoziationen etc. und ordnen diese dann in einem zweiten Schritt, sodass eine der Aufgabe entsprechende Struktur entsteht.
Beispiel: Comment on how the British Empire shaped its former colonies and discuss whether you think it has had a positive or negative effect.

British Empire shaped colonies through: ▸ ▸	positive effects: ▸ ▸
negative effects: ▸ ▸	my opinion: ▸ ▸

Überblick

Entwickeln Sie eine eigene Mitschreibe-Technik, verwenden Sie Abkürzungen und Symbole, damit Sie effizient und schnell arbeiten können. Ordnen Sie ihr Wissen und entwickeln Sie ein System, um auf dieses Wissen schnell und unkompliziert zugreifen zu können.
Verinnerlichen Sie die verschiedenen Methoden wie *scanning*, *skimming* und *intensive reading*, um ihr Ziel zu erreichen. Machen Sie sich mit *tables/grid*, *flow charts* und *mind maps* vertraut, indem Sie diese Techniken immer wieder anwenden, und so herausfiltern, für welche Art der Information welche Art der Anordnung oder Gruppierung ratsam ist.

Grammar

3

Es gibt Aspekte der englischen Grammatik, die einem Schüler Unannehmlichkeiten bereiten können. Wann zum Beispiel verwenden Sie die „simple"-Formen, wann die „progressive"-Formen des Verbs oder gar das Perfekt? Dieses Kapitel gibt Ihnen einen Überblick über die gebräuchlichen grammatikalischen Strukturen und veranschaulicht durch Beispielsätze, in welchem Kontext sie verwendet werden können. So haben Sie die Möglichkeit, diese Strukturen nochmals zu festigen und die schlimmsten „Stolpersteine" zu vermeiden.

3.1 Use of the tenses

Below you will find a brief overview of the different tenses in English and examples of how to use them.

Simple and progressive forms

The **simple present** is used:
- when something is generally true:
  Many people **drink** coffee.
  Cars **run** on fuel.
- for natural facts and scientific laws:
  Cats **have** four legs.
  The Thames **flows** through London.
- regular, repeated actions and routines:
  I **walk** my dog *every* morning and evening.
  Tom *usually* **cycles** to school.
- permanent situations:
  The "Mona Lisa" **hangs** in the Louvre.
  Berlin **is** the capital of Germany.
- for state verbs, which are generally used only in the simple form:
  This soup **tastes** delicious!
  I **don't want** to go out this evening – I **want** to stay at home.
- in time clauses after when, if, as soon as, until, etc:
  Emma will be very surprised when she **hears** our news!
  I'll wait here until **you're** ready to go.

This is often used with adverbs such as *always, usually, often, sometimes, occasionally, never, every* etc.

State verbs include *be, believe, belong, consist, contain, depend, hate, know, like, love, mean, need, prefer, realise, remember, seem, smell, taste, want.*

The **present progressive** is used:
- for actions happening at the time of speaking or actions incomplete at the time of speaking:
  It**'s raining** quite heavily – you'd better take an umbrella.
  We**'re learning** about the Cold War at school.
- for temporary situations:
  I**'m looking** after my grandmother's dog while she's in hospital.
  The sun **is shining** now, but it's going to rain later.
- for changing or developing situations:
  The average temperature of the globe **is** slowly **rising**.
  People in many Arab countries **are** now **demanding** democracy.

The **simple past** is used:
- for permanent or long-lasting situations in the past:
  His family **lived** in the same house for over 200 years.
  The old tree **stood** in a dark corner of the garden.
- for repeated actions or routines:
  We always **spent** Christmas at my grandparents' house.
  They **met** in the same café every Thursday afternoon.
- for completed actions:
  I **went** to school in a small village in Cornwall.
  The hospital **closed** down in 2009.
- for actions in a sequence:
  The referee **blew** his whistle and the match **began**.
  She **pressed** the button, the doors **opened** and she **stepped** into the lift.
- for state verbs:
  The food **smelt** so terrible that nobody even **wanted** to try it.
  They say this pen once **belonged** to William Shakespeare.

The **past progressive** is used:
- for temporary situations in the past:
  "Why didn't you come with us last night?" "I **wasn't feeling** well."
  He **was lying** on his bed, **listening** to music.
- for activities happening at a definite time in the past:
  At this time last week I **was taking** my final exam.
  She wasn't at home on Saturday – she **was visiting** Angie.
- for actions that were not complete at a certain time in the past:
  I **was surfing** the internet when my computer crashed.
  They **were talking** about Gina, but stopped when she came into the room.

We often use this in combination with the simple past to show that one action interrupted another.

The perfect tenses

Very common in English, the perfect tenses are not always easy to use correctly. The examples below illustrate some of the different situations in which they are used.

The **present perfect simple** is used:
- for recent events, without saying exactly when they took place:
  I**'ve** already **seen** that Harry Potter film, so let's go and see a different one instead.
  I'm sorry – Chris **has** just **left**. I don't know what time he'll be back.
- for the results of past actions that have an effect on the present:
  Oh no! The cat **has licked** all the cream off the top of the cake! What are we going to give granddad when he comes round later?
  I **haven't studied** hard enough this week – I'm sure I'm going to fail my test.
- for things that someone has experienced at some time in their life; the exact time when the event took place is not mentioned
  She**'s visited** New York several times but **has** never **climbed** to the top of the Statue of Liberty.
  I**'ve eaten** sushi before, but it didn't taste as good as this!
- for situations that began in the past and have continued until the present:
  He**'s had** the same jacket for over 10 years – it's time he got a new one!
  We**'ve lived** in this part of town since I was a baby.
- for routines or repeated actions that began in the past and have continued until the present:
  I**'ve read** all of her books – she's my favourite writer.
  Tim**'s played** football every Saturday since he was about 10 years old.
- for time expressions that indicate unfinished time:
  There **hasn't been** as much snow as usual this winter.
  My train **has been** over half an hour late three times this week – the service is terrible!
- for state verbs:
  We **haven't known** each other for very long, but we're already close friends.
  I**'ve** just **remembered** where I put my purse!

This includes expressions such as *today, this week, this month, this year.*

The present perfect simple and the present perfect progressive

In some cases, there is no real difference in meaning between the simple and progressive forms of the present perfect:

This applies in particular to the verbs live and work.

I'**ve worked** here for several years.
I'**ve been working** here for several years.

However, the focus of the sentence is different, depending on whether the simple or progressive form is used:

- The **present perfect progressive** focuses on the activity, while the **simple** form focuses on the result:
  I'**ve been studying** very hard for my test.
  I'**ve** just **found out** that I'**ve passed** my test – I'm so relieved!
- As with other tenses, the **progressive** form often shows that an action is not complete, whereas the **simple** form is used for finished activities:
  They'**ve been renovating** our school in the last few months, but the work won't be finished for a couple more weeks.
  The building looks so much better now that they'**ve renovated** it.
- The **progressive** form often shows how long something has been going on, while the **simple** form expresses how often something has happened or how much of something has been done:
  You'**ve been sitting** at your computer all afternoon. Why don't you go out and get some fresh air?
  I'**ve** already **taken** the dog for two walks today – now it's your turn!
- As with the other tenses, the **progressive** form is used to show that something is temporary, while the **simple** form indicates a situation that is permanent or long-lasting:
  I'**ve been looking** everywhere for my phone – I really need to find it.
  It seems that I'**ve** really **lost** my phone. I can't find it anywhere.

The present perfect and the simple past

It is not always easy to decide whether to use the present perfect or the simple past. Below are some pointers:

- The **present perfect** can be used to talk about things that happened at sometime in the past, but without saying exactly when. However, if a specific past time expression is used, the simple past is needed:

For example: yesterday, last week/month/year, last June/Wednesday/weekend, ago, and so on.

  She'**s worked** with many Hollywood legends, most recently with Leonardo Dicaprio, whose new film she **directed** last year.
  "I'**ve** never **been** to the States. **Have** you?" "No, but I **visited** Canada a couple of years ago."

3.1 Use of the tenses

- Expressions that indicate "unfinished" time (today, this week, etc.) cannot be used with the present perfect if they refer to short, completed actions.
  When **did** Tom **leave** this morning? not: ~~When has Tom left this morning?~~
  (at 10 a.m.): I'**ve sent** a lot of texts this morning.
  (at 5 p.m.): I **sent** a lot of texts this morning.
- The **simple past** is used if there is no connection to the present:
  Marilyn Monroe **starred** in several films. (As she is now dead, she will not star in any more films.) Compare:
  Although she is still young, Kristen Stewart **has** already **starred** in several films.
- The **present perfect** is often used to introduce new information, followed by the **simple past** to continue the topic:
  After a break of more than five years, heart-throb boy group Voicebox **has recorded** a new album. The band **split** up three years ago, during which time all four members **made** solo albums, none of which **were** very successful.

The past perfect simple and the past perfect progressive

The **past perfect simple** is used:
- for past events that occurred before other past events:
  The accident happened because it **had snowed** heavily in the night, making the roads dangerously icy.
  When she **had finished** working, she switched off her computer.

The **past perfect progressive** is used:
- for events that happened before another past event, the results of which could still be seen at a later stage:
  It **had been raining** for days, so the water level in the river was much higher than usual.
  I could tell that Danny **had been studying** hard: he did much better on his last test.
- for situations that continued for a while up to a certain time in the past:
  I saw a TV show about a woman who **had been searching** for her twin sister for several years, and was finally reunited with her last March.
  We were relieved when Ben finally phoned, as we **had been waiting** to hear from him all day.
- for talking about how long an activity or event went on:
  Jane **had been drinking** coffee all afternoon – it's not surprising that she didn't sleep well that night!
  He **had been saving** up for weeks to buy tickets to the concert.

Future forms

There are several different ways of talking about the future in English. Here are some examples:

Will/won't is used:
- for the future in general, but not things that have already been decided or arranged:
  *It's better to go clothes shopping after Christmas: everything **will be** cheaper then.*
  *I know my mum **will like** this DVD because it's one of her favourite films.*
- for making future predictions:
  *The next few months **will be** a busy time for me.*
  *Britain **won't leave** the European Union any time soon, no matter what the Prime Minister says.*
- for spontaneous offers, promises or decisions made at the time of speaking:
  *I**'ll buy** some bread while I'm out and we can have it for lunch.*
  *If you like, I**'ll help** with your maths homework.*

The **future progressive** is used:
- for activities that will be incomplete at a certain time in the future:
  *Come round at 8 o'clock – I**'ll be waiting** for you!*
  *There's no need to hurry. They**'ll** still **be having** dinner when we get there.*
- for things that are definitely going to happen at a certain time in the future:
  *The Olympic Games **will be taking** place in London this summer.*
  *This Friday evening at Bookworms: the author Richard Goodman **will be reading** from his latest novel from 7.30 p.m.*

> You need to mention when the action will be taking place.

Present tenses can be used with a future meaning:
- the **present progressive** is used to talk about things that have been arranged for the future:
  *I**'m going** to the dentist's on Tuesday morning and I'm really not looking forward to it!*
  *Chase **isn't having** a party on his birthday after all – some of us **are going** bowling instead.*
- the **simple present** is used to talk about timetables or other schedules:
  *"What time **does** Karen's train **get** in?" "At half past two."*
  *The concert **begins** at 9 p.m., but we should get there early if we want a good place.*

3.1 Use of the tenses

Going to is used to express the future:
- for plans or intentions:
  *This is the year that I'm really **going to get** fit and **take** up tennis again.*
  *They're **going to move** to France in a few months.*
- for making predictions about the future based on evidence that can be seen in the present:
  *There **are going to be** a lot of changes in our company in the next few months because they need to save money.*
  *We need to cut down that tree, otherwise it's **going to fall** down the next time there's a big storm.*

The **future perfect simple** and **progressive** are used:
- for actions that will be complete by a certain time in the future:
  *By the end of June, my brother **will have completed** his 7th marathon.*
  *I can't believe we'll **have been living** in France for 10 years by the end of April – time flies!*

> These forms are normally used in combination with *by*, e.g. *by the time, by next March, by the end of the year* and so on to show when the action will be complete.

To help improve your awareness of English grammar, try playing **grammar detective**. Choose an authentic English text and a grammatical structure (e.g. present simple, present perfect and simple past, future forms etc) and highlight each example of the structure you can find. This will help you to become more aware of how the different forms are used.	**Tipp** Grammar detective

3.2 The passive voice

In English, the passive is formed using the verb "to be" in the relevant tense plus the past participle. When using the passive, focus is placed on the action rather than the person who carried out the action. However, if it is necessary to mention the person, "by" is used, e.g. "The 'Mona Lisa' was painted by Leonardo Da Vinci". Below are some examples of the passive voice:

Present simple and **progressive**:
*Breakfast **is included** in the price of an overnight stay.*
*Tickets for the open-air festival **are being sold** through the event website.*

Past simple and **progressive**:
*The stolen jewels **were found** in the thief's car.*
*The thief managed to escape while he **was being taken** to the police station.*

Perfect tenses:
*Has Tina **been invited** to the party?*
*By the end of the month, her song **had been downloaded** more than 50,000 times.*

Note: the perfect progressive forms are not used in the passive voice.

Future forms:
*Your personal information **won't be made** public unless you tick this box.*
*His blog **is going to be published** as a book later this year.*
*If we don't hurry up, all of the nice food **will have been eaten** by the time we get there!*

As with the other perfect tenses, the progressive form of the future perfect is not used in the passive.

The passive with **modal verbs**:
*Mobile phones **cannot be taken** into the examination room.*
*Why didn't you lock your bike? It **could have been stolen**!*
*Bags **should not be left** unattended at any time.*
*The pictures **must have been posted** straight after the party, but we don't know who took them.*

Modal verbs include *can, could, would, might, may, should, ought, must, would.*

3.3 Conditional sentences

Consisting of two clauses, conditional sentences are used when we talk about what happens, or could happen, or could have happened in certain situations, depending on which tenses are used. Although conditional sentences are often referred to as "if clauses", other words can also be used to link conditional clauses, such as *when, unless, until, even if,* or *as long as*.

- The **zero conditional** is used to talk about things that always happen in a given situation. The **present simple** is used in both clauses:
  *When it **is** winter in Britain, it **is** summer in South Africa.*
  *If you **click** here, you **can** download photos.*
- The **first conditional** is used to talk about things that are likely to happen. Use **will/won't** in the main clause and a **present** tense in the subordinate clause:
  *I'**ll go swimming** after work if I **have** time.*
  *Unless you **work** harder, you **won't finish** your essay on time.*

  > In conditional sentences, will or would are not used in the *if-clause*.

- The **second conditional** is used to talk about things that are impossible, or that are very unlikely to happen. **Would/wouldn't + present** is used in the main clause and the **past simple/progressive** is used in the subordinate clause. Note, however, that the second conditional refers to future time:
  *My father **would go** crazy if he **found out** what really happened last weekend!*
  *I don't trust Brian. If I **were** you, I **wouldn't give** him your phone number.*
- The **third conditional** is used to talk about past situations that did not happen, although they were possible, or something that should not have happened, but did. Use **would/wouldn't have + past participle** in the main clause and the **past perfect** in the subordinate clause:
  *He **would have become** the new world champion if he **had won** the race.*
  *If I **hadn't forgotten** to put petrol in the car, it **wouldn't have broken down**.*

  > *If I were you* is a standard phrase often used to give someone advice or tell them your opinion. The combination of *I* and *were* may seem strange, but it is perfectly correct. In other examples, either *If I were rich ...* or *If I was rich ...* is correct.

- **Modal verbs** can also be used in the main clause of a conditional sentence instead of will or would:
  *You **could get** a better job if you **spoke** a foreign language.*
  *If they **hadn't repaired** that fence, somebody **might have been injured**.*
  ***Let** me know if you can **come** to the cinema with us.*

3.4 Use of the gerund

A gerund is a verb that is used as a noun, and is the same as the present participle ("-ing" form) of the verb. The gerund is used:
- as the subject or object of a sentence:
  Snowboarding is more popular than ever this winter.
  Reading when out and about is even easier since the invention of the e-reader.
  I enjoy **cooking** – I find it very relaxing.
  He can't seem to stop **texting**, no matter where he is. It can be really irritating!
- Gerunds can also have their own object:
  Travelling by public transport is becoming more expensive every year.
  Taking photos in the museum is forbidden.
  My father doesn't like **eating** foreign food.
  Our parents want us to stop **watching** so much television.

Gerunds are used after certain verbs:
- some common verbs that are always followed by the gerund are:
  admit, appreciate, can't help, can't stand, consider, delay, deny, dislike, enjoy, escape, excuse, feel like, finish, forgive, give up, imagine, involve, mention, mind, miss, postpone, practise, put off, resent, risk, suggest, understand
  I still haven't finished **writing** this essay!
  Would you mind **closing** the window? It's freezing in here!
  She considered **studying** medicine, but the course was too expensive.
  My cousin really enjoys **travelling** – he's going to Argentina next month.
- some common verbs that can be followed by the gerund are:
  forget, hate, like, love, prefer, remember, stop, try
  When it comes to exercise, I prefer **cycling** to **jogging**.
  Stop **telling** me what to do! I can make my own decisions.
- Notice how the meaning of the verbs listed above changes, depending on whether they are followed by a gerund or an infinitive:
  Remember to check your messages later so that you know where we're meeting. = don't forget to do it
  I **remember checking** my messages but I didn't see yours. = I know that I did it
  She **tried to work** in a corner of the café but found she couldn't concentrate. = she attempted to work but did not succeed
  Why don't you **try working** in the library? It's a lot quieter in there. = this is a suggestion of something that might work for you

3.4 Use of the gerund

Gerunds are used after certain preposition combinations:
- some common examples of verb + preposition followed by the gerund are: *More examples: dream of, succeed in*
I'm **fed up with listening** to her complain about her boyfriend. Why doesn't she just break up with him?
They're **thinking about moving** to France for a couple of years.
She **apologised for losing** my book and offered to buy me a new copy.
- some common examples of adjective + preposition followed by the gerund are: *More examples: keen on, nervous about*
I'm **interested in learning** how to windsurf.
My brother will probably never visit the States as he is **afraid of flying**.
I'm really **tired of asking** him to turn his music down. He's so selfish!
Mel is very **good at singing**.
We're very **excited about meeting** the president.
- some other common prepositions followed by the gerund are: *More examples: despite, thank you for*
In spite of having a terrible cold, Tony went to the football match.
Besides playing the piano and cello, she also sings beautifully.
Please check that you have completed the form **before handing** it in.
After winning an Olympic gold medal, she decided to end her career as a sportswoman.
I couldn't believe it when they all went on holiday together **without telling** me.

Gerunds are used as part of some compound nouns:
Although our town is only small, we still have our own **swimming** pool.
Lunch will be served in the **dining** room.
It's terrible that so many young girls today suffer from **eating** disorders.
Next week we're going on a **shopping** trip to London.
The gym has lots of equipment, including several **rowing** machines.
He wants to be a **racing** car driver when he grows up!
There is a **waiting** room inside the station.
The government has said it will improve **working** conditions for people with young children.

Another common use of this form is in notices or instructions about things that are not permitted:
No smoking.
Emergency access road: no parking here.
No diving from the side of the pool.
No talking while the exam is in progress.

3.5 Phrasal verbs

In English there are a large number of verbs consisting of verb + preposition, verb + adverb or verb + particle. Below are some common examples:

- phrasal verbs with **break:**
  Even though Josh and Cindy **broke up** three weeks ago, he still phones her every night.
  Somebody **broke into** our school at the weekend, but they don't think anything was stolen.
  Many cars **break down** in cold weather, causing long delays on the motorways.

- phrasal verbs with **bring:**
  Joanna was **brought up** by her father after her parents divorced.
  I would also like to **bring up** the subject of new library books at tomorrow's meeting.
  Please don't forget to **bring back** my dictionary when you've finished using it.

- phrasal verbs with **come:**
  I **came across** an interesting article about climate change in an online magazine.
  Why don't you **come over** tonight and we can watch the DVD together.
  They've been living in Spain for the last five years and only **came back** to England last week.
  At first I couldn't remember what had happened, but when I saw the photos it all started to **come back** to me.
  Come on! We should have left ten minutes ago!
  There was a power cut in our part of town last night, and the electricity didn't **come** back **on** for nearly three hours.
  Come in and sit down. You must be tired after your journey.
  The restaurant bill **came to** nearly £ 100. I'm glad my grandfather was paying!
  "How on earth did you break that door handle?" "I didn't! It just **came off** in my hand."
  They **came up with** several good suggestions for the new club house.
  Poor David has **come down with** chicken pox! He's got to stay at home for the next two weeks.

- phrasal verbs with **drop:**
  My aunt lives just round the corner, so she often **drops in** for a chat.
  I've asked Sandra to **drop** the books **off** at your house this afternoon.
  Simon **dropped out** of university after just three months and decided to train as a chef instead.

Note that some phrasal verbs can have more than one meaning.

3.5 Phrasal verbs

- phrasal verbs with **fall**:
  When I was 6, I **fell off** my bike and broke my arm.
  I once bought a T-shirt that was so badly made it **fell apart** the first time I washed it.
  We were hoping to go to the States last year, but our plans **fell through** as we didn't have enough money.
  Katie and Stella have **fallen out** again – they've haven't spoken to each other for 3 days.
  I **fell for** Mike the first time we ever met. It really was love at first sight!
- phrasal verbs with **get**:
  I hate having to **get up** so early during the week – I wish I could just stay in bed!
  She couldn't find our house because she **got off** the bus at the wrong stop.
  This book is very special to me, as it helped me to **get through** a difficult time in my life.
  When we were younger, we didn't **get on** at all, but now we're best friends.
  I need to **get on with** my work now, otherwise I'll never finish this essay!
  Don't make your presentation too complicated if you want to **get** your ideas **across** clearly.
  He had a very traumatic experience when he was 15 – it took him years to **get over** it.
  Hurry up and **get in** the car! I don't have much time!
- phrasal verbs with **go**:
  We're **going away** for a few days, but we'll be back on Thursday.
  Shall we **go for** a coffee after class?
  We stayed on the beach after the sun had **gone down**, just listening to the sound of the waves.
  Nicola has been **going out** with Mark for nearly three months now.
  A bomb has **gone off** in the centre of Belfast. It is not yet known how many people have been injured.
  The price of food has continued to **go up** in the last couple of years, making things even more difficult for low-income families.
- phrasal verbs with **keep**:
  Can you **keep** the noise **down**, please? I'm trying to work.
  I really wish I'd never accepted Jack's friend request – he **keeps on** sending me really boring messages!
  Frank cycles so fast that I can never **keep up** with him.
  Please **keep away** from that wall – the paint is still wet.
  I don't believe that Mae told us the whole truth. I'm sure she was **keeping** something **back.**

> It is a good idea to note down phrasal verbs in a sentence. This makes it easier to remember how to use them in context.

- phrasal verbs with **look:**
  I've dropped my earring somewhere here. Can you help me **look for** it?
  My grandma used to **look after** us while our parents were at work.
  She found the text very hard to understand, and had to **look up** more than half of the words.
  I'm really **looking forward to** my holiday – just two more days, then I'm flying to Florida!
  Look out! You nearly knocked that glass over!
  We all sat together on the sofa, **looking at** Lily's holiday photos on her laptop.
- phrasal verbs with **make:**
  He used to **make up** wonderful stories for his younger brothers. That's partly why he decided to become a writer.
  Alex **made up for** forgetting my birthday by taking me out for a meal.
  Sally and Pete fight a lot, but they always kiss and **make up** afterwards.
  He spoke so quietly that we could hardly **make out** what he was saying.
- phrasal verbs with **put:**
  She told the children to **put** their toys **away** in the cupboard when they'd finished playing with them.
  The longer you **put off** going to the dentist, the more your tooth is going to hurt.
  I wish I hadn't **put on** these shoes today. They're really hurting my feet!
  Although the fire spread quickly, the firefighters were able to **put** it **out** before too much damage was done.
  Ellie asked if we can **put** her **up** for the night on Wednesday, because she's coming to town for a job interview.
  Tom is always late and never apologises for it. I don't know why Carole **puts up with** his behaviour – I wouldn't!

Another way to organise phrasal verbs in your vocabulary notebook is to list several verbs with *off*, *on*, *up*, etc.

- phrasal verbs with **run:**
  We had to change our lunch order because the restaurant had **run out of** chicken.
  When he was 15, he **ran away** from home and lived on the streets for a while.
  My mum saw I'd left my homework on the table, and she actually **ran after** me all the way to the bus stop to give it to me!
  You'll never guess who we **ran into** in town yesterday – our old maths teacher, Mr Smith!
  They hoped the new building would be finished by now, but they've **run up against** a lot of problems with the construction company.

3.5 Phrasal verbs

▶ phrasal verbs with **take:**
*Paul really **takes after** his dad: they both love telling jokes and making people laugh.*
*She was so surprised to hear she'd won the competition that she couldn't **take** it **in** at first – she couldn't believe her luck!*
*I'm going to **take off** my jacket. It's really warm today!*
*Due to bad weather, the plane **took off** nearly three hours late.*
*The work's finished now. Why don't you **take** the rest of the day **off**?*
*It's never too late to **take up** a new hobby: my grandmother was 78 when she started learning Spanish!*
*My teacher **took** my phone **away** because I was sending texts in class.*
*I'd like to **take** you **out** for a meal to thank you for all your help.*
*Their new printer didn't work properly, so they **took** it **back** to the shop.*
*The company has just been **taken over** by a Japanese firm, and a lot of people are afraid of losing their job.*

Überblick

Grammatik ist ein wichtiger Teil jeder Sprache. Dieses Kapitel hat eine Übersicht über die wichtigsten Strukturen angeboten. Nutzen Sie das Angebot, grammatikalische Strukturen über den in den Beispielsätzen gebotenen Kontext zu erlernen. Zusätzlich sollten Sie so viel Englisch wie möglich hören, lesen und natürlich auch sprechen: Lesen Sie englische Zeitungen, suchen Sie englischsprachige Infos im Internet, schauen Sie sich Filme in der englischen Fassung an (ohne Untertitel). Dies sind nur einige der Möglichkeiten, die Ihnen helfen können, Grammatik nicht nur zu „wissen", sondern auch ein Gefühl für die Sprache zu entwickeln und ihre Sprachfertigkeiten auf diese Weise zu „automatisieren".

4 Landeskunde „Great Britain"

Großbritannien ist ein Land, in dem Traditionen noch eine große Rolle spielen. An der Spitze des Staates steht ein Monarch, der gleichzeitig an der Spitze der „Church of England" steht. Hier sind zwei der ältesten Universitäten der Welt, Oxford und Cambridge, sowie einige exklusive Privatschulen wie Eton oder Harrow, beheimatet. Es gibt auch Aspekte im parlamentarischen System, die sich seit der Gründung des Parlaments kaum verändert haben. Viele Menschen vertreten die Meinung, dass es in der modernen Welt keinen Platz mehr für Institutionen wie die Monarchie gibt, aber gerade diese Traditionen und Institutionen machen Großbritannien zu dem, was es heute ist.

4.1 Politics in Britain

Political system

Britain's political system is a parliamentary democracy, which means that parliament has supreme authority in all political matters. This is where new laws are made and all political issues are discussed.

The role of the monarch

Although Britain is still a monarchy, nowadays the monarch (currently Queen Elizabeth II) has no real political power. She is the Head of State, but this is chiefly a ceremonial position. One of the most important functions of the monarch today is to represent her country, both at home and abroad. However, she does still have a small part to play in the political sphere:

- She officially opens Parliament each year after the summer recess.
- She signs all bills before they become law and could, in fact, prevent a law from being passed by refusing to sign it. However, this is extremely unlikely to happen.
- She officially appoints the Prime Minister after a general election.
- She usually meets with the Prime Minister once a week to discuss current issues and give advice.

In 2012, the Queen celebrated her Diamond Jubilee: 60 years as monarch. Only Queen Victoria reigned for longer in Britain (63 years and 7 months).

Parliament

The British Parliament consists of two chambers, the **House of Commons** and the **House of Lords**.

The House of Commons

- This is where the Members of Parliament (MPs), elected by the citizens of Britain, meet to debate current issues, discuss policy, and make laws.
- After the last general election (May 2010) there were 650 MPs, each representing a constituency. The number of constituencies in the country can vary slightly from election to election, as the borders are redrawn if the population of an area changes. This is to make sure that all parts of the country have fair representation in Parliament.
- The best-known aspect of parliamentary sittings is the Prime Minister's Question Time. This takes place once a week and consists of half an hour of questions directed at the Prime Minister from both his or her own party and the opposition parties. Nowadays it can be watched live on the internet, and it owes its popularity to the lively nature of this question and answer session.
- There is a strict seating plan. The Prime Minister and the Cabinet sit on the front bench, and face the Leader of the Opposition and the Shadow Cabinet across a table. The other MPs sit behind them, and are therefore referred to as "back-benchers".

There are currently 145 women MPs.

The House of Lords

- Traditionally, the members of the upper house in the British Parliament were not elected, but had a right to a seat there.
- In the past, the members consisted of the Lords Spiritual, i.e. the Archbishops and other senior bishops of the Church of England, hereditary peers, i.e. aristocrats whose seat had been passed down through the generations and life peers (e.g. former politicians who have a right to a seat in their own lifetime, but which is not passed on to their descendents).
- In 1999, the governing Labour Party passed a law to reform the House of Lords. One aim was to take away the right of hereditary peers to have a seat there, although a compromise was reached allowing 92 hereditary peers to remain initially. The number of members has been reduced from 1,330 in 1999 to 827 today, the majority of which are life peers.
- The Lords have limited powers to influence the political decisions made in the House of Commons. They can suggest amendments to legislation, and can delay the passing of a new law for twelve months.
- The House of Lords used to be the highest court of appeal in Britain. However, since 2009, Britain has had a Supreme Court which has taken over these duties.

Since 2000 there has been an independent public body, the House of Lords Appointments Commission, which recommends people for peerages with no connections to a particular political party and checks that the people nominated are suitable for the position.

The electoral system

- A general election is normally held in Britain every four to five years. The exact timing is not fixed: it is up to the Prime Minister to choose the date for the election, as long as it is a maximum of five years after the previous one. This gives the Prime Minister a certain amount of freedom to call an election at a time that is advantageous to his party and when the chances of winning may be higher.
- The voting system at general elections is known as "first-past-the-post". This means that the candidate with the largest number of votes in each constituency wins the seat in Parliament, even if that person only receives a few more votes than the candidate in second place and the majority of the people in fact voted for other candidates.
- In practical terms, this means that it is almost impossible for small parties to win seats and gain representation in Parliament, and that British politics are dominated by a few large parties.

The main political parties

The site www.parliament.uk has a wide range of useful information about the British parliament.

There are three main political parties in Britain today, which together account for 616 of the 646 seats in Parliament. The smaller parties with seats tend to be regional parties such as the Scottish National Party or Sinn Féin.

The Conservative Party

- The Conservatives, also known as the Tories, returned to power at the 2010 general election. However, as they did not win enough seats for an overall majority in Parliament, they formed a coalition with the Liberal Democrats. The party leader, David Cameron, became Prime Minister.
- Traditionally they are a right-wing party that attracts middle and upper class voters.
- In the 1980s, under Margaret Thatcher, Conservative policy was characterised by its support of free enterprise and private businesses (e.g. with lower taxes) and privatisation of state-owned industries. Individuals were to help themselves rather than get lots of benefits from the welfare state, and the powers of the trade unions were severely limited. The policies of this time came to be known as "Thatcherism".
- During his time as opposition leader, Cameron steered Tory policy more towards the centre-right in an attempt to make it more attractive to younger and more liberal voters. It was more tailored to the issues of the day, such as improvements in the educational system, the health service and the environment. Since coming to power, the party has

made several unpopular decisions, including widespread cuts in public spending and a controversial Health and Social Care Bill, which will bring about considerable changes in the NHS.
- The party remains "Eurosceptic" in its foreign policy, as was illustrated by Cameron's veto, in December 2011, of a treaty to give the EU more influence over member states' budgets. In the past, the Tories were known for their close ties to the USA; the current Tory party has stated that they wish to continue a "strong, close and frank relationship with the United States".

NHS = National Health Service (see page 57)

More detailed information about Tory Party policies can be found at www.conservatives.com

The Labour Party
- Labour last governed Britain from 1997 to 2010, when they lost after three terms in power.
- Traditionally Labour is a left-wing party of the working classes with close connections to the trade unions.
- The increasing influence of the more radical left-wing members of the party during the 1970s and early 80s alienated the voters and led to a fundamental reform of the party's policies that started at the end of the 1980s and continued into the 1990s.
- As a result of four defeats in a row by the Conservatives between 1979 and 1997, Labour elected a young, dynamic leader called Tony Blair (only 43 years old at the time) and relaunched itself as "New Labour". In so doing, the party managed to attract a more middle class vote in addition to their traditional working class supporters.
- New Labour stands for social justice, equality and a strong sense of community. Its policies place emphasis on the importance of education, health, employment and the reduction of crime.
- The Labour Party tends to be more pro-Europe than the Conservatives; however, the protection of British interests always takes priority.
- Tony Blair's government also received widespread criticism in Britain for its support of George Bush's "war on terrorism".
- Since 2010, Labour has been led by Ed Miliband.

After Tony Blair's resignation in 2007, the party was led by Gordon Brown for three years.

The Liberal Democrats
- The Liberal Democratic Party was founded in 1988 when the Liberal Party and Social Democratic Party, a breakaway group from Labour, merged. They are now the third largest party in the country and formed a coalition government with the Conservatives following the 2010 general election. The Liberal Democrat leader, Nick Clegg, is also the Deputy Prime Minister.

- Their supporters include both former Labour and more liberal Conservative voters, as they have policies that appeal to both these camps. They are often described as a "centre left" party, although not all their policies fit this description.
- The Lib Dems, as they are often known, wish to change the electoral system to one of proportional representation, which would result in a more accurate reflection of the votes cast and, of course, would mean a greater chance for a party such as theirs to win an election outright.
- Other policies include the decentralisation of government power, the abolition of university tuition fees and opposition to very strict anti-terrorism laws, seeing them as an infringement of civil liberties. They are pro-Europe.
- The party has stated that around 65% of its manifesto for the general election was included in the coalition agreement with the Tories. However, many supporters feel that, since becoming part of the government, the Liberal Democrats have compromised some of their principles, such as voting for measures that would raise university tuition fees. This has been reflected in losses for the party at various by-elections held since the general election.

Scottish National Party

Even if the majority of Scottish people voted for independence, the country would not be able to simply leave the UK. The matter would have to be discussed in the UK Parliament and there would have to be an Act of Parliament to allow Scotland to separate.

- The SNP campaigns to make Scotland an independent country and a seperate member state of the European Union.
- Their political orientation is centre-left wing.
- They have six seats in the House of Commons and 68 out of 129 in the devolved Scottish Parliament (see below).
- In recent years, the party has been pushing towards independence even more strongly, especially after winning the majority in the Scottish Parliament in 2011. A referendum on the subject is being planned for 2014, although polls show that currently the majority of Scottish people would vote against separating from the United Kingdom.

Plaid Cymru

- "Plaid Cymru" means "The Party of Wales" and, like the SNP, campaigns for Welsh independence from the United Kingdom and membership of the EU as a separate country.
- Their position on the political spectrum is centre-left.
- As part of the promotion of Welsh interests, they work towards a bilingual society where the Welsh language has equal status to English.
- They currently hold three seats in the House of Commons and eleven out of 60 seats in the devolved National Assembly for Wales (see below).

Sinn Féin
- Sinn Féin, meaning "ourselves", is the main Republican party in Northern Ireland.
- Their main goal is to achieve the reunification of Northern Ireland and the Republic of Ireland.
- Due to their close links to the Provisional IRA, the Republican terrorist organisation, Sinn Féin has always been surrounded by controversy. However, both Sinn Féin and the IRA claim to be independent from each other, although their aims are very similar.
- Although they currently have three seats in the House of Commons, Sinn Féin MPs do not take their seats there in protest to what they see as the occupation of Northern Ireland by Britain. They also have seats in the devolved Northern Ireland Assembly (see below) and in Dáil Éireann, the Republic of Ireland parliament.

In 2011 Sinn Féin increased their number of seats in the Irish Parliament, showing that the party continues to have a strong political influence.

The Green Party
- The influence of the Green Party in Britain is growing strongly and the first Green MP was elected in 2010. As the first-past-the-post system makes it so difficult for small parties to win seats, this was a considerable achievement for the party, whose success is partly due to people's dissatisfaction with the way in which the large parties deal with environmental issues.
- The Greens are seen as a party that acts rather than one that just talks about the problems of the environment.

United Kingdom Independence Party (UKIP)
- This relatively new party (founded in 1993) is the subject of a great deal of controversy.
- Its main aim is to bring about the United Kingdom's withdrawal from the EU. Their mottos include "We can run our own country" and "Let's get our country back".
- Other central points in the party's manifesto include keeping the English pound instead of joining the single European currency, support for the National Health Service (NHS) and reduction of immigration.
- They are against devolution and would like to see the UK as "one country with one parliament".
- The main point of criticism from outsiders is that this is a racist party, although the members of UKIP deny this.
- The party does not currently hold any seats in the British Parliament, but has several local councillors and eleven seats in the European Parliament.

Devolution

At the end of the 1990s separate parliaments were established for Scotland, Wales and Northern Ireland. They do not, however, completely replace the central parliament in London, but have powers to deal with certain political matters on a more regional level.

England remains the only country in the United Kingdom without a parliament dealing solely with its own affairs.

- The Scottish Parliament was opened in July 1999. It deals with, among other things, education, health, agriculture, environment, food standards, sport, the arts, transport and tourism. The Parliament can also pass new laws, and, within certain limits, set the level of tax to be paid in Scotland.
- The National Assembly for Wales opened for business in 1999. It makes decisions about education, health, economic development and similar issues in Wales.
- The Northern Ireland Assembly was established in 1998. It deals with matters such as education, health, the environment and the arts. However, the Assembly was suspended from October 2002 to May 2007 as a result of a scandal involving allegations that members of Sinn Féin were spying for the IRA. In 2010, the Assembly received additional powers concerning justice and police matters.

Talking about: British politics

abolition – *Abschaffung*
by-election – *Nachwahl*
constituency – *Wahlkreis*
devolution – *Dezentralisierung*
first-past-the-post-system – *Mehrheitswahlsystem*
general election – *landesweite Wahlen*
legislation – *Gesetzgebung*
manifesto – *Wahlprogramm*
poll – *Umfrage*
proportional representation – *Verhältniswahlsystem*
referendum – *Volksentscheid*
welfare state – *Sozialstaat*

4.2 Education

It is compulsory for children aged between five and 16 to be in full-time education. There are different types of schools, both state and private; the most common are described below.

State Education

There are various types of state schools, some working in close cooperation with the local education authority (LEA) while others have independent sources of funding and are able to make several important decisions without the input of the LEA. State schools follow the National Curriculum (see below), a government programme that specifies the subjects that are to be studied and the standards of education that children should have reached by certain stages in their schooling.

Primary schools
- For children aged from five to eleven.
- The children are tested during Year Two (ages six/seven) and at the end of Year Six (ages ten/eleven) (see table below for subjects studied).

Secondary schools
For ages eleven to 16. At the age of 16, young people in Britain have the following options: stay on at school for a further two years, leave school and attend a sixth form college for one or two years, leave school and do a practical training programme, or leave school and find a full-time job.

Most young people take some form of national examinations, such as GCSEs (see p. 47), at 16.

Comprehensive schools
- This is the most common kind of state secondary school. The pupils are of mixed ability, some going on to do A-levels and then to university, whereas others leave school at 16.
- Many comprehensive schools deal with the problem of having pupils of mixed ability in one class by setting them. This means that the pupils split up into different groups for each subject according to their skills in that subject. It is possible, for example, for a pupil to be in the top set for English but the bottom set for chemistry.
- Comprehensives also offer a range of vocational courses. These are a good opportunity for less academic pupils to gain practical skills (see "Examinations and qualifications", p. 47).

Around 90 % of British secondary school children attend a comprehensive school.

Grammar schools

There are currently 164 in Britain and 69 in Northern Ireland.

- There are not many state grammar schools left in Britain, as several of them were converted into or merged with comprehensive schools in the 1960s and 1970s. One reason for this was that the Labour government in the mid-1960s believed that grammar schools were too elitist, and wanted to introduce an educational system in which all schools were open to all pupils, regardless of ability.
- Grammar schools only take pupils with high academic abilities, who generally have to pass an entrance exam before being accepted.
- There is more focus on academic rather than vocational subjects, and it is more common for pupils to stay on into the sixth form and take A-levels. Many grammar school pupils also go on to higher education.

Sixth-form colleges

- Many young people leave school at 16 and continue their education at a sixth-form college. In the past, the last two years at school were referred to as the "sixth form", which is where the name comes from.
- Pupils can take A-levels or do vocational courses here.

Voluntary aided schools

- These are schools where the land and buildings are owned by a charitable organisation, usually a church, rather than the state. The school governors are responsible for employing teachers and other staff, and they decide which children can be given a place.
- Most voluntary aided schools are Church of England, Roman Catholic or Jewish, although there are a few belonging to other faiths, such as Muslim schools.

They follow the National Curriculum (see p. 51), but are allowed to teach Religious Education from the point of view of their own particular faith.

- They receive financial support from the state for equipment, but the running costs are covered by the organisation that owns them.
- Increasingly, church schools in particular are seen as the best option by many parents, as they tend to be smaller, have good educational standards, and are likely to have fewer "problem" students. However, these schools give priority to families who actively practise that particular religion. As a result, there are growing numbers of parents who admit that they have started to attend church services regularly simply in order to get their children a place at a certain school, even though they may not be believers.

Specialist schools
- These schools follow the National Curriculum, but also focus on a "specialist" area: technology, science and maths, languages, sports or the arts.
- There are now over 2000 specialist schools, which, however, can currently only be found in England and not in other parts of the UK. Many of them are to be found in disadvantaged areas.
- As well as getting extra money from the government, the schools get sponsorship from private businesses.

Academies
- These are secondary schools that are partly financed by sponsors, who cover costs of up to £2 million in return for the right to influence decisions regarding the buildings, curriculum and specialisation. The academies are equipped with the latest technology and facilities. *(The sponsors can be private individuals or an organisation.)*
- They often replace an existing school that was doing very badly, and are supposed to help weak pupils from disadvantaged backgrounds, although the academies can choose up to 10 % of pupils with very good academic abilities.
- Like the specialist schools, academies focus on specific subject areas such as technology or the arts.

Examinations and qualifications

General Certificate of Secondary Education (GCSE):
- Pupils normally study for GCSEs in Years Ten and Eleven. Most of the final mark is based on written exams, although some subjects also involve coursework. Practical subjects such as art and design have more coursework than exams. In addition to this, some courses are split up into units, with pupils taking an exam at the end of each unit. Most subjects, such as English, are also divided into two levels, or tiers, and pupils can take the "higher tier" or "foundation tier" course based on their abilities.
- It is compulsory to take exams in English, maths and science; it is also common at many schools to take a modern language, English Literature, a subject from the field of Design and Technology and ICT (Information and Communication Technology). The pupils are normally free to choose the remaining subjects themselves. *(Schools may now choose which languages to teach. While it is still common to offer European languages such as French, German or Spanish, some schools also teach e.g. Russian, Arabic or Japanese.)*

Vocational qualifications

There are various vocational (work-based) qualifications available, which can be taken in addition or as an alternative to GCSEs. Not all schools offer them, however; they are often done at sixth-form college, or can be studied part-time while working or doing an apprenticeship.

- **NVQs (National Vocational Qualifications)**: pupils learn practical skills that enable them to do a job effectively. Subject areas include Business and Management, Sales, Marketing and Distribution, and Food, Catering and Leisure Services.
- **BTECs and Cambridge Nationals:** pupils learn a lot about particular business sectors or industries. They are designed to provide the knowledge and skills that employers are looking for in particular fields. Subject areas include Art and Design, Health and Social Care, Media, Public Services, Science and Sport.

A-Levels (Advanced Level Exams)

- Normally taken at the age of 18, these are the more traditional kind of academic examinations, although it is now also possible to take "applied", i.e. vocational, A-levels.
- At the end of the first year, students take an "AS" (advanced subsidiary) exam in their chosen subjects. This can be counted as a qualification in its own right, or the student can go on to complete a second year of study and obtain a full A-level at the end of it.

A-levels or an equivalent qualification, such as NVQs, are a requirement for studying at university.

International Baccalaureate Diploma

- This is an internationally recognised qualification aimed at students aged between 16 and 19. More and more schools in Britain are now offering this option.
- Students study a variety of subjects from the fields of languages, the arts, science, maths, history and geography.
- The course is assessed by written exams, coursework and an extended essay on a subject chosen by the student.
- In addition to the academic aspects of the course, students are expected to get involved in their local community, e.g. through theatre or music activities, sports and community service.

The National Curriculum

Key Stage Age School year	1 5–7 1–2	2 7–11 3–6	3 11–14 7–9	4 14–16 10–11
English	✓	✓	✓	✓
Mathematics	✓	✓	✓	✓
Science	✓	✓	✓	✓
Design and Technology	✓	✓	✓	
Information and Communication Technology (ICT)	✓	✓	✓	✓
History	✓	✓	✓	
Geography	✓	✓	✓	
Modern foreign languages			✓	
Art and Design	✓	✓	✓	
Music	✓	✓	✓	
Physical Education	✓	✓	✓	✓
Citizenship			✓	✓
Religious Education	✓	✓	✓	✓
Careers Education			✓	✓
Sex and Relationships Education (SRE)			✓	✓
Work-related Learning				✓
Personal, Social and Health Education	✓*	✓*	✓*	✓*

✓ = required by law; ✓* = not required by law
Source: www.nc.uk.net (Department for Education. © Crown copyright 2011)

This standard curriculum was introduced in 1989 and applies to all state schools. There are four "Key stages" when the pupils are tested; the table above shows which subjects must be studied at each stage. Other subjects can be studied at these stages but are not compulsory. In addition to this, parents have the right to withdraw their children from sex education and religious education lessons if they feel that these are not in keeping with the family's beliefs.

Private Education

- There are more than 2,200 independent schools in Britain, which cost from £700–£5600 per term. These fees do not include items such as books, uniforms and extra-curricular activities, all of which can add to the costs considerably.

Around 7% of children in the UK go to an independent school.

- The number of pupils in private education continues to rise as more parents are becoming dissatisfied with the standards of state schools. In private schools, the class sizes are smaller and the pupils can expect to get more individual attention. Academic standards are also generally higher.
- Independent schools do not have to follow the National Curriculum, but can devise their own teaching programme (within certain limits).

Preparatory (or "prep") schools
- These schools, traditionally for 8- to 13-year-olds, are often a first step towards attending a public school, and "prepare" the pupils for taking this step.
- Some of them are boarding schools.

Public schools
- The term "public school" in Britain refers to a very traditional type of private school, often a boarding school.
- Most public schools have a long history: the most famous among them are several centuries old, such as Winchester (founded in 1382), Eton (1440), or Harrow (1572).
- Public schools have a reputation of being very elite: people with high positions in public life in Britain, or even members of the royal family such as Princes William and Harry, attended public school. The very high fees charged also add to their exclusive nature.

These three famous public schools are still single-sex boys' schools; one of the most famous girls' public schools is Cheltenham Ladies' College, founded in 1853.

Higher Education

About 43% of school leavers in Britain go on to some form of higher education, either at university or a college of further education (e.g. an art school or technical college).

Universities
- There are approximately 200 universities in Britain. Oxford and Cambridge are the oldest, and have the best international reputation. Prospective students have to take an entrance exam and attend an interview, and there is a great deal of competition for the limited number of places there. As well as attracting the academic elite, the two universities with their beautiful old buildings and many traditions are very popular with tourists.

The term "Oxbridge" means 'either Oxford or Cambridge', e.g. 'Many Conservative MPs went to Oxbridge'.

4.2 Education

- The universities built during the Industrial Revolution are known as Redbrick Universities (referring to the material that some of them were built of). They were intended to provide more practical courses for the students, such as engineering or medicine. They were built in industrial centres such as Birmingham and Manchester.
- Undergraduates normally study for three or four years for a Bachelor's degree. Postgraduate qualifications include Masters degrees and PhDs (doctorates).
- The subject of tuition fees has caused a lot of controversy in recent years. Up until 1998, tuition was free, with the costs being covered by the student's LEA (local education authority). For the university year 2012/2013, however, students have to pay up to a maximum of £9,000 per year for tuition, in addition to living costs. This can be financed with a student loan, which has to be paid back once the graduate is earning more than £21,000 a year. However, this means that the majority of graduates start their working lives with large debts.

Talking about: Education

boarding school – *Internat*
coursework – *schriftliche Arbeit*
curriculum – *Lehrplan*
entrance exam – *Aufnahmeprüfung*
extra-curricular – *außerhalb des Lehrplans*
fees – *Gebühren*
graduate – *Hochschulabsolvent*
National Curriculum – *staatlicher Lehrplan/Bildungsplan*
to set – *in Leistungsgruppen einteilen*
school governors – *Schulbeirat*
sixth form – *die Oberstufe*
student loan – *Darlehen für Studiengebühren*
tuition fees – *Studiengebühren*
undergraduate – *Student (vor dem Abschluss)*
vocational course – *berufsbildender Kurs/Unterricht*

4.3 Working life in Britain

Like many industrial countries, the focus of the British economy and the various fields of employment have changed throughout the last decades. Whereas in the 19th century work opportunities were based in industry and manufacturing, today the emphasis is on services and the leisure industry. However, Britain still has a strong economy and a lower rate of unemployment than other large European economies.

The Industrial Revolution
Britain's economy became very strong during the 19th century due to:
- an abundant supply of natural resources and raw materials *(E.g. coal, natural gas, iron, oil)*
- cheap raw materials from its colonies throughout the world *(E.g. rubber, tin and palm oil from Africa)*
- a large number of trading partners throughout the British Empire
- the development of new, more efficient manufacturing techniques
- numerous new factories and a large workforce to manufacture goods (often at very low wages, which increased profits and made the economy stronger)
- improved infrastructure (e.g. railways and canals) to transport and distribute the products faster.

Changes in the job market
- Since the mid-20th century there has been a decline in traditional industries such as shipbuilding and coal mining.
- Manufacturing is also less important now than 50 years ago, although manufactured goods still make up a significant part of British exports.
- A large percentage of the goods manufactured in Britain today are still made for the motor industry and other types of transportation, but there has also been an increase in light and high-tech industries, such as computers and electronic goods. . *(Many items in the fields of food, drink, publishing and clothing are also produced.)*
- The largest growth area since the end of the 20th century has been in the service industries. These include retailing, catering, education, health services and tourism.
- Another area of strong economic growth in recent years has been the creative industries. Advertising, television, film and book publishing are just some of the fields in this sector.
- Finance plays an important role in the economy, with London as the world's largest financial centre.

The British workforce

The following table shows the main distribution of the British workforce.

Percentage of workforce	
Percentage of people in work (as of February 2012)	70.3 %
Percentage of people unemployed (as of February 2012)	8.4 %
Fields of employment	
Hotels and catering, repairs and distribution	24 %
Financial and business services	19.5 %
Education, social work and health services	19 %
Manufacturing	14 %
Transport, storage and communication	6 %
Public administration and defence	5 %
Construction (building)	5 %
Electricity, gas and water	5 %
Other	6 %

Source: www.statistics.gov.uk – Adapted from data from the Office for National Statistics licensed under the Open Government Licence v.1.0.

Working conditions

- The minimum wage for people over 21 is £6.08 an hour. For 18- to 20-year-olds it is £4.98; for 16- to 17-year-olds £3.68 an hour.
- As in many western countries, fewer people now have a traditional "nine-to-five" job. Longer working hours and (unpaid) overtime are the norm for white-collar workers (see p. 54).
- The statutory holiday is at least four weeks a year.
- In the last few years, laws have been passed to make working conditions easier for people with young children:
  - women have the right to 52 weeks maternity leave, up to 39 weeks of which are paid
  - men can take up to two weeks paid paternity leave
  - both parents can take parental leave, a total of 13 weeks unpaid holiday, to look after a child aged five or under.
  - both parents have the right to ask their employer to provide flexible working arrangements.

Nowadays, fathers are increasingly likely to take time off work or to work more flexible hours in order to look after their children.

Unemployment

- Due to the changes in the economy over the last few decades, there tend to be fewer blue-collar and unskilled jobs available than in the past, as many companies have transferred production overseas.

- There is a north-south divide in Britain with regard to unemployment rates. Generally speaking, there are more people out of work in the middle and north of the country, especially in places which, in the past, depended heavily on industries such as coal mining or steel-making.
- Unemployment benefit is available, but is not very high and depends on various factors such as family status or length of time without a job. There are various other schemes, however, such as the Jobseeker's Allowance for people who are actively looking for work.
- The unemployment rate amongst young people is higher than in the population as a whole. This is partly because the school system allows young people to finish their full-time education without any qualifications at all.
- There is higher unemployment among the ethnic minorities.

The lack of unskilled jobs makes finding work more difficult.

The role of language skills
- Many people in Britain believe that it is not very important to speak a foreign language. Globalisation and the spread of English as a world language has led to the attitude that "everyone speaks English". As a result of this, fewer young people are choosing to study a language at school or college than ever before.
- The government has recognised the seriousness of this lack of language skills, but has not done much to prevent the situation from getting worse. For example, it is not compulsory to study a language at school even up to GCSE level.
- However, if Britain is to remain competitive within Europe, more emphasis must be placed on learning foreign languages. Anyone from within the EU can apply for a job in Britain, and graduates will increasingly find themselves having to compete with highly qualified graduates from other European countries, who have the added bonus that they can speak more than one language fluently.

However, the current Education Minister wishes to reintroduce compulsory foreign languages for students who are 15 to 16 years or older.

Talking about: Work

blue-collar worker – *Arbeiter*	paternity leave – *Vaterschaftsurlaub*
catering – *die Gastronomie*	raw materials – *Rohstoffe*
to dismiss someone – *jmdn. entlassen*	retailing – *Einzelhandel*
flexi-time – *Gleitzeit*	statutory – *gesetzlich*
maternity leave – *Mutterschaftsurlaub*	unemployment benefit – *Arbeitslosengeld*
nine-to-five job – *normaler Büro-/Acht-Stunden-Job*	unskilled worker – *ungelernte Arbeitskraft*
notice – *Kündigungsfrist*	white-collar worker – *Angestelle/r*

4.4 British society

The British people

Population facts and figures

Population	62.3 million
Population aged 16 and under	11.6 million
Population aged 65 and over	10.3 million

Source: www.statistics.gov.uk – Adapted from data from the Office for National Statistics licensed under the Open Government Licence v.1.0.

- The population of Britain has continued to increase since the end of the Second World War.
- As in other European countries, the population as a whole is getting older, as people live longer and the birth rate declines.
- The number of people of working age will decrease over the next few decades, as more people retire and there are fewer young people to replace them. It has been estimated that, by 2031, a quarter of the population will be 65 or over.

As in many European countries, the official retirement age is likely to increase in the coming years to help to balance out this problem.

Effects of an ageing population
- More pressure on health service resources.
- More need for care facilities (old people's homes and private nurses in the home).
- More and more people reduce their working hours or give up work altogether to care for an elderly relative.
- More pressure on the state pension funds, which results in more elderly people living below the poverty line.
- However, people aged over 65 who have a good source of income have a positive effect on the economy. Many retired people now like to do what is light-heartedly referred to as "SKI", short for "Spend the Kids' Inheritance". This means that, instead of saving their money to pass on to their children, they spend it on themselves, mostly on leisure activities, holidays, meals and consumer goods.

Families

- The number of people getting married each year is gradually increasing, but the total is still far lower than 30 years ago.
- Nowadays more people have a civil wedding than a religious one. The main reason for this is that there are now a large number of places throughout the country, such as castles, historic buildings and hotels, where a civil wedding may be held. Therefore it is no longer necessary to choose a church wedding simply in order to have an attractive backdrop.
- A large number of people, especially those aged under 35, cohabit.
- One in four children lives with just one of their parents, usually with their mother.
- One in five women is childless.
- The divorce rate is now starting to rise again.

Ethnic background of the population

Ethnic background	% of population	Ethnic background	% of population
White	92.1	Black Caribbean	1.0
Mixed race	1.2	Black African	0.8
Indian	1.8	Black Other	0.2
Pakistani	1.3	Chinese	0.4
Bangladeshi	0.5	Other	0.4
Other Asian	0.4		

Source: www.statistics.gov.uk – Adapted from data from the Office for National Statistics licensed under the Open Government Licence v.1.0.

Social institutions

The welfare state

- The welfare state in Britain dates from the early 20th century. Before that time, the poor and needy generally had to get help from their families, churches and other charities. Anyone who was truly destitute could get a little money, called relief, or, quite often, was sent to a workhouse. Here they were given very basic food and shelter in return for manual labour. In the 19th century in particular it was considered shameful to be poor, and those who were well off tended to believe that people were poor through their own fault, because they did not work hard enough. This was seen as a justification for making conditions in workhouses bad to appalling. Understandably, most needy people did whatever they could to avoid being sent there.

Children aged two and over were even separated from their parents, as poor people were seen as not being able to take responsibility for their families.

- 1905–1911: The Liberal government began to introduce a series of public services with the intention of taking away the shame of poverty. These included:
  - old age pensions
  - free school meals
  - labour exchanges, i.e. places where unemployed people could go to find information about available jobs
  - the National Insurance Act was set up to provide money for healthcare and unemployment
- 1918–1941: Various new services to provide financial help were introduced, including unemployment benefits and council housing.
- The **Beveridge Report** of 1942: Sir William Beveridge recommended the introduction of a National Insurance scheme to finance healthcare, education, family allowance (financial benefits for families) and other social security payments. All workers were to contribute to this insurance. His ideas were implemented over the next six years.

  Beveridge was an economist and social reformer who set up a national system of labour exchanges while working on the Board of Trade under Winston Churchill.

- 1948: The National Health Service (NHS) was the first such scheme in the world, and was intended to allow every citizen to have access to free healthcare. It was to be paid for by national insurance contributions and government funding.

The NHS today
- Every British citizen still has the right to free treatment by a general practitioner (GP) in their local area.
- Due to the heavy financial demands on the system, many services that were free in the past, such as dental or eye care, now have to be paid for or at least subsidised by the patient. However, children under 16, young people aged 16, 17 or 18 in full-education, pregnant women and women who have had a child in the last 12 months, people on low incomes and people with certain medical conditions do not have to pay anything.

  This includes diseases such as diabetes or cancer.

- NHS hospitals can vary greatly in terms of conditions for the patients or services available, depending on the area in which they are situated.
- There are long waiting lists for routine operations, with patients waiting several months or even years for non-urgent treatment.
- As a result of this, many people in Britain now have private health insurance or individual policies for particular types of treatment, e.g. in case they need hospital treatment. However, even people with private insurance must continue to pay national insurance contributions.
- Several reforms have been introduced in recent years in an attempt to make the system more efficient and increase patient satisfaction. These include:

- A Patient's Charter, which details patients' rights and the standards of care they can expect. It lists their rights to information and gives details of the complaints procedure.
- Patients today are generally encouraged to become more actively involved in their healthcare and to make suggestions about how the day-to-day running of health services can be improved.
- NHS Foundation Trusts are hospitals that, instead of being controlled by the central government, are managed by local people, patients and staff, who are able to influence how these services are run so that they benefit the local community.

Health issues

- The increasingly elderly population is putting more and more strain on NHS resources.
- The problem of obesity, especially amongst children, is the subject of heated discussion in the UK. The population as a whole has become heavier over the last few decades, and a growing percentage of children and young people are overweight, some seriously so. This is blamed on the combination of eating the wrong kind of food and lack of exercise (too much time spent in front of the TV or at the computer), which is seen as typical of today's society.
- Several solutions have been suggested to tackle this problem. These include a focus on the kind of food school canteens serve and banning the advertisement of unhealthy snacks and drinks. It has even been suggested that, in cases of serious obesity, the NHS should pay for stomach reduction operations in order to force people to lose weight and therefore be less likely to suffer from typical diseases of the overweight, such as diabetes, when they are older. This, in turn, would save the NHS money in the long run. This idea is, however, controversial.

A campaign to improve school dinners is led by a well-known British TV chef.

Social security

Social security consists of:

- Income support: this guarantees a minimum income for people with little or no other financial means. Extra payments for housing costs can be made if necessary.
- Job Seeker's Allowance: this has replaced unemployment benefit. It is part of a wider scheme of advice, training and supervision intended to encourage unemployed people to actively look for work.
- State pensions
- Benefits for sick and disabled people
- Child benefit

Child benefit is currently £20.30 a week for the eldest child and £13.40 a week for each additional child.

The system of benefits is complicated, and many people find it difficult to work out exactly what benefits they are entitled to.

Social services
These include:
- Caring for elderly and disabled people, either in their own home or in some form of nursing home.
- Providing care for children and young people who are not able to live with their families.
- Providing care for the mentally ill.

Social issues

Crime and punishment
The most common types of crime in Britain are:
- theft and handling stolen goods
- drug offences
- violence against another person
- burglary
- criminal damage
- robbery
- sexual offences
- fraud and forgery

In recent years there has been a fall in crime rates overall, while the numbers of certain types of crime have risen. These include "new" offences such as internet-related crime (internet fraud, spam, viruses, hacking, paedophilia) and identity theft. The latter occurs when someone finds out another person's personal details (name, address, bank details, credit card details) and uses them to buy goods, take out bank loans or even apply for a new passport.

Courts
- A person accused of committing a crime normally has to go to court to be tried.
- Less serious crimes and civil cases are usually tried by a magistrate.
- Serious criminal cases are tried by a jury.
- Juries consist of citizens aged between 18 and 70 who are selected randomly for jury service.

Anyone who has lived in the UK for at least 5 years since the age of 13 can be called up for jury service. People with certain mental health conditions, or who have served long prison sentences, are exempt.

Punishment

Depending on the seriousness of the crime, the person who has been found guilty can be sentenced to:
- pay a fine
- do community service
- a prison sentence
- a suspended prison sentence

If the accused is found not guilty, he or she will be released.

Crime prevention

- Neighbourhood Watch scheme: groups of neighbours, led by a volunteer coordinator, come together to discuss ways to make their neighbourhood a safer place to live. The groups also work together with local police. There are two main ideas behind the scheme: to reduce crime locally and to encourage people to be good neighbours with a strong sense of community.
- Anti-social behaviour: there are now special local coordinators to help communities tackle problems of anti-social behaviour in their area. Examples of this include noisy neighbours, vandalism, graffiti and intimidation from groups of people, all of which can make it unpleasant or even frightening to live in a certain neighbourhood.
- Acceptable Behaviour Contracts (ABCs) are written agreements between a person causing anti-social behaviour and their local authority, landlord or the police. The idea is that the person should admit his/her anti-social behaviour and agree to stop it. The agreement also states the consequences of breaking the contract. They were originally intended for young offenders, but can be used for people of any age.
- Anti-social Behaviour Orders (ASBOs) are court orders designed to protect the public by, for example, banning continual offenders from certain places. The ASBOs last for a minimum of two years, and are also intended to encourage local people to report crime and anti-social behaviour.
- The "Respect" campaign for local communities aims to tackle problems such as truancy and anti-social behaviour in schools, as well as providing out-of-school activities for young people, making local communities stronger and supporting anyone who wishes to challenge anti-social behaviour.

ASBOs are, however, controversial, as they are often breached, and studies have shown that a number of people who receive them are suffering from mental health problems.

Immigration and race relations

Immigration to Britain
Around 1 in 8 people living in Britain were born in another country. The largest groups of immigrants come from Asia, especially the Indian subcontinent, the Caribbean, and Europe. In recent years, immigration has continued to increase, despite promises by the Conservative government to significantly reduce the number of immigrants by 2015. However, in 2010 241,000 foreigners were allowed to settle in the United Kingdom, while fewer failed asylum seekers and illegal immigrants were forced to leave. The increase is due in part to the expanding European Union, whose citizens have a right to settle in a member country if they wish to do so.

Nearly 250,000 people migrated to the United Kingdom in 2011. There are different categories of migrants. On the one hand there are temporary migrants, including students and skilled workers who are allowed to remain in the country to work for a certain number of years, but are then expected to return to their home country. Permanent migrants are allowed to settle in the UK indefinitely. The government is currently working on plans to make it more difficult for temporary workers to apply to settle permanently in the UK, and to reduce the length of some temporary visas to 12 months.

There are also plans to reduce the number of visas, such as student visas, issued to foreigners.

Reasons for immigration
The main reasons that foreigners are allowed to settle in Britain are:
- asylum
- to work
- to study
- to rejoin members of their family who already live there.
- Since EU nationals can now live in Britain for as long as they wish, provided that they have a job or can support themselves financially, they are no longer included in statistics of this kind.
- In the 1950s and 1960s, there was an urgent need for workers in the UK, and foreigners, especially from former British colonies such as the Caribbean, India and Pakistan, were encouraged to come to fill the gap.
- The number of asylum seekers increased sharply at the end of the 1980s as people fled international trouble spots such as Somalia and former Yugoslavia. However, although the percentage of asylum seekers in the UK is slightly above the EU average, the number decreased overall during 2003 and 2004.
- The latest influx of immigrants is from eastern European countries that joined the EU in 2004, and from European countries still outside the EU.

- The government dealt with this new wave of immigrants by establishing a Workers Registration Scheme, which ensured that such people entered Britain in order to work rather than to claim social security benefits. This scheme allowed migrants to fill gaps in the job market; however, the scheme closed in April 2011. Citizens from Bulgaria or Romania still need authorisation to work in Britain.

Problems for ethnic minorities
- Integration is difficult, especially among immigrants who do not speak good English.
- They are more likely to have low-paid, unskilled jobs and to live in areas where the housing is poor.
- Their presence causes feelings of resentment among some British people, who believe that immigrants have only come to the country in order to live off social security benefits.
- Due to recent terrorist attacks in Britain carried out by Muslim extremists, Muslims or "Muslim-looking" people are now often regarded with suspicion. This is partly fuelled by government warnings, e.g. that universities and colleges should be on the lookout for Islamic extremists on their campuses.

Such as the suicide bomb attacks that took place on 7th July 2005 on the London Underground and a bus during the rush hour.

- The ethnic minorities are generally underrepresented in public life, whether in politics, the police force and the army and similar fields. This also applies to the trade unions, which means that they have fewer people representing their needs in a working environment.

Working against discrimination
- The 1976 Race Relations Act makes it illegal to discriminate against anyone on the basis of race, colour, nationality or ethnic origin. This applies to employment, housing and education, as well as to the provision of goods, facilities and services.
- The Equality and Human Rights Commission is an organisation set up to promote a just and integrated society, where diversity is seen positively. They monitor the media for positive and negative reporting, give input to proposed changes in laws connected to immigration and ethnic minorities, offer legal advice to people who have suffered discrimination, and provide guidelines for schools and employers, among much else.

Set up in 2007, the Commission combines the responsibilities of the former Commission for Racial Equality, the Equal Opportunities Commission and the Disability Rights Commission.

4.4 British society

Integration and acceptance

- People from ethnic minorities have a much higher public profile nowadays, especially on television. Children's programmes and soap operas in particular take care to show a broad cross-section of the community.
- There are more celebrities from ethnic backgrounds, for example in the fields of sport and music. As these stars are normally quite young, they serve as positive role models for other young people.
- Ethnic restaurants are extremely popular and dishes from other cultures have become integrated into British cooking. This is supported by celebrity TV chefs from a variety of backgrounds.
- There has been a definite increase in marriages between people from different ethnic backgrounds, showing greater integration, at least on a personal level.

Talking about: Social issues

the accused – *Angeklagte/r*
anti-social behaviour – *asoziales Verhalten*
asylum seeker – *Asylbewerber/in*
burglary – *Einbruchdiebstahl*
to care for someone – *jemanden pflegen*
celebrity – *Prominente/r*
civil wedding – *standesamtl. Hochzeit*
to cohabit – *zusammenleben*
council housing – *Sozialwohnungen*
court – *Gericht*
destitute – *mittellos*
EEA – *Europäische Wirtschaftsraum*
fine – *Geldstrafe*
forgery – *Fälschung*
fraud – *Betrug*
general practitioner – *Allgemeinarzt*
intimidation – *Einschüchterung*
jury – *Geschworene*
landlord – *Vermieter*
magistrate – *Richter*
national insurance – *staatliche Krankenversicherung*
needy – *bedürftig*
obesity – *Fettleibigkeit*
offence – *Verbrechen*
continual offender – *Wiederholungstäter/in*
pension – *Rente*
poverty line – *Armutsgrenze*
to retire – *in Ruhestand gehen*
to sentence – *verurteilen*
social security – *Sozialversicherung*
suspended sentence – *Haftstrafe auf Bewährung*
theft – *Diebstahl*
truancy – *Schuleschwänzen*
to try – *vor Gericht stellen*
welfare state – *Sozialstaat*
workhouse – *Armenhaus*

4.5 Religion

The main religions in the UK

There are six main religions represented in the UK. The following table shows the representation of these groups throughout the population as a whole:

Religion	Number who stated this as their religion	Percentage of population	Religion	Number who stated this as their religion	Percentage of population
Christian	42,079,471	75 %	Jewish	266,875	0.5 %
no religion	9,220,653	15.6 %	Buddhist	151,883	0.25 %
Muslim	1,589,183	2.7 %	other religions	178,544	0.3 %
Hindu	558,485	0.9 %	not stated	4,405,646	7.5 %
Sikh	336,430	0.8 %			

Source: www.statistics.gov.uk/census/default.asp – Adapted from data from the Office for National Statistics licensed under the Open Government Licence v.1.0

- Britain is officially a Christian country, where the head of state is also the official religious head.
- The main Christian religions in the UK are: the Church of England, the Roman Catholic Church, the Presbyterian, Methodist and Baptist Churches, the Church of Scotland and the Church of Ireland.
- The data from the census above refers to the religion that people identify themselves with, that they were brought up with. It does not necessarily reflect the number of people who actively practise their given religion.
- According to a survey taken in 2009, 44 % of people living in Britain define themselves as Christian, around 5 % said they belong to a non-Christian religion, and over 50 % claimed to have no religion. However, many people who say they do not believe still state that they have an affiliation to a certain religion, normally because it has been passed down to them by their parents. This is sometimes referred to as "cultural Christianity", where religion has the role of being part of a person's cultural identity rather than having a spiritual function.
- People belonging to the Church of England are among the least likely to go to church regularly. However, church attendance normally rises considerably at important feasts such as Christmas or Easter, and many Anglicans marry in church or have their children christened, again illustrating the social and cultural aspect of religion: it still has a part to play in British tradition.

Source: British Social Attitudes Survey

The Church of England
- England's official established church is also known as the Anglican Church.
- Up until 1534, England was a Catholic country. However, King Henry VIII asked for the Pope's permission to divorce his first wife, Catherine of Aragon, because she had not managed to give birth to a male heir, and the king had fallen in love with a younger woman, Anne Boleyn. When the Pope turned down his request, he decided to split from the Catholic Church and declare himself Supreme Head of the Church in England. The title is significant: Henry had not founded a new religion, but simply enabled himself to be in charge of religious matters in England, and to adapt the state religion to suit his own purposes.
- Gradually, the Church of England developed into a Protestant religion, and was established as such during the reign of Elizabeth I (1558–1603).

Elizabeth's predecessor, her half-sister Mary Tudor, was Catholic and refused to give up that religion as Queen.

The Church and the State
- One criticism of the Church of England is that it is not separate from the state. For example, the Prime Minister is involved in the appointment of the Archbishop of Canterbury (the highest-ranking bishop in the Church) and other senior bishops.
- In addition to this, decisions made by the General Synod (the Church's governing body) have to be approved by Parliament, although the politicians are not allowed to make any changes.
- Senior bishops currently still have seats in the House of Lords, which means that they are actively involved in the political life of the country.
- All Anglican clergy have to swear allegiance to the Crown.
- However, the Church does not receive any funding from the government. Most of its finances come from donations and various historic funds.

Different kinds of Anglicans
There are two main Church of England groups:
- The High Church, or Anglo-Catholics: its church services are very similar to the Roman Catholic mass. The ritual of the service is of central importance, as is the authority of the clergy.
- The Low Church, or Evangelicals: the Bible is seen as the only source of authority, and church services tend to be simple ones of prayer rather than the celebration of Holy Communion. Preaching also plays an important role, and lay preachers are common.

Other issues

- The first Anglican women priests were ordained in 1994, after many years of disagreements and under a great deal of protest. Today, the number of women priests continues to increase: nearly half of the new clergy ordained in 2009 were women. In 2000, a new, equally controversial discussion started about whether the Church should permit women to be ordained bishop. After several years of debate, the majority of Church members would now agree to the ordination of women bishops; a new vote on the legislation that will finally make this possible is due in November 2012.
- Another extremely controversial issue in recent years has been the question of homosexual priests. The Church of England allows gay people to be ordained as long as they are celibate. However, the recent appointments of openly homosexual priests to high positions within the Church caused a lot of disagreement. This, together with the connected issue of whether blessings of same-sex couples should be approved by the Church, is causing great division in the Anglican Communion (a world-wide affiliation of Anglican Churches). Members of the Anglican Communion in Nigeria, South East Asia and South America in particular have threatened to break away from the group of churches that allow same-sex blessings and homosexual priests.
- Church attendance has declined in recent decades, with fewer young people going to church regularly. However, the number of women at services has significantly increased since the ordination of women priests, as many feel that female priests can identify better with their needs and concerns.

For more information on the Church of England, its beliefs and activities, see www.churchofengland.org

The Church of Scotland (the "Kirk")

- The official national church in Scotland is completely independent from the state.
- It is a Presbyterian church, which is governed democratically by church councils consisting of ministers, elders (also known as "presbyters") and deacons, but it does not have any bishops.
- A General Assembly is held once a year, where the Moderator, the head of the church for one year, is elected.
- The services normally consist of prayers and hymns, with a long sermon. Holy Communion is often only celebrated a few times a year.
- The services can be conducted either by a minister or a lay preacher.
- The "Kirk" has had women ministers since 1968; today most of the people training to be a minister are women. 2004 saw the first woman Moderator.

The second woman Moderator to date held office in 2007.

The Church in Wales
- Wales does not have its own official church, but is part of the Anglican Communion.
- The Church tends to be more High Church-oriented, although conscious attempts are being made to make the liturgy more relevant to a wider range of people.
- Other Christian churches, such as the Presbyterian Church of Wales, also have a large membership.

Northern Ireland
- The terms "Protestant" and "Catholic" have strong political overtones in Northern Ireland, and are often used to represent a set of attitudes that now have little to do with religious beliefs.
- Most Unionists, who want Northern Ireland to remain part of the United Kingdom, tend to be Protestants who are often of English, Scottish or Welsh descent.
- Most Nationalists tend to be Catholics. Their aim is that their country should once again become part of the Republic of Ireland. However, according to a recent survey, 24% of Northern Irish Catholics wish their country to remain part of the UK, which shows that the issue is not as clear-cut along religious lines as it is often claimed.
- For many people, the term "Catholic" or "Protestant" is one of identity, a way of expressing a sense of community and affiliation with a particular group rather than strictly following certain religious practices.
- Despite initiatives to promote understanding between the two main religions, a large percentage of Catholics in Northern Ireland still have a deep-seated mistrust of Protestants, and vice-versa. Even if the issues in the country can be resolved through negotiations in the foreseeable future, it is obvious that it will take much longer for these prejudices to disappear.

The peace process in Northern Ireland began in the mid-1990s; the British military campaign in the country officially ended in 2007.

The Free Churches
- These are Protestant Churches which, at various times, broke away from the Church of England due to disagreements over doctrine or ritual.
- The main churches in this group are the Methodists, Presbyterians, Baptists, the United Reform Church, the Quakers and the Salvation Army.
- Although there are differences between them, they also have several similarities, including emphasis on the authority of the Bible rather than that of religious leaders, the fact that both men and women can be ordained minister, and the simplicity of their chapels and services.

The Catholic Church in Britain

- The Catholic Church suffered several centuries of persecution in Britain after Henry VIII broke with Rome in the 1530s.
- It was not until 1829 that the Church was granted full civic rights again, and from the 19th century onwards membership increased, helped along by numerous immigrants from Catholic countries such as Ireland.
- Throughout the UK there are about 3,300 parish churches.
- There are approximately five million baptised Catholics in Britain, of which about one million attend mass regularly. Although numbers have dropped considerably over the last decades, this still makes Catholics the largest actively practising religious group in the country.

Attendence has been boosted again in recent years by immigrants from Poland and Lithuania.

Non-Christian religions

- The main non-Christian religious groups represented in Britain today are Muslims, Hindus, Sikhs, Jews and Buddhists.
- These groups have their own places of worship (there are, for example, over 600 mosques in the UK) and, often, their own community centres.
- The Jewish community has a long history in Britain, although Jews have had to deal with anti-Semitism there, too.
- The number of Jews increased in the early 20th century as thousands fled from the pogroms in Russia. Jewish refugees from Europe were allowed to settle in Britain before 1938, but not during World War II, except for approximately 10,000 Jewish children who were rescued from Nazi Germany. However, many European Jews were allowed to immigrate to Palestine during the 1930s, which was controlled by Britain at the time.
- Nowadays there are around 350,000 Jews in Britain, who are generally well integrated into life there.
- Many Muslim communities are now afraid that they may be suspected of preaching extremist attitudes. These suspicions are seen by many as a form of discrimination, and an injury of their rights to practise their religion freely.
- As a result of this, religious leaders from all faiths emphasize the importance of dialogue to increase tolerance and understanding between the religions.

There are also around 140 Muslim schools in the UK, although only a handful of these are state-run; the others are attended by pupils who are registered as home-schooled.

Talking about: Religion

celibate – *im Zölibat leben*
clergy – *die Geistlichen/der Klerus*
deacon – *Diakon*
lay – *Laien*
to ordain – *zum Priester weihen*

parish – *Pfarrbezirk*
persecution – *Verfolgung*
preacher – *Prediger*
sermon – *Predigt*

4.6 Foreign affairs

The British Empire

Britain's colonial empire, which lasted from the late 16th to the mid 20th century, was the largest ever in the world. At its height in the early 1900s it comprised over 20% of the world's land area and about 458 million people. It was said that "The sun never sets on the British Empire"; in other words, the empire was so extensive that there would always be daylight in at least one of the colonies.

Reasons for empire-building
- Since it is an island, Britain has long been a seafaring nation. The first great explorations took place during the reign of Elizabeth I (1558–1603) when Sir Francis Drake sailed around the world (1588) and Walter Raleigh explored the Americas between 1578 and 1595. However, the first long-term colonies were not founded until the beginning of the 17th century.
- Economic factors played a large role from the start: the idea was to establish foreign trade in order to bring wealth to the mother country. Colonies were a source of cheap raw materials and provided a market for exports. Large trading companies were established as early as the 17th century, e.g. the East India Company (1600) and the London (Virginia) Company (1606).

The main goods traded included silk, cotton, salt, opium and tea.

The first empire
The first British colonies were in:
- the West Indies (Jamaica, the Bahamas, the Bermudas)
- India (although it was not directly ruled by Britain until 1858)
- North America
- Canada (Newfoundland, Hudson Bay)
- Gibraltar

Britain acquired some of this land during wars with France (Canada, India) and Spain (West Indies, Gibraltar). After gaining control of Gibraltar, Britain was permitted to supply slaves and trade goods to the Spanish Americas, which established the country as a major overseas power.

The North American colonies

These can be split into three groups:

- The New England Colonies: the area around Boston settled by the Puritans.
- The Middle Colonies: the area around New York settled by various European immigrants attracted by the religious and political freedom to be found there.
- The Southern Colonies: producers of tobacco and cotton. This is where slavery was introduced.

The Plymouth Colony in today's Massachusetts was founded in 1620.

Britain expanded its North American territory when it gained control of the French parts of Canada in 1763. To pay for the increasing costs of a growing empire, it decided to impose taxes on the North American colonies (the Stamp Act of 1765). The colonists resisted this, arguing that they should not have to pay taxes until they were represented in the British Parliament. The Boston Tea Party (1773) protested against tea taxes, leading ultimately to the War of Independence and the founding of the United States of America as a country in its own right.

The Second Empire

After America became independent, Britain concentrated on extending its empire towards the east. Trade still played the most important role in the earlier stages, especially during the Industrial Revolution when there was a huge increase in goods available for export and in the need for raw materials.

Imperialism

As the British Empire expanded, the colonists felt it was their mission to "civilize" the native populations of the countries they settled. It was seen as being in the best interests of the local people to impose Western values, beliefs, and white society in general on them. However, this was often done with a lack of sensitivity towards native cultures that led to resentment, resistance and, in the end, the fight for independence.

Some important colonies

- **India:** This was already a vital trading post, and the British consolidated their position there by playing a more active role in Indian politics. During the 19th century, large areas of the country were conquered, English established as the official language, and Queen Victoria was proclaimed Empress of India.

- **Australia:** The explorations of Captain Cook in the 1770s led the British to believe that they had discovered a rich, fertile land which, although a long way away, could form a valuable part of the empire. It was first mainly used as a penal colony for convicts to ease some of the pressure on Britain's overcrowded prisons. Although, as it turned out, much of the country consisted of desert, it still proved to be a source of wealth when gold was discovered there. Australia, along with New Zealand and Canada, became Britain's main colonies with mostly European settlers.
- **Africa:** The British conquered Cape Colony from the Dutch during the Napoleonic Wars, which gave them a stronghold in South Africa. By the beginning of the 20th century Britain controlled one third of the African continent.

> Although prisoners were sentenced to be transported for perhaps 5 years, once in Australia they were unlikely to be able to afford to return to Britain, at least not in the early days of the colony.

The break-up of the Empire
This was a gradual process, which happened for many reasons:
- Australia, New Zealand and Canada demanded the right to govern themselves.
- rebellions in India (Great Sepoy Mutiny in 1857, passive resistance under Gandhi from 1920)
- growing nationalism and demands for independence in various states (e.g. Ireland from 1916; Kenya 1952)
- conscription: citizens of British dependencies were expected to fight for Britain during the two World Wars, which many colonies rejected
- economic reasons: after World War I independence was given to some colonies (e.g. Egypt) to ease the financial strain on Britain.

Procedure
- Initially all colonies were known as "crown colonies" and were governed from London.
- They then became "self-governing colonies" that were run by local governments, but some elements, such as defence, remained the responsibility of Britain.
- The former colonies finally became "dominions", which were free nations that kept the British Monarch as Head of State. This transition first took place in the "white colonies", e.g. Canada (1867) and Australia (1900). Most African and Asian colonies, however, did not gain their independence until after the Second World War.

> Despite decade-long discussions about whether Australia should become a republic, the British monarch remains Head of State, which seems unlikely to change in the foreseeable future.

British Dependencies
This is the name given to the remaining British colonies, 15 self-governing nations that still depend on Britain for defence and foreign affairs. They

include the Bermudas, the Falkland Islands and Gibraltar. Some of these dependencies have caused serious problems, such as when the Falkland Islands were seized by Argentina in 1982 after Britain cut back on their defence. The Falklands were only regained after two months of costly war.
It is not clear what the long-term future of these last remainders of the British Empire will be.

The British Commonwealth

Many of the former colonies remain part of an organisation called the Commonwealth of Nations. Initially this was a way of maintaining economic ties with former colonies that were now independent states; today it allows member states to interact at a more informal level, states that, at least in the past, had certain things in common, such as language and culture, due to their association with Britain.

Foundation of the Commonwealth
- 1931: The Commonwealth of Nations was established as an association of all dominions, which were now declared equal in all matters. These states had the right to reject any laws passed by the British government and to pass legislation on domestic affairs.
- Former colonies that had become republics (e.g. India) and therefore did not recognise the monarch as head of state joined the Commonwealth later; they saw the monarch as the symbolic head of the Commonwealth but not of their own individual country.
- Economic ties between Commonwealth countries remained important.

The Commonwealth today
- There are 54 member states including Britain.
- The heads of government or state meet every two years to discuss international issues.
- There are many Commonwealth institutes, societies, professional associations and university exchange programmes.
- English remains the common language.
- The Commonwealth Games, a large sporting event, are held every four years. The athletes compete in a wide variety of sports, including some that are only really played in Commonwealth countries, such as netball and lawn bowls.
- There are joint British/Commonwealth programmes in agriculture, engineering, health and education.

- Commonwealth citizens get some special privileges that are not available to all foreigners. These include the right to vote or to be able to take part in certain immigration programmes.

Principles of the Commonwealth
- 1971 Singapore Declaration: commitments to peace, equality, fighting racism, economic and social development.
- 1991 Harare Declaration: reconfirmed these principles and placed additional emphasis on democracy, human rights and social justice.
- Member states that violate these principles can be punished by economic sanctions or even suspension from the Commonwealth. For example, Zimbabwe was suspended in 2002 due to the electoral and land reform policies, and human rights violations that occurred under the leadership of President Mugabe.
- Commonwealth members are free to leave the association if they wish to do so, as membership is voluntary. Zimbabwe left in 2003 after the other members refused to lift the suspension; other states have left in protest at particular issues, but rejoined at a later stage.
- Although the Commonwealth has been able to encourage democracy in some countries, it has had little effect in other conflicts, and its long-term future is doubtful. Economic ties with Britain have weakened in recent years as the importance of the European Union grows, and the traditional sense of solidarity among Commonwealth countries has been lost: many no longer have very much in common with each other.

In 2011, the Commonwealth was accused of not taking enough action against human rights violations by its members. This lack of interest by the member states is seen as just one example of how the Commonwealth is coming to the end of its natural life.

Britain and Europe

Britain's relationship with continental Europe is not always an easy one. Being an island, it is physically separate from mainland Europe, and the Empire allowed Britain to develop close ties with more distant countries. In addition to this, there is a special connection with the USA: the two countries share a common language, culture and a history of political cooperation.

Post-war Britain
The Second World War changed the balance of world power, and in many areas Britain could no longer keep up:
- It had to get financial help from the USA and Canada because it was so badly in debt.
- There were shortages and rationing of food and everyday goods, and a lack of housing, which would continue for some years.

Food rationing did not end until 1954.

- Many of its colonies wanted to become independent, signalling the end of the Empire.
- The new world powers were the USA and the USSR.

European division and unity

In the post-war years, Europe was rebuilt from two sides and in two quite distinct ways: the western countries followed a capitalist, democratic ideology, whereas the eastern bloc took on the communism of the USSR. Some western countries felt that they could become stronger again, both economically and politically, if they formed some kind of union. They wanted to prevent another war and boost the economies of European countries. Britain, however, felt that its political ties were closer to the USA. This is illustrated by the fact that it joined NATO in 1949, but did not join the European Community (EC) until 1973.

Other key dates

- 1975: in a referendum, two-thirds of Britons voted to remain in the EC, despite huge opposition when the country joined.
- 1991: although Britain signed the Maastricht Treaty that allowed the start of the single European market, Prime Minister John Major made sure that the country had the option to remain outside the single currency, and did not sign the Social Charter which guaranteed certain minimum conditions of employment throughout the EC.
- 2002: Britain, along with Denmark and Sweden, did not change its currency to the euro when the other 12 member states did.
- from 2003: Britain has been widely criticised by other EU states for its role in supporting the war in Iraq.

Opposition to the euro remains strong in Britain

The EU – for or against?

British politicians are divided over the question of whether the EU is a good thing for Britain or not. There are, of course, voices for and against in all the big parties, but, generally speaking, the Conservatives tend to have more "Eurosceptics", whereas the Labour government and smaller parties such as the Liberal Democrats are usually more pro-Europe. However, there is a large percentage of Eurosceptics among the general public in Britain, which is one reason why parties such as UKIP (see "Politics") have had some success among the voters.

Eurosceptic attitudes

- There is a loss of sovereignty and national identity (e.g. the monarch's picture would no longer appear on the currency).

4.6 Foreign affairs

- Britain has to pay too much into the EU and doesn't get an equal share out.
- Many laws made in Brussels are seen as interference in the way in which the country is run – Britain should be able to run its own affairs.
- As the EU grows and more people from poorer countries receive the right to live anywhere they choose within the EU, Britain will end up having to support more immigrants, with negative effects on the economy.

Pro-Europe attitudes
- Britain is a European country and will increasingly come to rely on the EU economically in the future.
- There are various EU subsidies that are also good for Britain.
- Britain can make a positive contribution to EU policy by taking an active part in decision-making.
- British people have the freedom to live and work in all other EU countries.
- Britain can take advantage of the free trading conditions within the EU.
- Immigrants from "new" EU countries do not have to become a problem. It is possible to limit the numbers that come, they can fill gaps in the job market, and statistics have shown that many do not, in fact, stay long term.

Talking about: Foreign affairs

to conquer – *erobern*
conscription – *Einberufung*
convict – *Strafgefangene/r*
penal colony – *Strafkolonie*
rationing – *Rationierung*
referendum – *Volksentscheid*
to settle – *siedeln*
slavery – *Sklaverei*
sovereignty – *Staatshoheit*
subsidies – *Subventionen*

Im 21. Jahrhundert ist Großbritannien nicht mehr die Weltmacht, die es einmal war. Die meisten Kolonien sind inzwischen unabhängig – auch wenn einige, wie zum Beispiel Australien, noch immer den Britischen Monarchen als Staatsoberhaupt anerkennen. Es ist offensichtlich, dass die Verbindungen aus der damaligen Zeit dazu führten, Großbritannien zu der multikulturellen Gesellschaft zu formen, die es heute ist. Auch die Tage der industriellen Vormachtstellung sind vorüber. Im Bereich der internationalen Beziehungen spielt Großbritannien jedoch noch immer eine wichtige Rolle. Und nicht zuletzt aufgrund der faszinierenden Geschichte ist das Land ein sehr beliebtes Reiseziel.

5 Landeskunde „The USA"

Im Laufe der letzten 500 Jahre haben sich die Vereinigten Staaten von Amerika zu einer Weltmacht entwickelt. Eine der großen Errungenschaften in den Anfängen war die Gründung eines demokratischen Staates. Dieser fußt auf einer Verfassung, die noch heute als eines der wichtigsten politischen Dokumente der Geschichte angesehen wird. Die Menschen, die nach und nach einwanderten, bildeten die Grundlage der lebendigen, vielseitigen Gesellschaft von heute – mit all den Vor- und Nachteilen, die eine solche breite ethnische und kulturelle Durchmischung mit sich bringt. Heute, im 21. Jahrhundert, ist der Einfluss der Vereinigten Staaten von Amerika auf Politik, Kultur und Gesellschaft noch immer enorm.

5.1 Politics in the USA

Political system

The political system in the United States is made up of three parts: the Legislative Branch, the Executive Branch and the Judicial Branch.

Legislative Branch

Congress is located in the Capitol Building in Washington D.C. The name "Capitol" comes from the Capitoline Hill in Ancient Rome.

This branch consists of Congress, which is divided into two chambers: the House of Representatives and the Senate.
- Both chambers have equal power.
- Both are elected directly by the citizens of the USA.
- Both chambers must agree before a bill can become law. This can cause difficulties if one political party has the majority in the House of Representatives, and the other has the majority in the Senate.

House of Representatives	Senate
435 members	100 members
each member represents a congressional district of about 600,000 people	each state elects two senators
Representatives serve for two years	Senators serve for six years
all House seats are re-elected every two years	one third of the Senate is re-elected every two years

Powers of Congress:
- to make laws
- to impose and collect taxes, and control federal spending
- to control trade with other countries and within the States
- to print money and regulate its value
- to declare war and make peace agreements
- to maintain, arm and discipline the armed forces
- to promote science
- to oversee and check the activities of the Executive Branch

Executive Branch

The Executive Branch consists of the President and Vice President of the United States and an organisation of approximately four million people, including one million military staff.
- In order to be elected president, candidates must have been born in the USA, be at least 35 years of age and have lived in the US for at least 14 years.
- Until the election of Barack Obama in 2008, all US presidents were white males.
- A president serves a 4-year term of office and cannot serve more than two terms overall.
- He and the Vice President are elected by the Electoral College (see p. 82), and are the only political figures to be elected nationally, all other elections taking place at state or district level.
- They do not have to be members of the political party that holds the majority in Congress.

The role of the President

The President is Head of State, Head of Government, Commander-in-Chief of the military and Chief Diplomat. In addition to this, his powers include:
- suggesting new laws to Congress
- signing or vetoing laws passed by Congress. A veto can be overturned by a two-thirds majority in Congress.
- appointing federal judges (including Supreme Court judges); however, these must be approved by the Senate
- appointing members of the Cabinet, of federal agencies (e.g. the CIA), and other federal employees and diplomats. Again, these appointments have to be agreed by the Senate.
- managing national affairs and the federal government
- pardoning criminals (except those who have committed a crime against the State)

Since 1990, the citizens of the USA have alternately voted a Republican then a Democrat as president. Currently, a Democrat is in power.

- influencing foreign policy
- having control over military strategy and matters of national security

However, the President needs the approval of Congress for most decisions he makes. Therefore things can become very difficult for him if his political party no longer has the majority in Congress, as happened in November 2006, in the middle of the Republican President George W. Bush's second term in office, when his party lost their majority both in the House of Representatives and in the Senate.

Judicial Branch

The USA has two types of courts: the federal courts and the courts of each individual state. These two systems are separate from each other, except for certain cases that start at state level but go through several appeals, the last of these being the Supreme Court.

State Courts

The autonomy of each individual state is a very important aspect of American politics.

- Each state in America has its own laws and legal procedures.
- They deal with civil cases involving private individuals or between citizens and local or state governments.
- Each state has its own supreme court, which has the final say in matters concerning that particular state's laws and constitution, and is the final court of appeal in such matters.
- However, if the case involves a federal question, i.e. is connected to the US Constitution or laws concerning the USA on a national level, it may be taken to a federal court on appeal.

Federal system – the Supreme Court

- This is the highest court in the land, where the final judgements are given regarding constitutional and legal matters.
- The court has nine judges who are nominated by the President, subject to approval from the Senate. The judges have the job for life, but can retire or resign if they wish to do so.
- The appointment of judges can be controversial, as the President is likely to choose people who are sympathetic to his views. This can then have an effect on judgements that are passed, especially on matters concerning the interpretation of or changes to the Constitution, although the judges should, theoretically, be neutral.
- The most important job for the Supreme Court is to rule on whether certain laws or government policies are unconstitutional or not. In so doing, it can overrule government decisions.

- All federal courts must follow the rulings made by the Supreme Court in matters concerning the Constitution and federal laws.
- The Supreme Court is not permitted to make judgements concerning the laws and constitutions of individual states.
- The Supreme Court only hears a small number of the cases that are sent there for appeal, choosing those with the greatest importance for the nation or the Constitution.

The American Constitution
The United States' system of government is based on its Constitution. Britain's American colonies had gained their independence in 1776, and in the years that followed it became clear that the central government needed more power if the country was to become and remain united. The Constitution was formulated in 1787 and ratified in 1788. It is still considered to be one of the great political documents of the western world today.

The Constitutional Convention, where the Constitution was drawn up, took place in Philadelphia and was attended by representatives of 12 of the country's 13 states.

Most important points of the Constitution
- The government must have the agreement of its citizens for the decisions it makes on their behalf, i.e. the citizens have an active say in how they are governed.
- The citizens have the power to elect the people who govern them. Politicians therefore have to answer to the people who elected them, and are responsible for representing their needs.
- The importance of the separation of powers, which is why the US government has its three individual branches.
- The system of checks and balances. Each of the three branches of government has some powers over the others, so that no one branch can become too strong.
- Federalism, which means that the national government and the individual states share authority. Once again, this is to ensure that neither one becomes more powerful than the other.
- Flexibility. In other words, amendments can be made to the Constitution as necessary.

The Bill of Rights
The first ten amendments to the Constitution were added in 1791 and are known collectively as the Bill of Rights. They set down certain civil rights that every citizen should have, including:
- freedom of speech, the press and religion
- the right to hold meetings as long as they are peaceful
- the right to lobby the government to bring about changes

- the right to have and use weapons for protection
- the right to a fair trial, and freedom from cruel punishment

There have been a total of 27 amendments to the Constitution to date. An amendment can be suggested either by Congress or by the states, and must be ratified by at least three-quarters of all states. The President cannot make any changes to the Constitution.

> Torture is an example of "cruel punishment". Opponents of the death penalty also argue that this counts as "cruel and unusual punishment".

The political parties

The USA is basically a two-party state, consisting of the Democratic Party and the Republican Party. Although there are some smaller parties such as the Green Party, the Reform Party and the Libertarian Party, which have increased their number of supporters in recent years, they tend to be more successful at local or state level. All seats in Congress are currently held by either Republicans or Democrats.

The main principles of the two biggest parties are shown below. Naturally, there are a number of factions within these huge organisations, so the following is simply a general overview of the main points.

The Democrats

The party is generally in favour of:
- a higher minimum wage
- more government finance for healthcare; possibly the introduction of a national health system
- more investment into alternative and renewable energy sources
- stricter anti-pollution laws
- lower tuition fees for colleges to make higher education more affordable
- equal opportunities and affirmative action (actively giving advantages to minority groups, e.g. in the field of employment)
- same-sex marriage and rights for homosexuals
- the right of every woman to birth control and abortion
- stem cell research

> The colour blue is used to represent the Democrats in the USA, and red is used for the Republicans. This can be confusing, as in many other countries, such as Britain, blue represents right-wing politics and red left-wing.

The party is generally against:
- the continued American military presence in Iraq: the troops were finally withdrawn at the end of 2011 under the Democrat President Obama
- unilateralism, i.e. the idea that if the USA feels its security is being threatened, it can take military action without the agreement of other nations.
- the use of torture against prisoners
- violations of the right to privacy
- the free availability of guns

The Republicans

The party is generally in favour of:

- free-market policies and the importance of individual companies and entrepreneurs being able to run their own businesses without government interference. This means, for example, that issues such as how much workers are paid should be settled by the individual employers.
- tax cuts, especially for people who create jobs
- making it more difficult for people to get welfare money, and therefore encouraging more people to look for a job
- capital punishment
- the right to own guns
- the teaching of creationism and intelligent design on the same level as evolution
- US military action in the Middle East with the aim of spreading democracy to that part of the world
- stricter anti-terrorism laws

The nickname for the Republicans is the "Grand Old Party", GOP for short. Their symbol is an elephant.

The party is generally against:

- an increase in the minimum wage
- the forming of trade unions
- a national health insurance scheme
- abortion
- same-sex marriage
- stem cell research
- measures to stop global warming such as those set down in the Kyoto Protocol

There is also increasing pressure from the more conservative factions of the party to limit people's access to birth control and to teach sex education in schools without mentioning contraception.

Election campaigns

Elections play a very important part in American political life, mainly because there are so many of them, which means that the results can be used to gauge the mood of the electorate. Every four years a new president is elected, and there is some form of Congressional election every two years. Election campaigns tend to be lavish displays of party unity, often with personal appearances by celebrities and making extensive use of the media. The idea of television debates between presidential candidates, for example, comes from the USA, but has now spread to other parts of the world.

Presidential candidates

Candidates for the two parties are chosen in one of two ways, depending on the state:
- Through primary elections held in some states: the candidates are selected by the voters.
- Through party conventions, where representatives of the parties meet to choose delegates to be sent to their party's National Convention. The presidential candidate is then chosen at the convention.

The Electoral College

The President and Vice President are not elected directly by the people, but through the complicated system of the Electoral College. This idea of the Electoral College originally came about because, in the early years of the USA, people living outside the cities normally did not have much information about individual presidential candidates: communications were not very good, and the poor transport connections did not allow candidates to travel widely and visit the people. It was also thought that ordinary, and often uneducated, citizens did not have the skilled judgement necessary for choosing a good president.

Therefore, respected local people were nominated as "electors" to represent presidential candidates. The rest of the citizens voted for one of the electors, who would in turn give the votes to the candidate of their choice.

The system today

- There are the same number of electors for each state as the total number of Senators and Representatives for that state.
- The people cast their vote for one of the presidential candidates.
- The votes cast in each state are collected, and the candidate with the most votes receives all of the electors' votes for that state. This is known as a "majority" or "winner-takes-all" system.
- There are 538 electoral votes in the country as a whole, so a candidate needs at least 270 votes to win.
- The main disadvantage of this system is that the candidate who received the largest number of individual votes from the people does not necessarily win.

In some states, the electors are not legally obliged to give their vote to the candidate who gets the most votes from the people.

Talking about: American politics

amendment – *Verfassungszusatz*
appeal – *Berufung*
appellate court – *Berufungsgericht*
constitution – *Verfassung*
faction – *Parteigruppe*
federal – *Bundes-*
judicial – *juristisch*
legislative – *gesetzgebend*
unilateralism – *Politik des Alleingangs*
to veto – *Einspruch erheben*

5.2 Education

Schools

Public Education
In the USA, "public" education means free, state-run education. About 85% of pupils attend public schools; the rest go to private schools. Education is not controlled by the federal government: Each individual state decides on its curriculum. Children must attend school from the ages of five or six to 16, although they can stay on until they are 18. Depending on the state, the pupils will go to either two or three different schools until they graduate:

As in Britain, it is possible for parents to homeschool their children if they wish.

Elementary school	Grades 1 – 6
Junior High School	Grades 7 – 9
Senior High School	Grades 10 – 12
Elementary School	Grades 1 – 8
High School	Grades 9 – 12
Elementary School	Grades 1 – 6
High School	Grades 7 – 12

Elementary schools
- Pupils are taught reading, writing, basic grammar, spelling and vocabulary, basic maths, and basic history and science.
- They also study art, music, sport and handicrafts.

High schools
- Pupils follow a general course of study, which includes science (physics, biology and chemistry), mathematics, English, social science (including subjects such as American history) and physical education. These courses are the minimum requirement for high school graduation.
- At most schools it is also possible to do "electives", which are more specialised courses and help to prepare pupils who want to take a certain career path.
- Additionally, high schools offer a range of extra-curricular activities which pupils are encouraged to get involved in. These include sports, bands and music activities, school newspapers, writing clubs and many more besides.

Some examples of electives are computer science and IT, performing arts, visual arts or foreign languages.

Grading and testing
- The standards of testing vary from state to state. In some states, 70 out of 100 is a passing grade; in others it is 60, or as high as 75.

- However, standardised tests do exist in the form of SATs (Scholastic Assessment Tests) and ACT (American College Testing). These tests are part of the entry requirements for most universities in the States.

"Magnet" schools
- These specialist public schools are usually found in big cities.
- They aim to attract pupils with a particular talent in the fields of science, engineering, the humanities, fine arts or performing arts.
- Competition to get a place at some of these schools is fierce, as they are thought to offer better opportunities than "ordinary" public schools.

Private schools
- These are often affiliated with a particular church or religious group.
- Trade or vocational schools are usually private, where pupils learn the skills necessary for a particular job.
- The fees vary: more expensive schools have better teaching.

Higher education

There are many types of college and university, both public and private.

Some private universities, such as some Bible colleges, are unaccredited. This means that the degrees they award are not recognised by many employers.

Universities
- To get a place at university, applicants need good SAT results and good average grades at high school. The universities also consider the applicant's involvement and abilities in extra-curricular activities such as sport. He or she may have to write an essay, and/or go to the university for an interview before being given a place.
- The best-known and most prestigious universities in the States belong to the so-called Ivy League.
- Students first take a bachelor's degree, a four-year course normally leading to a BA (Bachelor of Arts) or a BSc (Bachelor of Science).
- Students can then go on to do graduate studies. It is not possible to do an undergraduate degree in law or medicine, as is the case in Britain. Students wishing to study either of these subjects have to do a bachelor's degree first.
- Tuition fees at American universities can be as high as $50,000 a year for the most exclusive institutions. This does not include living expenses. However, scholarships and student loans are available.

The Ivy League consists of Harvard, Yale, Princeton, Dartmouth College, Brown University, Columbia University, Cornell University and the University of Pennsylvania.

Community colleges
- These are also known as technical, junior or city colleges.

- Anyone with a high school diploma can enrol.
- Part-time courses for people who already work are also available.
- Students can prepare for university, and earn credits that count towards a bachelor's degree.
- As well as this, it is possible to take a vocational course: people can train for professions such as electrician.
- In addition, these colleges offer other programmes, such as the opportunity for people who dropped out of high school for some reason to take or complete their high school diploma.

Educational issues

Religion and evolution
One of the most controversial issues in recent years is whether evolution should be taught in schools as scientific fact or simply as one possible explanation of how the world came into being.
- In some (mostly Southern) states, fundamentalist and family values pressure groups do not want pupils to be taught about evolution as fact. Instead, they favour one of two alternative explanations about the origins of the world:
  Creationism = a literal interpretation of the Bible, which states that God created the world in seven days no more than 10,000 years ago. Not all Creationists believe in this timeframe, but all think that evolution cannot adequately explain how the Earth came to exist.
  Intelligent design = the idea of natural selection and chance extinction of species, as stated in the theory of evolution, is rejected. Instead, it is thought that all biological developments happened for a reason, and that the natural world was "designed" by an external being, i.e. God, in order to arrive at our current point of development.
- As a result of pressure from these groups, in some states the science textbooks must stress that evolution is an unproven theory, not scientific fact, and must also include a discussion of creationism and/or intelligent design.

Sex education
- Many people, often those from strict religious backgrounds, do not want their children to be taught about sex and sexual health at school. Some feel that children learn about sexual matters when they are too young, or are taught things that do not match their family's views on the subject.

- Some people take the view that teaching children and young people about sexual health matters, such as methods of contraception, encourages them to become sexually active at a younger age.
- Many groups strongly support teaching the concept of abstinence, i.e. that young people should not have sexual relations at all before getting married. However, studies have shown that this does not significantly reduce the number of sexually active teenagers or teenage pregnancies.

In March 2012 a law was passed in Utah which will allow schools to stop teaching sex education and prevent them from teaching about contraception and discussing homosexuality. Several other states have similar laws.

Literacy rate
- Compared with other developed countries, American schools have a high dropout rate. In addition to this, the US has a lower literacy rate than most other western countries, with below-average skills in the areas of reading, maths and science.
- This has led to initiatives such as the "No Child Left Behind" Act of 2001. The law aims to raise skills levels in all schools, and to provide assessment to make sure that the aims are being achieved.
- The law specifies the minimum qualifications that teachers must have; teachers are tested to ensure that they fulfil the requirements.
- Since the introduction of the law, the test scores for African-American and Hispanic children have risen dramatically; previously white children had much higher scores than pupils from other ethnic groups.

Security
- A number of schools in the USA, especially in poorer areas, have many problems with crime. Some have to deal with gangs or drug dealing; there is also the threat of weapons such as guns or knives being used.
- To try and deal with these problems, some schools have installed metal detectors and have their own security guards.
- Some schools have also worked out a plan of action in case of a shooting incident within the school grounds.

Talking about: Education in the USA

abstinence – *Enthaltsamkeit*
elective – *Wahlfach*
the humanities – *Geisteswissenschaften*
literacy – *Lese- und Schreibfähigkeit*
scholarship – *Stipendium*

5.3 Working life in the USA

Historical background

Like in Britain, the USA's economic power increased dramatically during the first half of the 19th century, when manufacturing became widespread. However, at first only the north-east of the country was really industrialised, with the south and west relying mainly on agriculture as a source of income. It was not until after the Civil War (1861–1865) that America grew to become one of the world's top economic powers, a position that it still holds today.

This economic growth was due to a number of factors:
- The country discovered that it had plentiful resources of raw materials (e.g. iron, coal, oil, copper).
- Large amounts of precious metals were found (gold in California, silver).
- The second half of the 19th century was the age of invention: large numbers of new products, e.g. the telephone, the fridge, the sewing machine, the typewriter, the camera, the elevator and many more besides were invented and manufactured in the States.
- Electric light and ways to use electricity commercially were invented, increasing the efficiency of manufacturing procedures.
- Mass production became possible, and was perfected by Henry Ford in the form of the assembly line.
- From the beginning of the 19th century onwards there was a steady stream of immigrants to provide cheap labour.
- The idea of starting with nothing and working one's way up to become a wealthy citizen of good social standing is an essential part of the American Dream, and one that was often realised at that time: a new class of rich businessmen arose, who then boosted the economy further by buying consumer goods.
- Improved transportation, e.g. through the railway system, meant that goods could be distributed more easily throughout the country.

The California Gold Rush was from 1849–1855, when around 300,000 people flocked to California hoping to make their fortune.

Main fields of employment today

The American economy is based on a variety of industries and fields of employment. Different industries are concentrated in different areas:
- New York City: finance, publishing, broadcasting and advertising
- Los Angeles: film and television
- San Francisco Bay Area and Pacific North-West: technology
- The Midwest: manufacturing and heavy industry
- Detroit: car manufacture

The Ford Motor Company was founded in Detroit in 1903, followed by other famous car manufacturers such as Chrysler.

- The Great Plains: agriculture (known as "the breadbasket of the world" due to all the wheat, corn, soy beans and rice grown there)
- The South-east: tourism, agriculture (cotton, tobacco) and lumber
- Throughout the country as a whole, three-quarters of the workforce are employed in the service industries, including tourism – the country has the third largest tourist industry worldwide.

Working conditions

The government in the USA has always played a minor role in regulating working conditions. Throughout the 19th century the country's economy could perhaps best be described as "laissez-faire capitalism": employers were free to run their companies, and decide on working conditions within them, without any real outside interference from the government. On the one hand, this meant that businesses were able to achieve higher profits as they could adapt more easily to meet market requirements. However, this also meant that they could treat their workers as they wished. The workers were powerless, often having to suffer terrible conditions, or be made redundant when times were bad.

During the Great Depression of the 1930s, however, the government was forced to introduce some programmes to help the unemployed, who made up nearly 25% of the workforce at that time. Later, laws were introduced to reduce monopolies and enable competition. Additionally, the government set down standards of business practice and introduced laws that gave workers certain rights.

The influence of labor unions

- The idea of free enterprise for businesses still holds strong today: companies in the States generally have far greater freedom in running their business than in other countries.
- It is therefore often left up to labor unions to negotiate terms and conditions of employment with individual companies. These include wages and working conditions.
- Labor unions are strictly regulated, and it is not always easy for workers to form one. Either the employer must agree to the founding of a union, or the majority of workers must want to form one.
- In some states, government employees are not allowed to form a union.
- Despite the existence of labor unions, workers in the USA often do not have a sense of job security. Employers still have the right to "hire and fire" their employees fairly freely, as the laws regarding the firing of workers are not particularly strict.

Many employers have the right to fire their employees without giving them much notice. The employee may be given a "separation bonus", i.e. are paid for one or two weeks but have to leave their job immediately.

5.3 Working life in the USA

- The country had an overall unemployment rate of 8.3% as of January 2012. However, the rate for African-American people was 13.6%; for people of Hispanic or Latino origin it was 10.5%.

Pay, holidays and benefits
- There is no fixed minimum wage for the country as a whole: this is a matter for the individual states, and there is always a great deal of opposition whenever it is suggested that the minimum wage should be raised.
- One of the effects of this is a large gap in earnings between different social groups: although the average annual salary for the country as a whole is higher than in western Europe, in reality 90% of households have an average income of around $31,000 or less, with the remaining 10% of the population controlling nearly 75% of the country's wealth. This shows that the gap between rich and poor has become even more obvious in recent years.   *Just under $50,000 in 2010*
- Due to the low wages at the bottom end of the job market, many unskilled workers have two jobs in order to make ends meet.
- Workers in the USA do not tend to have very much paid holiday, with many companies allowing their workers only ten days or less each year. In addition to this, there are ten public holidays in the country as a whole, which most states recognise; there are some other holidays that only certain states have.
- Shops and many other businesses are open on most public holidays.   *The exceptions are Thanksgiving and Christmas Day*
- Conditions for women with babies are not as good as in other western countries. Paid maternity leave is not usual, although it is possible for a new mother to apply for other payments, such as sick leave, to cover the weeks immediately before and after the birth. Some women have a total of just twelve weeks leave before and after the baby is born, returning to work a couple of months after giving birth.
- Many companies have a range of benefits that their employees can take advantage of. These include health insurance (which is important in a country where there is no national health insurance scheme), additional insurance for dental care or eye care, pension plans, and life insurance.

---

agriculture – *Landwirtschaft*
assembly line – *Fließband*
free enterprise – *freie Marktwirtschaft*
invention – *Erfindung*
labor union (AE) – *Gewerkschaft*

lumber – *Bauholz*
make someone redundant – *jmd. entlassen*
service industry – *Dienstleistungsgewerbe*

Talking about: Working life

5.4 American society

The American people

Population facts and figures

Estimated age structure (2012)

Age	Percentage of population
0 – 14 years	20.1 %
15 – 64 years	66.8 %
65 and over	13.1 %

Source: CIA World Factbook 2012, Washington, DC: Central Intelligence Agency, 2012

- The population of the USA is estimated to rise to nearly 314,000,000 by mid-2012.
- This figure includes an estimated 11.2 million illegal immigrants.
- Although, like in most western countries, people are living longer in the States, the birth rate continues to increase slowly. This, along with immigration, helps to balance out the older population.

The largest group, around 62 %, come from Mexico.

The American middle class

The professional middle class has become the most influential group in the States. There are several reasons for this:

- They have good incomes, and tend to spend them on houses, cars, appliances for their homes and other consumer goods, therefore having a positive effect on the economy.
- Typical professions for this group include business managers, teachers and professors, economists, political scientists, journalists, engineers, doctors, lawyers, architects and writers. These are the sorts of occupations where people have a lot of power to make their own decisions, put their own ideas into action, and to influence public opinion.
- Education is important: middle class parents want good schools and universities so that their children, in turn, can go on to find high-status jobs and continue to live a middle-class lifestyle.
- Because they are one of the strongest groups financially, they have considerable political influence: politicians know that they must listen to the concerns and wishes of this group if they want to be re-elected.

Ethnic background of the population

The ethnic make-up of the USA is rooted in the many waves of immigrants who have settled in the country in the last four centuries (see below). The following table shows the main racial groups in the country today:

Racial ancestry	Percentage of the population
White American (including people from Europe, North Africa, the Middle East, Central Asia and white Hispanics)	79.96 %
Hispanics (of any race)	15.1 %
Black or African American	12.85 %
Asian American	4.43 %
Amerindian and Alaska native	0.97 %
Native Hawaiian or other Pacific Islander	0.18 %
Two or more races	1.61 %

Source: U.S. Census Bureau

- The most common ancestries among people of European descent are:
  - German (19.2 %)
  - Irish (10.8 %)
  - English (7.7 %)
  - Italian (5.6 %) and
  - Scandinavian (3.7 %).
- Although, at the moment, the majority of the population are descendents of white European immigrants, these demographics are changing. It has been estimated that, by 2040, this will no longer be the largest group.
- The fastest-growing minority groups are Hispanics and Asian Americans.

> The indigenous peoples of the USA are also known as Native Americans.

Immigration

The population of the USA is made up of a wide variety of different races. The majority of the people came – and still come today – in the hope of making a better life for themselves in America. However, this ethnic mix also includes the Native Americans, who had already settled throughout the country when the first Europeans came along, and the natives of Africa who were brought against their will to work as slaves.

There have been several waves of immigrants since the first permanent settlements in the early 17th century. The following is an overview:

Date	Main countries of origin
1600–1790	England; Scotland; Ireland; Holland; Germany
1790–1849	Ireland; Germany; Italy; Britain; France; Russia; China; Mexico; South America
1850–1930	Germany; Britain; Ireland; French Canada; Italy; Scandinavia; Poland; Eastern European Jews;
1930 – present	the Philippines; Europe (post World War II, including refugees); Canada; Mexico; Korea; Hungary; Japan; Cuba; Vietnam; Latin America

By far the largest group of immigrants today is from Mexico, followed by Asian countries such as the Philippines, Vietnam and China.

Reasons for immigration

1st group:
- Members of religious groups that had broken away from the mainstream churches in their home country came to escape religious persecution (e.g. the Puritans from England).
- Colonies were settled to grow tobacco.
- Land was cheap and economic conditions were better than at home.

2nd group:
- The Great Famine in Ireland drove the Irish to leave their home country in their thousands.
- There was political instability in other parts of Europe, e.g. during and after the French Revolution.
- In 1849, gold was found in California, which signalled the start of the gold rush, when thousands of people travelled to the newly discovered gold fields in the hope of making their fortune.
- There was the prospect of finding work; others came to join members of their family already living in the States.

Also known as the Potato Famine, this refers to a period from around 1845 to 1852 when a disease called potato blight killed a large number of potato plants throughout Europe. The effects in Ireland were particularly devastating, as, due to many other economic and political factors, a large part of the population lived mainly on potatoes. As a result, the country lost up to 25% of its population through starvation and emigration.

3rd group:
- People came to escape poverty in Europe.
- Between 1880 and 1924, approximately two million Jews emigrated to escape the pogroms in Eastern Europe.
- The Mexican Revolution from 1911–1929 resulted in more than one million refugees entering the USA, although many returned to Mexico in the following decades.
- The economic boom that America underwent in the second half of the 19th century made many people see the country as the land of opportunity – they went there to live the "American Dream".

4th group:
- Most immigrants came to escape war and oppression in their home countries.

5.4 American society

- Jobs were plentiful after the end of the Second World War, when many women who had worked as part of the wartime effort went back to being housewives.
- From 1948, displaced people, especially from Europe, were allowed to immigrate to the States.
- People fleeing from Communist countries (e.g. Hungary, Cuba) were able to move to America.

With its strict anti-Communist stance, the US was very supportive of the victims of Communist regimes.

The "melting pot" theory

The term "melting pot" has often been used to describe the integration process of immigrants in the States. The idea was that the new immigrants would gradually assimilate into life in America by giving up their old lifestyles, thereby helping to form a national identity. This is certainly what Americans in the 18th and 19th centuries desired for their country; this can be seen by the motto "e pluribus unum" ("from many to one"), which is still printed on American coins today.

- This worked fairly well for the first waves of immigrants, up to the mid 19th century, as the majority of them were white, northern European Protestants who could identify with the ideas and values of the Puritan descendents and therefore assimilated well.
- From the mid 19th century, the immigrants came from a far wider range of countries, and as a result assimilation became more difficult.
- American citizens today do, to a certain extent, share a national identity, e.g. with regard to language (over 80% of Americans speak only English at home) and patriotic feelings (there is a sense of national pride that has become more widespread since the terrorist attacks of 11 September 2001).
- However, a large number of people refer to their ethnic or linguistic origins when asked to describe themselves: they are African American, or Irish American, or German American, rather than just "American".
- American social make-up today is often described as the "salad bowl", "mosaic" or "symphony". In other words, it consists of separate parts that make up a whole and work together, yet at the same time keeping their individual identities.

People take interest and pride in their ethnic background. For example, many cities have their own "Octoberfest" run by people with a German background.

Immigration policies

- Until the end of the 19th century, there were no restrictions on immigration to the States. There were plenty of jobs, and ship fares from Europe were cheap enough for almost everybody to afford. Settlers were encouraged, especially after independence, as a higher population would help to establish America as a country in its own right.

▸ Since the end of the 19th century, various laws and policies to control immigration have been introduced:
  – 1882: Chinese Exclusion Act, which was intended to ban Chinese labourers.
  – 1917: All new immigrants were tested to see if they could read and write to restrict the number of unskilled workers.
  – 1921: The Emergency Quota Act limited the number of new immigrants from each nation, depending on how many people from that nation were already living in the country.
  – 1924: The Immigration Act set quotas to further limit immigration, especially of unskilled immigrants, and to ensure that there was an even distribution of different ethnic groups.
  – 1938: America was still suffering through the Great Depression; in addition to this, there was a strong mood of anti-Semitism and fear of foreigners. As a result, the government's immigration policy placed severe restrictions on the number of people allowed to stay in the country, including refugees hoping to flee Nazi Germany.
  – 1948: These restrictions were relaxed for refugees and displaced persons following the Second World War.
  – 1965: The quota system for different nationalities was abolished. Instead, limits were set: 120,000 visas a year for the Western Hemisphere, and 170,000 visas for the Eastern Hemisphere. Visa applications from people with family already resident in the States were additional to these quotas.
  – 1986: The Immigration Reform and Control Act meant that employers could be punished for hiring illegal immigrants. However, this did not stop illegal immigration, as the law is not often enforced and it is easy to produce fake documents.
  – 1990: Total immigration was increased to 700,000 per year, with visas being granted mainly to reunite families or for workers with certain skills that were needed.
  – 1996: Stricter laws expanded the list of criminal activities for which immigrants can be deported. Since then, over one million immigrants have been sent back to their home countries.

Starting with the Wall Street Crash in 1929, this period of economic recession and high unemployment did not really end until America entered the Second World War.

Work was begun on the project, and 640 miles of fencing interspersed with a system of cameras and sensors were set up until the project was cancelled in 2010 due to high costs and technical problems.

Present day issues

▸ Discussions revolve around how best to limit the number of illegal immigrants entering the country. Suggestions have included building a wall or barrier along the whole of the border between the USA and Mexico.

- Some politicians would like to pass laws that allow long-term illegal immigrants to gain legal status in the country. Many of these immigrants have children who were born in the States and attend school there; they protest that the economy of the USA would suffer without people like them who are prepared to do the kinds of dirty, low-paid jobs that many Americans refuse to do.
- Opinion polls have shown that, since the 9/11 attacks, a larger percentage of American citizens support the idea of stricter immigration controls, believing that this would make the country a safer place.

The Civil Rights Movement

The history of black people in the USA is an integral part of the country's social history, and has helped to shape American society as it is today. African Americans first arrived in the country involuntarily as slaves. After the abolition of slavery, they faced decades of oppression and discrimination, which even the Civil Rights Movement could not completely eradicate.

History of slavery and abolition
- 1619–1808: Approximately 300,000 people were shipped from Africa to work as slaves in the USA. They lived mainly in the southern states and worked on the cotton, tobacco and sugar cane plantations. These crops made the plantation owners extremely rich, as well as being major products for export. After 1808, no more slaves were transported to the USA, but many were born in the country.
- 1833: The National Anti-Slavery Society, an abolitionist movement, was founded, although most of its supporters came from the northern states rather than those in the south where large numbers of slaves existed.
- 1865: Slavery was abolished after the American Civil War.
- 1868: The 14th Amendment of the Constitution gave black Americans the status of citizens.
- 1870: All male American citizens were given the right to vote, no matter what their race.

Freedom and discrimination

Although African Americans technically had the same rights as other citizens after the Civil War ended, in practice they had to suffer widespread, often officially approved, discrimination and intimidation, particularly in the southern states.
- Segregation was practised in all walks of life. This was permitted by laws known as "Jim Crow Laws" (1880s); in a famous case brought to

Segregation ranged from separate schools for black and white children to black people not being allowed to eat in the same restaurants or even drink from the same water fountains as whites.

the Supreme Court in 1896, the judges ruled that segregation was not unconstitutional.
- Black people were not allowed to exercise their right to vote.
- They were not given equal access to job opportunities, so they remained poor and dependent.
- They were subjected to acts of violence, both private and within a more organised framework, led by groups such as the Ku Klux Klan.
- From the early 20th century onwards, many African Americans left the southern states in hope of finding a better life in the more liberal northern and western states. To a certain extent, their hopes were realised, but even in these abolitionist areas discrimination was widespread.

The Civil Rights Movement

The 20th century saw the rise of several organisations working to end segregation and ensure equal rights for people of all races. These included:
- The National Association for the Advancement of Colored People (NAACP), founded in 1909, which took several cases of segregation to court.
- The Congress of Racial Equality (CORE), founded in 1942, organised peaceful demonstrations against segregation.
- The Southern Christian Leadership Conference, founded in 1957 by Martin Luther King, Jr., and other black Protestant ministers, used boycotts and peaceful demonstrations to try to end segregation.
- The goal of the "Black Muslims", or Nation of Islam, founded in 1930, was a separate black state within the USA, and not integration. Malcolm X was the best-known representative of this group; he was assassinated in 1965.
- The Black Panther Party, founded in 1966, aimed to end discrimination by violent means.

Key events in the Civil Rights Movement

This protest was highly effective because a large number of black citizens used the buses, and the boycott therefore cost the bus companies a lot of money.

- 1954: The NAACP won a famous court case, Brown v. Board of Education, which ruled that it was illegal to have separate schools for different races.
- 1955: A woman called Rosa Parks refused to give up her seat to white passengers on a public bus in Montgomery, Alabama. She was arrested and convicted for this. In protest, black people boycotted the buses for over a year in Montgomery, until segregation on public buses was lifted.

- 1961: Student volunteers took trips on interstate buses in the south to try and end segregation on public transport: the journeys were known as Freedom Rides.
- 1963: The March on Washington for Jobs and Freedom. Between 200,000 and 500,000 people from throughout the country staged a peaceful protest for civil rights. Martin Luther King made his famous "I have a dream" speech, where he spoke of his hope that one day all Americans would be equal.
- 1965: The Voting Rights Act made it easier for minorities to register to vote.
- 1968: Martin Luther King was assassinated.
- 1970–1976: As a measure to end segregation in schools, white children were taken by bus to schools in black areas, and visa versa.
- 1972: Laws were passed to encourage positive discrimination for ethnic minorities in the field of employment.
- 1984 and 1988: The Reverend Jesse Jackson, a black minister, was nominated as a presidential candidate for the Democratic Party. Although he did not win the nomination battle, he inspired more people from ethnic minorities to play an active role in politics. His son, Jesse Jackson Jr., is a member of the House of Representatives.

African Americans today
- More African Americans are members of national and local governments, notably Colin Powell, who was Secretary of State from 2001 to 2005, and Condoleezza Rice, Secretary of State from 2005.
- Barack Obama (Democrat) is the first African American President (elected in 2008).
- There are far more black celebrities today in the fields of sport, film and music.
- More young African Americans complete high school and college or university, and have better chances of getting a good job. However, the high school drop-out rate among this ethnic group is still high.
- Many black people still live in deprived areas, where unemployment is high, and, especially for young people, it is easy to become involved in criminal activities such as drug dealing or gang membership.
- Prejudice and discrimination is still fairly widespread. One example is the aftermath of Hurricane Katrina, which hit the south-eastern states of the USA in August 2005. The disastrous lack of organisation of evacuation and relief for the affected areas led some people to claim that this was, in part, due to the fact that a large percentage of those affected were black and living in poor areas. They felt that relief would

The same applies to all races living in poverty, of course, but people from ethnic minorities are more likely to be doing so.

have arrived more quickly for a predominantly white area. Whether or not this is true, it illustrates the mistrust and the feelings of "them and us" that still exist for many people today.

Native Americans

It is not known how many Native Americans lived in North America before the first Europeans arrived, but there are likely to have been at least two million. There were hundreds of different tribes, with their own languages and culture, although all believed that they were an integral part of the cycle of nature. The idea of property and ownership of land was foreign to them, which became one of the many reasons for tension between native tribes and the new inhabitants of their country.

The first British settlers would probably all have died in their new country if a friendly local tribe had not helped them. Ironically, because the Indians had shown them how to survive, more and more Europeans were able to settle in the country; in return, the new settlers contributed to the dramatic fall in the number of Native Americans, both accidentally and through deliberate persecution.

The Native Americans and the new settlers
- The Europeans did not respect Native American beliefs and customs; some even tried to convert them to Christianity.
- The Indians had little resistance to European diseases such as smallpox and measles, and often died from them.
- Because many Native American tribes were nomadic, it was easier for the settlers to occupy their land.
- Many tribes were forced to live on reservations, and were not allowed to leave them without permission. The reservations were often in areas that were not particularly good for farming, hunting and fishing. These conditions further weakened the tribes.
- There were wars between the Indians and the white settlers in which many natives were killed.
- Although the government made several treaties with the Native American tribes with regard to land ownership, they were quick to break them if, for example, they wanted to build something on that land.
- Many attempts were made to assimilate them into white society by making it almost impossible for them to continue to live their traditional lifestyles: the long-term result was widespread poverty and depression among them.

However, one famous example of a battle won by the Native Americans was the Battle of Little Bighorn in 1876, where the Americans under General Custer suffered a humiliating defeat.

5.4 American society

- Native Americans were not given American citizenship until 1924.
- It was only in the 1970s that tribes were finally recognised as self-determining associations with the same rights as other ethnic groups.

Native Americans today
- There are approximately 1.8 million registered tribal members in the USA.
- The federal government recognises 563 different tribal governments throughout the country.
- Native Americans still suffer from the long-term negative effects of European occupation, which can, for example, be seen in the fact that large numbers of them suffer from mental health problems, alcoholism and heart disease.
- Many Native American governments get a large part of their income from casinos situated on their reservations. While some tribes feel that using gambling to get revenue conflicts with their traditional culture, others use the money to build up a stronger economy for themselves in order to improve their situation.

Social welfare

Compared to other developed countries, only limited welfare services are available to the poor and needy. There are historical reasons for this: the country was founded by people who believed in the Protestant work ethic, i.e. that everyone is responsible for themselves, and must work hard to gain wealth and a good standard of living. There is the belief that too many welfare benefits from the state discourage people from looking for work and make them dependent. In addition to this, charity is an important aspect of this Protestant mentality: those with money should give part of it for good works. This means, however, that such donations were often made at a more local level, e.g. through a church, with little government interference. It was during the Great Depression that the government realised the need for some form of financial help for people who had fallen on hard times through no fault of their own, and some benefits were made available to the unemployed (see above) and for old-age insurance. However, it is still very much left up to the individual to make sure he or she is covered in case of financial need.

To name one example, many churches run soup kitchens where homeless people can get a free meal.

Healthcare

In 2010, President Obama introduced a new healthcare act to be implemented gradually over 4 years which will, among other things, help the poor to get health insurance.

- The USA does not have a national health insurance system, and it is not compulsory to have health insurance.
- Americans have to take out private health insurance, or have insurance schemes that their employers pay for, either partially or completely. Over 16 % of Americans have no health insurance at all.
- There are two government-funded healthcare programmes for the poor (Medicaid) and for the elderly and some disabled groups (Medicare). However, these systems do not cover all costs, and there has been a decrease in the number of doctors who accept these types of insurance. It can therefore be difficult for those in need to get good medical treatment.
- One reason that costs for medical treatment are so high is the large number of people who sue their doctors or hospitals if something goes wrong. As a result, more is charged for treatment to cover possible legal costs if a patient decides to sue.

Social security

- Most employed and self-employed people pay social security taxes on their earnings.
- These taxes cover retirement, disability, survivorship (benefits for the spouse or children of a worker covered by social security who has died) and death. Unemployment insurance is no longer covered by this scheme.
- Unemployment insurance benefits are available to people who have lost their job, and is based on what that person earned in their last year of employment. Only people who have earned above a certain amount qualify for this benefit.
- Other programmes provide help such as of rent subsidies, healthcare subsidies and food stamps.
- The Temporary Assistance for Needy Families programme, introduced in 1996, gives help to poor families so that their children can be cared for in their own homes rather than having to go into a state institution. Recipients must try to find work as soon as possible, no later than two years after beginning to receive benefits. People on this programme can receive benefits for a maximum of 60 months within their lifetime. The idea is to encourage people to work rather than to accept temporary benefits, and it has reduced the number of people receiving such benefits. Statistics show, however, that the poverty rate in the country as a whole has not really changed.

Social issues

Crime and punishment
- The most common types of crime in the USA are: homicide, rape, robbery, assault, burglary, theft and motor vehicle theft.
- The rate of violent crimes, especially murder and crimes involving guns, is higher than in other developed countries.
- The homicide rate has decreased steadily in the last few years, and is now at a rate of 4.8 victims per 100,000 people.
- African Americans are far more likely to be victims of murder than people of other races: in 2005, nearly half of all murder victims were black.
- Furthermore, 79 % of all homicide victims are male, and in general men are far more likely to become a victim of crime than women.
- Other social factors that play a role are age and financial position: people from poor backgrounds and young people are more likely to suffer from the effects of crime.

> Partly due to the Second Amendment to the Constitution, which states that citizens have the right to keep and bear arms, a large number of people in the US own guns. Illegal gun ownership is also widespread.

The war on drugs
America takes the problem of drug and alcohol abuse very seriously, with severe punishments for drug-related crimes. As well as focussing on the problem at home, the USA tries to put pressure on drug-producing countries (e.g. Peru, Bolivia, Colombia) to prevent drugs from being smuggled into the country in the first place. However, despite tight controls and heavy penalties, statistics show that these measures have not been very effective in cutting drug and alcohol use.

- The best-known historical example of an attempt to control drug use was Prohibition (1920–1933), when alcohol was banned. It is now known that sales of alcohol actually increased during this period, and a black market developed to meet the demand, as a result of which many people became extremely rich.
- The USA has a higher legal drinking age than many other countries: in several states alcohol may only be sold to people aged 21 and over.
- Today the war on drugs tends to focus more on narcotics, especially the possession and sale of marijuana. Almost half of the arrests made for drug crimes are related to marijuana.
- Prison sentences are very common for drug-related crimes, even relatively mild ones, which in turn puts a great deal of pressure on the prison system.
- Many companies now test their employees for drug and alcohol usage; members of staff who fail these tests can be fired.

> This has not, however, significantly reduced underage drinking.

Capital punishment

The USA is one of the 42 countries in the world that still retains and actively uses the death penalty as a means of punishment. The issue is an extremely controversial one, with emotional arguments on both sides. For a time, the death penalty was abolished in the States, but was reinstated in 1976, since which time 1,056 people have been executed.

Death penalty facts

38 of the 50 states have the death penalty on their statute books, although not all of them actively use this option. Some states now have a moratorium on the death penalty, which means that no executions are currently being carried out there. The table below lists the ten states with the highest number of death row inmates. It shows that the ratios between the number of people on death row and the number of people who are actually executed vary from state to state.

State	Number of inmates on death row (2011)	Number of executions (2011)	State	Number of inmates on death row (2011)	Number of executions (2011)
California	719	0	Alabama	205	5
Florida	405	2	North Carolina	165	0
Texas	322	9	Ohio	155	4
Pennsylvania	216	0	Arizona	135	3
Georgia	107	3	Tennessee	89	0

Source: http://deathpenaltyinfo.org

- Due to the complicated appeal procedures, inmates often spend at least ten years on death row before they are executed; some are there for 20 years or more.
- The most common method of execution is the lethal injection, although other methods such as electric chair, gas chamber, hanging and firing squad have also been used.
- Death row inmates are usually kept apart from other prisoners, excluded from educational and employment opportunities within the prison, and are restricted with regard to having visitors and taking exercise, often spending up to 23 hours a day alone in their cells.
- Since 1990, the USA has executed more juvenile offenders (people who were under 18 years old at the time of the crime) than any other country.
- 140 death row inmates have been found innocent and released since 1973, in some cases after spending many years in prison.

The prisoner is first injected with a drug to send him or her to sleep, followed by a drug to paralyse the muscles and then one to stop the heart, leading to death.

The death penalty: for and against

It seems unlikely that the death penalty will be abolished in the USA in the near future, as the pro-death-penalty lobby has strong political influence. However, anti-death-penalty groups also make their voices heard, and often have the support of celebrities, especially in high-profile cases. The main arguments of the two groups are:

Pro:
- Anyone who deliberately kills another person does not deserve to live.
- The families of the victims are comforted by the fact that justice has been done.
- The death penalty acts as a deterrent, and makes society safer.
- Life imprisonment without parole is not a suitable alternative, as laws can change and a convicted murderer may be released on parole after all at a later stage.
- Human beings are not perfect and make mistakes, so it may be possible that a few of the people who have been executed were, in fact, innocent. However, this is balanced out by the thousands of innocent victims that are killed by convicted murderers who were released early from prison; this would not have happened if these murderers had been executed.
- If someone who takes a life is not executed, it implies that the victim's life was not worth very much, because their killer was not fully punished.

Contra:
- All human life is valuable, even that of killers, and the state does not have the right to take someone's life.
- Executing a murderer will not bring the victim back to life; in fact, it means that another family will lose a loved one.
- The death penalty does not act as a deterrent: homicide rates are not lower in countries where this is punishable by death than in countries without capital punishment. A large percentage of violent crimes are committed in rage on the spur of the moment, or under the influence of alcohol and drugs: the offender does not think about the consequences at the time of the crime.
- Life imprisonment without parole is a more suitable punishment, and is cheaper than execution in the long run because of the very expensive legal processes that have to take place before someone is put to death.
- The death penalty is not applied consistently. A convicted murderer is more likely to be sentenced to death if the victim was white rather than from another racial group. Furthermore, there is a financial aspect. Offenders who are able to pay for a first-class legal team are unlikely to be given the death penalty, but many people convicted of murder come from poor backgrounds and cannot afford a good lawyer.

- Some people who have been executed clearly suffered from mental illness, and were therefore not entirely responsible for their actions.
- As long as there is a risk of even one innocent person being executed, the death penalty should be banned.

Homeland Security

It was the worst terrorist attack on mainland USA to date: 3,000 people were killed on that day.

The Department of Homeland Security was established by President George W. Bush shortly after the terrorist attacks of September 11, 2001. The main functions of the department are to protect United States territory from terrorist attacks, and to provide the necessary aid for dealing with natural disasters. It aims to prepare for, prevent and react to emergencies within the US, at its borders and beyond, especially acts of terrorism.

Measures introduced by Homeland Security include a colour-coded, 5-step security alert system that ranges from "green" (low risk) to "red" (severe risk). Depending on the level of the alert, police presence in certain places can be increased, vehicles can be searched, or other security steps can be taken. In addition to this, the department advises citizens on how they can prepare for different kinds of emergencies, including the preparation of emergency survival kits.

The department has come under criticism for several reasons, including:
- The information about possible emergencies makes people unnecessarily anxious.
- The colour-coded system is unreliable, since the general public are not informed about the criteria for the different levels of alert, and therefore cannot know whether the current level of threat is accurate or not.
- The government has been accused of raising the threat level for political reasons, e.g. during elections, so that people will vote for the politicians who seem to take security threats the most seriously.
- The department was accused of incompetence for its delayed reaction to the Hurricane Katrina disaster of 2005.

Talking about: US society

abolitionist – *Sklavereigegner/in*
ancestry – *Herkunft*
assault – *Körperverletzung*
capital punishment – *die Todesstrafe*
to deport – *abschieben*
deprived – *sozial benachteiligt*
deterrent – *Abschreckungsmittel*
displaced people – *Vertriebene*
firing squad – *Exekutionskommando*
food stamps – *Essensmarken*
homicide – *Mord*
lethal injection – *Todesspritze*
narcotics – *Rauschgift*
parole – *vorzeitige Entlassung*
segregation – *Rassentrennung*

5.5 Religion

The majority of people in the USA who claim to have a religious affiliation belong to one of the Christian churches. The main religions represented are as follows:

Religion	Percentage of population	Religion	Percentage of population
Protestant	25.9 %	Buddhist	0.7 %
Roman Catholic	23.9 %	Muslim	0.6 %
Mormon/Church of the Latter-Day Saints	1.7 %	Other or unspecified	2.5 %
Other Christian	1.6 %	Unaffiliated	12.1 %
Jewish	1.7 %	No religion	4 %

Source: CIA World Factbook 2012, Washington, DC: Central Intelligence Agency, 2012

The number of people in the USA who state that they have no religious affiliation has more than doubled in the last 15 years. In contrast, a far larger percentage of the population (53 %) than in other developed countries say that religion is very important in their lives. In addition to this, religion plays a role in politics, even though, according to the Constitution, these two matters should be completely separate.

History of religion in the States

Many of the early settlers in America had left Europe for religious reasons: they were being persecuted for their beliefs and wanted to live in a place where they would be free to practise their religion in the way they wanted to. Signs of these religious foundations can still be seen in American society today.

- 1620: A group that came to be known as the Pilgrim Fathers were Protestant dissenters who had broken with the Church of England. They first moved to Holland, but later decided to start a new colony in North America where they could worship in their own way and maintain their cultural identity. Their ship was called the Mayflower, and their settlement was the Plymouth Colony.
- from 1630: The Puritans were Protestants who aimed to "purify" the Church of England of practises left over from the days before the split with the Roman Catholic Church. They first settled in New England, and then spread throughout the new colonies. They were intolerant of anyone who did not share their religious beliefs, even to the extent of punishing those who did not conform. Since only church members were allowed to become politicians in the colonies under Puritan rule,

There were 102 pilgrims plus crew on board when the Mayflower set sail from England; however, due to disease caught on the journey (which came from living in very cramped conditions for several weeks), more than half of them were dead by the time the ship returned to England, leaving the rest to start a colony.

- they were easily able to impose punishments, at times going as far as to execute dissenters or people belonging to other religions, such as Quakers.
- 1636: Roger Williams, a Puritan leader, was forced to leave Massachusetts because of his disagreements with the colonial government there. As a result, he founded a colony of his own in Rhode Island, based on principles of religious freedom rather than forced worship. Some of these principles, such as the separation of church and state, religious tolerance and freedom of religion, were written into the American Constitution.
- The North American colonies also became a refuge for other religious groups as the 17th century progressed. These included Catholics (in Maryland), Quakers (in Pennsylvania), Jews (in New York City, Rhode Island, and other coastal towns), and various German sects, e.g. Mennonites, who also settled in Pennsylvania.
- The Great Awakening, an early evangelical movement, began in the early 18th century and by the 1730s had spread throughout the American colonies. Huge open-air meetings were held, where influential preachers brought about a revival of religious feeling. There were many conversions, both of slaves and free people, who were regarded as equals. The main groups that supported the Awakening – the Baptists, Methodists and Presbyterians – had become the largest Protestant groups in the country by the early 19th century.
- Religious arguments were used in part to justify the American Revolution: they helped to convince American citizens that, morally, it was right for them to fight for independence from Britain. The defeat of the British led many Americans to believe that God was on their side, and wanted them to create a great, free nation.
- 1791: Religious freedom and the separation of church and state were written into the Bill of Rights.

It can be found in the First Amendment, which states that Congress must not make any laws to establish a particular religion or prevent a particular religion from being practised.

The Puritan Legacy

The American mentality today owes a lot to the country's Puritan beginnings:
- The concept of the "Protestant work ethic", which means hard work and self-discipline that leads to wealth and success, plays an important role in the American business world.
- The Puritans believed that they were very special in God's eyes, and that God had blessed their new country. They therefore felt that they had a moral right to defend their beliefs and way of life.

- In addition to this, they believed strongly in a fair and equal society, and refused to tolerate anyone who did not share their views on what that society should be like. Some people see this way of thinking reflected in certain current political policies: American society is believed to be the best in the world, and anyone who disagrees must be an enemy of the state.
- It was thought that personal wealth was a sign of God's blessing, which is one reason why making lots of money is still seen as important today.
- However, the Puritans believed that part of this money should be given to the needy; Americans are very generous when it comes to works of charity.

Religion and politics

Although constitutionally separate, the influence of certain religious groups on political issues is very strong:

- Except for John F. Kennedy, who was a Catholic, and Barack Obama, who is an African American, all American Presidents have been WASPs (White Anglo-Saxon Protestants). Kennedy's connection to the Catholic Church was seen as a huge disadvantage for many, who thought that he would be too much under the influence of the Pope to govern effectively.
- Certain religious groups, especially extremely conservative, Protestant fundamentalists, have gained considerable influence in the last few decades. They believe in traditional family values, no sex outside of marriage, and the traditional role of the woman in the home.
- They oppose, among other things, homosexuality, abortion, euthanasia and certain kinds of biotechnology, such as human cloning and stem cell research. All of these are current political issues in the US. Additionally, they would welcome prayer in schools and the teaching of creationism on an equal basis to evolution (see above under "Educational issues").
- Since the 1970s groups belonging to the Christian Right have been exerting influence on voters, seeing themselves as hitting back against liberal government policies. They were instrumental in helping the Republicans to win the 2000 election.

Increasingly, many fundamentalists would like to ban contraceptives.

Other churches and sects in the USA
Sects
- 1830: The Church of Jesus Christ of Latter-Day Saints, or the Mormons, was founded by Joseph Smith. After widespread persecution in other parts of the country, members of the church settled in Utah, where a high percentage of the population is still Mormon today.
- 1872: The Jehovah's Witnesses were founded; their influence has since spread throughout the world.

Black churches
- The earliest of these date back to the 19th century, and were founded by African Americans as a place where they were free to worship, as they were often made to feel unwelcome in other churches. One example is the African Methodist Episcopal Church.
- Black churches played a significant role in the Civil Rights Movement: for example, Martin Luther King was a minister.

Muslims in the USA
- There are an estimated six to seven million Muslims in the USA, most of whom are well integrated in American life. A large percentage of them have a university degree and a professional career where they earn a good salary.
- Some Muslim organisations work closely with the government to give advice about US policy in Afghanistan and Iraq. Others work with the community to promote tolerance and understanding between Muslims and non-Muslims.
- Most Muslim organisations in the States emphasize their moderate standpoint, and condemn any form of violence or terrorism. However, suspicion and mistrust of anything connected to Islam has grown since the attacks of September 11, and there are greater fears of acts of terrorism from possible Muslim extremists living in the country.

American Muslims say that they have to face greater discrimination and stereotyping since the attacks, while often experiencing other people's ignorance with regard to Islam.

Talking about: Religion

dissenter – *der Nonkonformist*
to presecute – *verfolgen*
to purify – *reinigen*
to worship – *eine Religion ausüben*

5.6 Foreign affairs

Isolationism and intervention

Since the early 20th century, the USA has been involved in numerous international incidents and conflicts. This was not always the case. After gaining independence from Britain, America distanced itself from international politics, concentrating on expanding its territories within North America.

The land to the west of the original 13 colonies was not part of the United States at first, but was gradually purchased over time.

The Monroe Doctrine of 1823 formed the basis of American foreign policy for many years that followed. Fearing that France and Spain would try to regain control of their former colonies in Latin America, President Monroe drew up the following doctrine:
- Europeans must not colonise any part of the American continent.
- The USA will not involve itself in European affairs, as long as there is no threat to American rights.
- Any attempts to colonise the continent will be seen as a hostile act towards the United States which will be dealt with appropriately.

However, by the end of the 19th century, America had become an economic power, and wanted to establish foreign trade partners for the export of goods. The country was also beginning to intervene in foreign affairs:
- 1904: The Roosevelt Corollary, an amendment to the Monroe Doctrine drawn up by President Theodore Roosevelt, put an end to the USA's political isolationism. It stated that the USA had a duty to intervene in politically and financially unstable countries on the American continent, in order to protect them from the threat of Colonisation.
- Another aspect of US interventionism has been so-called "dollar diplomacy". By investing in foreign countries, particularly in Latin America and Asia, the USA has been able to influence the politics in these places to suit its own economic purposes.
- There are several states that, at least for a time, became overseas territories of or were annexed to the USA. These include:
  - Puerto Rico (1898–1952), which is still a US commonwealth country
  - Cuba (1899–1902; 1906–1909); Guantánamo Bay is still controlled by the American army.

One example of this was support for Panama's battle for independence from Colombia in return for being allowed to build the Panama Canal – a vital trade link between east and west – and to control the Canal Zone.

First World War

In keeping with their policy of non-interference in European affairs, the USA did not enter World War I until a very late stage, although President Wilson offered to help negotiate a peaceful solution. However, in 1917, when it came to light that Germany had asked Mexico to enter the war as their ally, the United States declared war on Austria-Hungary.

After the war, the USA helped to draw up the Treaty of Versailles, but decided not to join the League of Nations that was founded at the time, believing that they should once again keep out of European affairs.

Second World War

- Again, the USA did not enter the war until a later stage, in this case after the Japanese bombed Pearl Harbor in 1941.
- In 1945, America dropped the world's first atomic bombs on targets in Japan, which effectively signalled the end of the war but the start of a new era, both of warfare and of world politics.

On the cities of Hiroshima and Nagasaki

Post World War II

When the war was over, the USA and the USSR emerged as the two new world superpowers. Much of US foreign policy in the years that followed focussed on trying to prevent the spread of communism.

- The Marshall Plan of 1947 meant that money was pumped into Europe, both in order to help rebuild the war-torn countries and to keep as much of Europe as possible a western, capitalist democracy. The USSR, however, wanted the countries under its jurisdiction to remain communist. Consequently, an economic, political and ideological barrier known as the Iron Curtain divided Europe until the 1990s.
- In 1949, the North Atlantic Treaty Organisation (NATO) was founded as an alliance of nations who would support each other if one of the members was under military attack.
- The American military took part in several conflicts throughout the world in order to fight communism:
  – the Korean War (1950 – 1953)
  – the Vietnam War (1959 – 1973)
  – the Cuban Missile Crisis (1961)

NATO's initial member states were the United States, Canada, the United Kingdom, France, Belgium, Luxembourg, the Netherlands, Norway, Italy, Portugal, Denmark and Iceland.

The end of the Cold War

The Cold War, which lasted from the end of the 1940s to the late 1980s, was a time when the USA and the USSR did their best to outdo each other in terms of military supremacy and nuclear armament. It was the real fear of nuclear war that finally brought the two sides to the negotiating table. They met several times during the 1970s and 1980s, and gradually agreed to reduce the number of nuclear missiles available to them. The agreements reached between the two superpowers made a major contribution to the fall of the Iron Curtain in 1989.

Since the mid-1990s, Russia has been a US ally. However, the potential for disagreement and conflict remain.

The war on terrorism

9/11 and the aftermath

On September 11, 2001, Islamic extremists carried out four more or less simultaneous suicide attacks. They hijacked four domestic flights; two of the planes were flown into the World Trade Center in New York City, one into the Pentagon, and one crashed in the Pennsylvania countryside. Most of the dead were either civilians or members of the emergency services.

- The reactions in the USA immediately after the attacks were those of shock that the country was not invulnerable to terrorist attacks on their own soil, gratitude and support for the members of the emergency services and the general public who risked their lives to save others, and a surge in displays of patriotism.
- The popularity ratings for President Bush rose dramatically.
- Most of the world expressed sympathy and support for the USA in the wake of this disaster.
- Several conspiracy theories arose, including claims that the US government had known about the attacks beforehand but did nothing to stop them, or that it even played a role in planning the attacks in order to have an excuse to take military action in the Middle East.

For example, sales of American flags soared.

US response

President Bush declared a war on terrorism that was to take place on an international scale. This took several forms:

- Homeland security and the US Patriot Act were introduced to prepare for, detect and prevent acts of terrorism.
- Military action was taken: 2001–2002 in Afghanistan – an attempt to defeat the Taliban and the Al Qaeda leader Osama bin Laden, who were thought to have been behind the 9/11 attacks; 2003–2011: the occupation of Iraq, to overthrow Saddam Hussein, who was also suspected of involvement in the attacks and was thought to have weapons of mass destruction intended for use against the West.

After years as one of America's most wanted criminals, Bin Laden was captured and killed by a US special forces unit in 2011 in Pakistan.

Saddam Hussein was captured in December 2003 and held as a prisoner of war by the Americans. He was handed over for trial to the interim Iraqi government the following year, who executed him in December 2006.

Points of controversy

Several points of criticism have been made about US policies following the 9/11 attacks, both at home and abroad:

- There have been serious infringements of civil liberties since the attacks, for example giving the authorities the right to secretly listen to phone calls and read e-mails between people in the US and abroad.
- Since no evidence of weapons of mass destruction was found in Iraq, the war there was unjustified.
- US troops have been in Iraq for too long and should withdraw.
- Several prisoners who are described as "enemy combatants" in the field of international terrorism are being held at the Guantánamo Bay prison in Cuba. Some of these people have been there since 2002. The prisoners have not been tried for any crimes, and there have also been allegations of torture. Several prisoners have gone on hunger strike, or attempted or committed suicide. It is difficult for them to have contact to a lawyer or to their families. In June 2006, the Supreme Court ruled that these prisoners must be given a fair trial. Some of the prisoners have been or will be released without being charged; some of those remaining are to face trial. At the beginning of 2009, President Obama signed orders to close the Guantanamo Bay prison within a year; however, as of early 2012, these orders had not yet been carried out.

Nevertheless, for the time being the US government stands by its anti-terrorism policies and international activities in this field as being the best way to fight the international terrorist threat.

US foreign affairs	conspiracy theory – *Verschwörungstheorie* intervention – *Einschreiten* isolationism – *Isolationspolitik* negotiating table – *Verhandlungstisch*	nuclear armament – *Atomrüstung* weapons of mass destruction – *Massenvernichtungswaffen*

Überblick

Die USA ist heute in vieler Hinsicht einer der mächtigsten Staaten der Welt. Dort getroffene Entscheidungen können andere Staaten nachhaltig beeinflussen, was wiederum ein Grund dafür ist, dass die Präsidentschaftswahlen der USA weltweites Interesse genießen. Einerseits ist die USA einer der modernsten Staaten, andererseits wundert sich die Welt gelegentlich über „Altmodisches", beispielsweise bei der Entscheidung einiger Staaten, im Unterricht den Schwerpunkt eher auf die Schöpfungsgeschichte als auf die Tatsachen der Evolution zu legen. Unter anderem aufgrund dieser Doppelgesichtigkeit bleiben die USA ein Faszinosum.

Focus on world issues – Globalisation   6

Die Globalisierung ist eines der Hauptthemen der Gegenwart, nicht nur, weil so viele Bereiche des Lebens davon betroffen sind. Es ist ein kontroverses Thema, da die Globalisierung gute Seiten hat – aber eben auch (teils heftige) Schattenseiten.
Dieses Kapitel liefert Informationen und Vokabular, um Texte zu „globalisation" verstehen zu können – aber auch, um Essays und „comments" rund um dieses Thema erarbeiten zu können.

6.1 What is globalisation?

Globalisation means that many aspects of life, such as economy and business issues, environmental issues, culture and people, are connected throughout the world. It is sometimes easy to forget that this is not a new phenomenon. On the contrary, throughout the ages people have always been interested in discovering new places and adopting the ideas that they found there, as well as bringing their own culture to those places.

globalisation (BE) – globalization (AE)

- The Ancient Greeks and Romans conquered large parts of the known world, spreading their culture throughout the places they invaded. For example, in Britain the Romans built roads and introduced technologies such as central heating in the home. Luxury goods such as wine and olive oil were also imported, although only the rich could afford them.
- The Silk Road was a collection of ancient trade routes that, at its height, connected the east coast of China, Indonesia, India, Persia, Iran, eastern Africa and Europe. Both land and sea routes were used to transport goods such as silk and other expensive fabrics, spices, perfumes and jewels, to name just a few. In addition to this, it helped to bring different kinds of technology to other parts of the world, and to spread religious and philosophical ideas from the varied societies along the way.

Trading along this route began in around 206 BC.

- The Islamic Golden Age (approx. 750 AD to 1257 AD) was a time when Islamic civilisation spread throughout northern Africa, the Arabian states and western Asia. Once again, art, philosophy, science, architecture and technology of all kinds were able to spread. For example, the hajj, the traditional pilgrimage to Mecca that Muslims are required to make, became a central place where people from a large variety of places were able to come together to exchange ideas and trade goods, as well as pray.

- Starting in the late 15th century, European explorers began to discover the wider world. Most of these explorers came from Portugal, Spain, Holland and Britain, and travelled many hundreds of thousands of miles by ship, often with the aim of discovering or establishing new trade routes. When they returned to Europe, they brought many things with them that were unknown in their home countries: different types of food and plants, animals and precious metals. *Two examples are tomatoes and potatoes* Some of the colonies established as a result of these voyages also produced goods for export to the Old World, notably tobacco and cotton. There were, of course, downsides to this: for example, colonisation also helped to spread diseases to which the native populations had no immunity. Moreover, the trade that took place between the old world and the new included the slave trade, where large numbers of Africans were sold and transported across the Atlantic Ocean to work as slaves in the Caribbean and, later, in the southern states of America.

- The Industrial Revolution can perhaps be seen as the beginning of modern globalisation. It first took off in Britain during the 19th century, when the number of factories dramatically increased, allowing the mass production of goods. Britain imported raw materials from its colonies around the world and exported the goods it produced, making it the world's first economic superpower. In America, industrialisation took a little longer to arrive, but once it had taken hold, the country soon outstripped the rest of the world with regard to manufacturing. *It was discovered that the country had a plentiful supply of coal, gas and iron, for example.* By the end of the 19th century, as a result of inexpensive raw materials, natural resources and a seemingly endless supply of cheap labour in the form of immigrants, the USA had become the new global superpower.

6.2 Globalisation today

Nowadays the world is connected in many different ways. Economic issues are just one aspect of this. In fact, globalisation now exists on a scale that would have been difficult to imagine even a few decades ago. The growth of global communications alone – through the internet and cheap, speedy phone connections via satellite, to name just two examples – has changed the way we live. International travel has become faster and easier, as has, in many cases, migration between different countries. The following discusses some important features of globalisation in more detail.

The role of the internet: global communication

Of all the global phenomena to have arisen in the last few decades, the internet is perhaps the one to have had the most dramatic effect on our everyday lives. It would not be going too far to say that life without it would be inconceivable, as it is now so deeply integrated into even ordinary activities. The internet, and therefore the World Wide Web that contains the world's websites, are now accessible nearly everywhere in the world and, thanks to technologies such as smart phones and wireless internet access, we can go online more or less any time and anywhere we wish. The advantages and disadvantages of the internet are always an interesting talking point: the information below summarises frequently discussed aspects of the internet, with examples of arguments for and against each point.

Availability of information

- *Pros:* The World Wide Web contains information on almost every subject that exists. Not everything is easy to find, but, in most cases, search engines enable users to track down the information they need.
  The internet has become a library that is accessible to everybody. There are online dictionaries and encyclopaedias, such as Wikipedia, that everybody can consult, but also contribute to. These resources often contain forums, where people can ask questions and get input from others.
- *Cons:* Naturally, websites also exist on subjects that most people do not want to see, or would not want their children to have access to, such as pornography or right-wing extremist sites. While it is possible for parents to use filtering or blocking software to control what can be viewed on a personal computer, the websites are still out there and older children or teenagers may be able to surf more freely at a friend's house, for example.

There is no guarantee that all of the information found online is accurate. If searching for information for an essay or project, for example, it is important to check more than one source.

- *Pros:* The internet helps people. They can look things up quickly and find the solution to all kinds of problems, saving time and money. For example, someone having trouble with an electrical appliance, or needing to solve a computer problem, can look up the answer online and find information on how to fix the problem themselves rather than taking it to be repaired. People also commonly search for advice on medical issues, perhaps to avoid going to the doctor's or to look for reassurance about symptoms they are suffering.
- *Cons:* Not all information found on the internet is accurate or reliable. It can be dangerous if, for example, somebody searches for information about a medical problem and works out a diagnosis for symptoms they have instead of going to see a doctor, or relies on the information provided by other people.

> Students should also beware of simply downloading and copying material they find online to use in their own essays, as they may be infringing another person's copyright.

The online community

- *Pros:* Many people enjoy being part of an online community where they can talk about a shared interest. Some of these communities also take the form of support groups, for example for people suffering from certain medical conditions. One advantage over a "real-life" support group is that online forums are available at all times, which means that members will always have someone to "talk" to. In addition to this, they can share their experiences with a much wider range of people and get fast answers to their questions. Some people find it helpful to be able to talk to others who understand their situation while remaining anonymous.
- *Cons:* Some people may come to rely too much on the advice given in forums rather than consulting a professional.

The convenience factor

- *Pros:* The internet allows people to shop, pay bills, do their banking and similar everyday activities from the comfort of their own home, at any hour of the day. The convenience of this is obvious: they are completely flexible as they are not tied to the opening hours of shops and other facilities. Goods are delivered to the door, an added bonus for people who work long hours, or who are perhaps unable to leave their homes due to old age or illness.

- *Cons:* There is the problem of security, especially when entering bank or credit card details onto a website. Despite security measures, websites can be hacked, giving victims an unpleasant surprise when they check their bank account or credit card statement.

The working world

- *Pros:* The internet has revolutionised the way we work. For many jobs, it is no longer necessary to sit in an office all day every day, as the work can be done from another location. It is also far easier for professionals working in a particular field to exchange knowledge and ideas without having to travel.
- *Cons:* Many people complain that working life is more stressful nowadays than in the past. Technologies such as e-mail and mobile phones mean that employees are always available, even outside working hours or when on holiday in some cases. It is often expected that e-mails should be answered immediately, increasing the pressure on workers.

The role of bloggers

- *Pros:* Far from being a passive medium, the internet is a source to which everybody can contribute. One very common way to do so is through blogging. While some blogs are merely personal, an online diary of their author's life and opinions intended mainly for friends and family, others reach a far wider audience, with hundreds of thousands of clicks per day. It can certainly be an effective way of getting a message across. Political bloggers, for example, can provide important information and comment on current situations. In countries with repressive regimes, such as China, blogging is often seen as a real threat to the state and is subject to censorship. Governments in countries like this are naturally afraid that a true picture of the political and social situation there will become known in the wider world. Therefore the internet makes it easier for people living in such regimes to practice freedom of speech.
- *Cons:* As mentioned above, some governments censor internet use in an attempt to stop bloggers from spreading information that they do not wish to be made public. In extreme cases, bloggers may even be arrested and imprisoned.

The term "blog" is a short form of "web log", a log being another word for a diary or journal.

Social media

- *Pros:* Social media connects people, allowing them to communicate easily. Friends and family can share news, photos and any items of interest that they come across. Users can join various groups connected to their interests and hobbies. For many people, social media sites are a hobby in themselves – they enjoy spending time surfing, posting and chatting to friends in their free time. In addition to this, sites such as Facebook or Twitter can be a good medium for promoting, for example, an event or cause, as a large number of people can be reached within a short space of time.

  Some networking sites are intended to be used in a work context, and allow users to link up with others working in their field, for example. Such sites play an increasingly important role today, in times of high unemployment, as networking can be an effective way of getting a job.

  In recent years, social media has also played a political role. During the "Arab Spring" of 2011, civil unrest that had started in Tunisia and Egypt spread through North Africa and the Middle East as more and more people took to the streets to express their dissatisfaction with their government. The successful organisation of these protests is put down in part to use of digital media. Facebook was used to arrange when the protests would take place, which were then coordinated through Twitter. Afterwards, those who had been there uploaded films they had taken with digital cameras and phones onto the internet, so that the rest of the world could see what was going on. This in turn had two results: it was impossible for the governments concerned to lie about what had happened, and citizens of other countries with similar regimes were inspired to take to the streets, too. Although it cannot be claimed that social media directly brought down the governments in these countries, it is clear that it will have an increasingly important role to play in places where authoritarian governments try to control and repress their citizens. Protests can be arranged during elections, making it more difficult for them to be rigged; corruption and human rights violations can be made public.

- *Cons:* Security settings are extremely important for anyone using social media sites. Users need to ensure that only certain people are permitted to view their profile. It is easy to be anonymous on the internet, and for people to disguise who they really are. It is therefore essential to think carefully about what kind of personal details can be viewed by the general public. Moreover, there are now employers, for example in America, who check up on the social media pages belonging to people who have applied for a job in their company. Depending on the kind of information they find there, they may well decide not to employ the person after all.

People nowadays, especially young people, have far less personal contact with their friends, spending their time chatting to them digitally rather than face to face.

The problem of cyberbullying (see below) is also connected to social media sites.

Cyber-bullying

Bullying is something that, unfortunately, has always existed in schools and among young people in particular. There always have been, and probably always will be, people who think it is all right to pick on others who they see as being different or weak in some way. In recent years, however, the internet, especially online chat rooms and social networking sites such as Facebook, have added a new dimension to this. It is now possible to make unkind or even threatening comments about someone else that will be seen, more or less instantly, by hundreds of other people. They may in turn add their own comments, or forward the original to others, spreading the message further. There is little that the victim of the bullying can do to stop this. It is often not clear to those commenting on the original post that they are helping to bully someone, as they may simply see it as a joke or a harmless bit of teasing. However, as in the case of all bullying, whether done online or not, the victim may not find it easy to laugh it off. In extreme cases, the victim may suffer from anxiety, depression, or even be driven to suicide.

Other negative points:

- Since there is no central governing body for the internet, online security will always be a problem. Hackers can manage to crack the most complicated codes, and there is the threat of identity theft.
- Computer viruses can be spread, for example through spam mails.

Other positive points:

- E-mail, e-learning, e-business: the internet makes many forms of everyday communication easier and more convenient.
- Programs such as Skype bring people together, making it possible to talk to friends and family "face to face", even if they live on the opposite side of the world.

6.3 Globalisation and the economy

The growth of international trade has affected the economies of most countries in the world. There will, of course, always be winners and losers as a result of this; more often than not, the economies of the developed world are the winners, whereas developing countries, being more vulnerable to exploitation, frequently lose out.

Working conditions

There is a considerable contrast between working conditions in the developed world and developing world, differences that many Western companies have been able to take advantage of:

Working conditions in developed countries:

- Workers have fixed weekly working hours.
- Many of these countries have a minimum wage.
- Most allow workers to form and join trade unions.
- Workers can go on strike to protest against unfair conditions or low pay.
- In most Western countries it is usually not possible to fire an employee with immediate effect: a period of notice must be given.
- Most have industrial tribunals, where employees can, for example, appeal if they feel they have been fired from their job for unfair or illegal reasons.
- Women usually have the right to paid maternity leave, although the amount of money they receive and for how many weeks varies.
- In some countries, such as Germany, women have the right to return to their job within a fixed period of time after being on maternity leave.
- An increasing number of countries allow fathers to take paternity leave.
- Conditions in offices and factories have to comply with certain safety standards.
- Some form of unemployment benefit is normally available, although, again, the amount and the period for which it is paid varies greatly from country to country.
- Employees are entitled to paid holiday and sick leave.
- Companies in many countries have to pay health insurance contributions for their employees or, for example in the USA, offer their employees health insurance packages.

Despite these generally positive factors, working conditions in the West are not always perfect:
- Whenever there is a recession, people fear for their jobs.
- Fewer low-skilled and unskilled jobs exist nowadays. This can, for example, be due to the use of technically sophisticated machinery that can perform tasks previously done by hand, or that can complete the work so quickly that fewer employees are necessary.
- Many companies have closed down some or all of their factories in developed countries and relocated production to places where they can manufacture their goods more cheaply (see below).
- It can be difficult for working parents, particularly mothers, to find a good "work/life balance". Many mothers need or want to work, yet would also like to spend quality time as with their family. A possible solution to this problem is the option of working part-time or job-sharing. However, not all companies allow this, and there are many part-time jobs that are unskilled and badly paid. Mothers who stay at home for a few years to look after their children may find it difficult to return to work, or at least to their former position. This is especially true if they had a highly skilled profession.

Working conditions in developing countries

The priority of most companies is to make a profit. To do so, they need to manufacture their products as cost-effectively as possible, and one way of doing this is to transfer some or all of their production overseas. For European companies, "overseas" can mean Eastern Europe or parts of Asia such as China or Vietnam. In the USA, many goods are likewise made in Asia, while others are produced south of the border, in Mexico or beyond. The advantages for the companies that do this are clear: they can increase their profits by producing their goods in countries where factory rental, amenities such as electricity and, most important of all, wages are lower than in their home country. However, the other side to this coin is that the working conditions in many of these countries are anything but ideal. This applies particularly to companies in so-called "export processing zones".

Export processing zones, or EPZs, are industrial parks in developing counties such as China where export goods are mass-produced. Foreign companies are often given tax breaks and other benefits to encourage them to set up business there.

- Employees are often expected to work long hours with just one short break.
- They are paid low wages that are barely enough to live off. In some cases, money may be deducted from their wages to pay for social security contributions, although the workers themselves do not necessarily benefit from these.

- Workers often have to meet targets, i.e. they have to complete a certain amount of work within a given time. If they do not manage this, they may have to work even longer hours until they have finished. This overtime is unpaid.
- The conditions inside the factories are often unhealthy and dangerous: the air becomes very hot because of the machines that are in constant use combined with poor ventilation.
- Proper safety clothing and equipment is often not provided.
- Sick pay and unemployment benefit frequently does not exist.
- Trade unions are often forbidden, so workers have no official way of protesting about their conditions.
- In areas with high unemployment, it is easy to find staff for these factories. Women are seen as ideal workers, e.g. in clothing factories, because they are easier to manipulate and less likely to complain about low pay.
- In extreme cases, teenagers or even children have to work in factories instead of going to school like their contemporaries in developed countries. Often, they come from large families that urgently need money.
- It is difficult for workers to negotiate better conditions for themselves, as they often do not have any real rights. If they are seen as causing trouble, they can be fired and other workers taken on to replace them.
- In some countries, such as Thailand or Bangladesh, there have been cases of people being arrested or even attacked for campaigning for better conditions for factory workers. In other cases, companies may decide to move their factory to another area or another country if workers demand their rights too strongly. As a result, many people, desperate for a job, accept the terrible working conditions to avoid losing their only source of income.

These conditions are a consequence of globalisation. Because the global economy enables companies to manufacture goods anywhere in the world, there is strong competition among governments to offer incentives, such as cheap utilities and cheap labour, to encourage foreign companies to set up business there. For the governments, this means additional sources of employment and foreign investment coming into the country. Logically, it is the workers at the bottom of the chain who will suffer the most. Clothing manufacturers tend to be among the worst culprits here.

What can be done?

One positive effect of globalisation is that it is more difficult for companies to hide the way in which they produce their goods. Media reports inform consumers about these practices making them think about the origins of the goods they buy. It is also easier to raise awareness using the internet. There are groups such as the Clean Clothes Campaign, which works to let people know how clothes and sportswear are produced. Such groups speak to companies and governments, lobbying them to improve conditions and stop worker exploitation. Furthermore, they offer support to workers and help them to fight for their rights.

Education of consumers in developed countries is essential if the situation is to be improved. These consumers are used to choosing from a wide range of goods at a low price. As long as there is demand for cheap goods, manufacturers will continue to produce them. However, it is possible to bring about changes by letting people know the true cost of their cheap T-shirt from Vietnam. If enough customers boycott companies whose clothes have been made in sweatshops, for example, the companies will have to rethink their policies if they want to win those customers back.

> There are many more such groups, including the SweatFree Communities, which works against sweatshops (www.sweatfree.org) or Women Working Worldwide (www.women-ww.org).

Fair trade products

One way to ensure that workers are paid a fair wage for goods they have made or food they have grown is to choose products with the Fair Trade label. Moreover, this is becoming increasingly easy to do, as more and more companies are switching to fair trade ingredients and materials for the manufacture of their products. To name just one example, Cadbury's, Britain's most famous chocolate company and one of the largest chocolate manufacturers in the world, now uses fair trade cocoa beans to make some of their best-selling chocolate bars. This decision supports cocoa farmers in countries like Ghana, allowing them to grow the beans sustainably.

What does fair trade mean?

- Fair trade products are ones that guarantee higher prices, good working conditions, local sustainability and trade on fair terms for workers and farmers in developing countries. Companies that buy fair trade goods have to agree to pay no less than the market price. This is different from the way trade, especially with developing countries, usually works. In order to produce as cheaply as possible, many companies impose conditions that take advantage of the weakest producers, making it difficult for them to break out of the cycle of poverty.
- Farmers working for fair trade organisations, however, are in control of their working conditions. They are paid sustainable prices for their products, so they can cover their costs and actually live off the money they earn.

More detailed information on this subject can be found at www.fairtrade.org.uk

- Fair trade associations can make money available for investment in social, enviromental and economic development projects.
- Some producers need money before they can produce their goods, for example farmers may need to buy fertilizer or seeds before they can begin growing. Fair trade organisations make it possible for them to get the money they need, which they can then repay when they start earning from the sale of their products.
- Fair trade allows long-term trading partnerships to be established in which all parties have a say in the way business is done.

The market for fair trade products has grown considerably in recent years. On the one hand, consumers are more aware of the conditions under which, for example, food is produced, and want to support farmers in developing countries. Purchase decisions of this kind help consumers to feel good about what they are buying. Likewise, many companies have discovered the power of the green dollar, knowing that fair trade products will attract a certain type of customer; this encourages them to use fair trade ingredients and materials in their goods. Nowadays all major supermarket chains carry a range of ethically sourced products. In addition to this, several food outlets use fair trade ingredients. For example, there are some coffee chains that offer coffee made with fair trade beans.

The "green dollar" means money that is spent on environmentally sound products and services. In Britain we can also talk about the "green pound".

The Celtic Tiger

Between 1995 and 2007 the Irish economy underwent a boom that was as dramatic as it was unexpected. This period of affluence came to be known as the "Celtic Tiger": Celtic after the country's native inhabitants, the Celts, and Tiger because Ireland was suddenly such a powerful force on the economic stage. Before the boom, Ireland had been one of the poorest countries in Europe, receiving a lot of financial support from the European Union. This aid was certainly a factor in the boom, as money was invested in education and infrastructure paving the way for companies to become more productive: workers were better educated and improved infrastructure and communications made Ireland a more attractive place to set up business. In addition to this, the state offered subsidies to international businesses to encourage them to come to Ireland. Several high-tech companies took up this offer, attracted by these and other incentives such as lower wages in comparison with much of Western Europe and lower tax rates.

>>

The economic boom had several consequences. One was that Ireland now became one of the wealthiest countries in Europe. People had far more disposable income, and spent their money on consumer goods, cars, second homes on the west coast and much more. Money was invested in improving cities and transport services. Many people who had emigrated from Ireland returned as it had now become an attractive place to work. In addition to this, immigrants from other parts of Europe started to arrive, particularly from the Baltic States and Poland, who worked in retail or in the lower-paid parts of the service sector. This was, of course, an interesting turn-around, as Ireland had long been a country that people left to find work rather than one that offered attractive job opportunities to foreigners. Many young Irish people living in the countryside moved to the cities to take advantage of the jobs on offer there.

In 2001 and 2002, there was a global economic which also negatively affected the Irish economy. Other factors such as the 9/11 terrorist attacks had a negative effect on the tourist industry, on which Ireland, despite the high-tech boom, still heavily relied. Moreover, Irish workers were now being paid higher salaries, which meant that several companies relocated their production lines to cheaper places such as Asia. However, after 2003, Ireland enjoyed another, albeit slower, period of economic growth. Tourism recovered, and more high-tech companies set up factories in the country, e. g. for manufacturing personal computers.

In the long term, however, Ireland was unable to maintain its competitive edge, and, like much of the rest of the world, once again slid into recession. Among other factors, professional salaries had become too high for the country to remain attractive for many businesses, while at the same time wages for unskilled and manufacturing jobs were lower than the European average, creating a two-class society. Unemployment has risen steeply, the property market has collapsed and, once again, the Irish government has had to look to the EU for financial aid. The Celtic Tiger is no longer a strong player in the global economy.

>> **The Celtic Tiger**

Your disposable income is the money you have left to spend after income tax has been paid.

6.4 Migration

A further effect of globalisation is that it has greatly increased the mobility of workers. Naturally, the concept of people leaving their home country to look for better job opportunities abroad is nothing new. For example, the idea of the "American dream" has inspired people from around the world to immigrate to the USA, hoping to make a good life for themselves in the country where nothing seems impossible. Canada and Australia have also long been popular destinations. Now, in the 21st century, moving abroad for work can be both easier and more difficult than in the past, depending on the circumstances:

For more details on the USA and immigration, see chapter 5.

- European Union nationals have the right to live and work in other EU countries without a work permit or visa. They can apply for any jobs advertised in the country of their choice, although their language skills and other qualifications will of course be taken into consideration.
- Thanks to the internet, it is easy to search for and apply for jobs in other countries. Many jobs are advertised online, either directly through the company or in the job search section of newspapers. In addition to this, there are a huge number of online recruitment sites where people can search for jobs at home and abroad. Some also allow job seekers to post their CV on the site to be viewed by prospective employers.
- Many countries have a lack of skilled workers in certain fields, for example in computer technology, and make up for this lack by offering highly qualified professionals from abroad incentives to come and work there for a certain period of time.
- Whereas some people choose to move abroad to work, for example in order to experience life in a different culture, others are driven more by economic necessity: if there are no jobs and no prospects in their native country, they often look elsewhere for a place to earn a living.
- However, unskilled jobs are more and more difficult to find in developed countries, due to technological developments that have enabled companies to cut back on workers, and due to the global recession, which means that fewer people are being taken on.
- Seasonal work, such as fruit picking, is often done by migrant workers, as they can be paid a lower wage than average and do not have to be offered a permanent job. It is common, for example, for workers from Eastern Europe to travel to Western Europe to do seasonal work, or for Mexicans to work as fruit pickers in California.

▶ Some people, driven to extreme measures by the desperate economic situation in their home country, go to dangerous lengths to emigrate to a country where they think they will have a better chance of getting work. For example, refugees from Africa undertake the perilous journey by boat across the Mediterranean Sea to southern Europe. Frequently, the boats run into difficulties when the sea turns rough, and many of the potential immigrants never make it, but drown or die in the terrible conditions on the overcrowded boat.

Another example are the many Mexicans who illegally cross the border to the USA. There are estimated to be at least 2 million illegal immigrants in California alone, many of whom are doing unskilled, low-paid jobs.

The global economy makes it easier and more attractive for highly qualified professionals to work abroad. They can take advantage of job opportunities in industry and commerce, or take up an academic post at a foreign university or college. For example, many specialists have left Western Europe for positions in the USA, attracted by higher salaries. The top American universities also appeal to academics due to their high-quality research facilities.

Brain drain

This can, however, become a problem when large numbers of highly skilled workers leave a country. In order to remain competitive, every country needs enough people with the right kind of professional skills and technical know-how, and the economy of the country suffers if this is not the case. This is the meaning of the term "brain drain": the best brain power is "drained" away and disappears. As well as the attractions of better pay and conditions, there are other reasons why such people leave their home countries. For example, when Eastern European countries such as Poland joined the European Union, for the first time scientists had the opportunity to look for jobs in the West, and many of them did so, although many returned later when Poland's economy became stronger. Likewise, at least half a million Russian computer scientists and other academics left the country after the collapse of the Soviet Union in 1991. Albania has been experiencing a similar brain drain since the fall of Communism there. Countries in the European Union that are not doing well economically, such as Greece, Spain and Portugal, are also seeing a significant increase in emigration, as people look for ways to escape the growing unemployment and provide financial security for themselves and their families. The flip side of the coin is, of course, that these highly educated people are necessary to help rebuild the country's economy and help it out of its recession.

>>

>> **Brain drain**

The "green card" is the document that allows foreigners to live and work permanently in the United States.

To make up for the loss of their own scientists, countries suffering from brain drain need to encourage others to come. In the European Union, for example, there is a so-called "blue card" scheme, similar to the American green card, which aims to attract skilled professionals from Asia, Latin America and Africa to come and work there. Partly as a result of this, there are now a large number of computer programmers from India working in Europe, to name just one example. When this happens, it is often referred to as a "brain gain". This is good for the economy of the host country, but can of course result in brain drain in other countries.

In addition to this, a further problem can arise when highly skilled workers immigrate to another country, for example if they have come as refugees or asylum seekers. Although they may have a high-level academic qualification, this may well not be recognised by their host country. As a result, they are not allowed to practise their profession in their new country, or are expected to gain additional qualifications before they can do so. Many are unable to get these qualifications (perhaps because it is too expensive for them to do so), and so are forced to do jobs that are far below their skills. For instance, somebody who had been a doctor in their home country in Africa might have to resort to working as a cleaner in Europe. This situation is known as "brain waste": the skills are available, but the host country does not make use of them.

6.5 Globalisation and environmental issues

It goes without saying that globalisation must have a significant effect on the ecology of our planet. We are able to travel far more freely than 100 years ago, and are no longer satisfied with local food and products: we want to be able to choose from goods originating from distant parts of the world, and to have them available at all times. This has been going on for a long time, and the damage to the earth has been considerable. However, people are slowly starting to rethink their behaviour and to consider what can be done to reverse some of these negative effects.

A planet on the move

Human beings love to travel, and increasing numbers of us can afford to do so. Air travel has become far cheaper, and the majority of adults in developed countries own a car. As a result, we need more and more fossil fuels to keep us mobile, using up the world's natural resources in the process. In addition to this, our planes and cars add to the pollution levels that so many of our activities cause, which in turn contributes to global warming.

Flying

- Nowadays more people travel by plane than ever before. Budget airlines encourage short trips both for business and pleasure, and the increasing popularity of exotic holiday destinations has contributed significantly to the increase in long-haul flights.
- Although planes nowadays have new technologies that allow them to use fuel more efficiently, and biofuels have been developed for aircraft use, the problem of pollution remains because of the increase in passenger numbers and freight transported by air.
- Some airlines now offer passengers the option to offset their carbon footprint when booking a flight. Passengers can pay an additional fee, and the money is used for carbon offset schemes, such as tree-planting initiatives. However, since the extra charge is voluntary, it is easy to choose not to pay it.
- As the volume of air travel continues to rise, many airports feel the need to expand, for example by building an additional runway, to cope with the higher number of flights. This in turn has an additional impact on the environment. On the one hand, part of the countryside has to be destroyed in order to build the runway and the necessary additional infrastructure, which in turn affects the natural habitats of animals and

> There were an estimated 2.75 billion air passengers in 2011.

plants in the area. Then there is the impact on the people living near the airport. An additional runway means an increase in air traffic, and therefore in noise and pollution. This is the reason that, whenever an airport proposes the building of a new runway, there are strong protests from local residents and environmental groups, which always delay any such plans, sometimes considerably, even if the airport expansion does often go ahead in the end. Those responsible for giving these building plans the go-ahead, for example politicians, will always weigh up the environmental issues against the economic benefits and often decide in favour of expansion for this reason.

Economic benefits include the creation of new jobs, and larger numbers of tourists and business people visiting the region.

- It seems unlikely that flying will become less popular any time soon. There are some things that can be done to reduce the need to fly, particularly for work reasons: as video conferencing technology improves, companies can be encourage to hold meetings with customers and staff in different locations online, rather than everyone flying to meet in one place. Another suggestion is to scrap frequent flyer programmes so that people have less incentive to fly more often to gain air miles that they can then exchange for a free flight. Reductions in flight numbers could also be made if more people could be encouraged to go on holiday in their home country, and to travel to their destination by train. However, it would be surprising if such measures had a significant effect on the number of people travelling by plane. Moreover, the amount of international freight being transported by air is unlikely to decrease, as it is so much faster than the alternative methods of shipping.

Cars

For many people in the western world, life without a car would be unimaginable. In North America they are perhaps most popular of all, with people even getting into their cars to travel what seems like ridiculously short distances of a few hundred metres. As with planes, our love of the motor car has considerable impact on our world.

- Carbon dioxide emissions from car exhaust fumes have added considerably to the amount of air pollution, which in its turn contributes to the greenhouse effect and therefore global warming.
- In some places, particularly in rural areas, it is becoming increasingly difficult to live without a car due to the lack of alternative means of transport. Bus and train services are often infrequent or non-existent, leaving residents with no choice but to drive wherever they need to go. In many cases, families need two cars so that parents can get to work, as well as taking their children to their activities, do their shopping ...

- However, car manufacturers have recognised the importance of producing vehicles that are more energy-efficient and can run on cleaner fuels. New models of cars have better fuel consumption and are fitted with catalytic converters to reduce exhaust fumes.
- There are an increasing number of hybrid cars on the market. These are vehicles with more than one source of power, for example an electric motor and an engine that runs on petrol. The idea is that the car should mainly run on electricity, which is of course a far cleaner source of power, but with a much smaller petrol tank as a back-up. Car manufacturers are working on developing the technology which will result in all-electric cars capable of driving long distances.
- To reduce pollution, many cities in Germany now have environmental green zones. Only cars with a low emission value can drive into these zones, and must be marked with a green environmental badge. In other countries, measures are taken to reduce the amount of fine dust from car exhausts in certain places. For example, London has a Congestion Charge Zone: vehicles have to pay a fee to drive into this area. The idea is to reduce the amount of traffic in central London which, in turn, reduces the amount of pollution being caused by these vehicles.

Climate change

The term 'climate change' is often used as a synonym for 'global warming', i.e. the fact that the average temperature of our planet has been rising over time and continues to do so. This is, of course, not the first time this has happened. In the course of the billions of years of earth's existence, the overall temperature has risen and fallen several times, causing ice ages followed by more temperate periods. In fact, we still live in an ice age today, with 10 % of the surface of the planet under ice, and icy, snowy winters in many parts of the world. It is natural for the Earth's temperature to rise after an ice age; the problem this time is the fact that human activities are contributing to the higher temperatures, making them rise more quickly. Climate change also has natural causes, such as the flow of water in the world's oceans, changes in solar radiation that reach the earth, plate tectonics or volcanic eruptions. This is one reason why there are people who do not believe that global warming is caused by human behaviour. They argue that temperatures will rise anyway, as they have in the past, and will then probably begin to fall again at some date in the future. Clearly, there are several factors that play a role in these changes, but there is enough evidence to suggest that human activities are the most significant of these. What is worse, it may be impossible to undo most of the damage we have done.

Human activities contributing to global warming

- The burning of fossil fuels (e.g. for vehicles and manufacturing purposes) has increased the amount of greenhouse gases in the atmosphere, which in turn make temperatures rise.
- Making significant changes to the surface of the planet, e.g. by wide-scale cutting down of forests. To name one example, the rainforests of Brazil are far smaller now as compared to a few decades ago, as they have been cut down to make way for farming or to provide wood for commercial activities. Trees play an important role in absorbing the greenhouse gas CO_2, so, clearly, if there are fewer trees, more of this gas can escape into the atmosphere.
- The use of aerosols and appliances containing CFC gases, such as fridges. These gases have been shown to considerably damage the ozone layer, which is needed to protect the planet from dangerous rays from the sun.

> CFC stands for chlorofluorocarbon, an organic compound of carbon, chlorine and fluorine.

Consequences of global warming

- A considerable amount of the world's ice will melt (e.g. the ice caps at the north and south poles, the Greenland and Antarctic Ice Sheets), causing sea levels to rise. This in turn will cause more flooding in lowland areas.
- Some parts of the globe will become far hotter, especially in the northern hemisphere. There will be more heat waves, and rainfall is likely to become far heavier than now, again leading to an increase in flooding.
- Higher levels of CO_2 and warmer temperatures will negatively affect certain ecosystems, leading to many species of plants and animals becoming extinct.
- People living in coastal areas will be far more vulnerable to flooding.
- The rising sea levels will threaten small islands in particular, making it difficult or impossible for people to continue to live there. Countries such as the Maldives would be affected in this way.
- The amount of clean water available will be reduced, which in turn will have a negative effect on the health of many groups of people.
- There will be a reduction in the amount of crops that can be grown, particularly in developing countries such as India. At the same time, the population in these countries is expected to rise dramatically. The result is likely to be a rise in diseases connected to malnutrition, as well as more famines.

> The crops that will be affected are the basis of many people's diets: rice, millet and maize.

What can be done to reduce the effects of global warming?

- In order to reduce the amount of fossil fuel used around the world, ways of using alternative energy sources more effectively will have to be found (see below).
- By reducing the amount of energy we use, we can reduce the amount of energy that is wasted. This is an area in which each individual can make a small contribution: we can switch off electrical appliances when they are not in use, and insulate our homes to make sure that heat does not escape.
- We can make a conscious choice to use our cars less, or not to travel by plane. Using public transport, going by bike or car-pooling may be options, at least some of the time.
- We can use renewable fuels in our vehicles.
- Reforestation: trees can be planted to replace those that have been cut down using sustainable forest management. Many such forests exist, and it is possible to buy paper products made from wood pulp that is certified as coming from a sustainable source.
- We can recycle our waste and choose recycled products. We can also reduce the amount of waste we create in the first place (e.g. by avoiding products that come with a large amount of packaging). This reduces greenhouses gases released by manufacturing and waste disposal.
- We can buy appliances, e.g. washing machines that are more energy-efficient, as newer models tend to be.
- We can turn down the heating in our homes by a couple of degrees.
- New buildings can be designed to be energy-efficient, using renewable energy sources for heating and electricity.
- Town planners can make urban development more energy-efficient, which in turn provides a better quality of life for the citizens (for example when pollution levels are reduced). Among other things, this can be achieved by ensuring that there are enough parks and green spaces, planning the location of amenities such as shops so that there is less need to travel long distances to reach them, or to travel to them by car. Public transport infrastructure can be improved, and it can be made less attractive (e.g. through expensive parking options) to drive private cars into the city centre. Safe cycle paths can be provided, and it can be made more pleasant to walk (e.g. by building wide pavements).
- Regarding transport, more freight could be transported by rail rather than by road or air. Public transport must be made more attractive to use, and could be run on biofuels or be powered by electricity.

> To "car-pool" means to share a car with one or more other people making the same journey.

However, individuals can clearly only do so much. In order to significantly counteract the effects of global warming, it is important that changes are also made at a national and international level, i.e. all governments around the world should be responsible for this world-wide problem. Some international agreements have been made to this end. For example there is the Kyoto Protocol, which has been signed and ratified by 191 states. The signatories are committed to reducing greenhouse emissions caused by certain gases, as well as making other changes to improve the overall situation. Unfortunately, many countries have failed to meet their agreed targets and, although they can be fined for doing so, cannot be forced to make the necessary changes. The USA, one of the greatest producers of greenhouse gases in the west, signed but did not ratify the protocol. Economics play a significant role here. Large companies have a strong lobby, especially in countries such as the USA, and they put pressure on the government not to pass laws that will force them to change the way they work, especially if it will cost them more. In addition to this, fuel, e.g. for cars, is far cheaper in the US as compared with most of the rest of the world, and people are not prepared to pay more, despite the fact that reducing emissions would mean cleaner air for everybody. It seems that it will remain difficult to reduce global warming on an international scale.

The Kyoto Protocol was agreed in December 1997 and came into force in February 2005.

Alternative energy sources

There are several reasons why it is becoming increasingly important to look for alternative sources of energy: fossil fuels such as oil and gas pollute the environment, are expensive and, in the case of oil and petroleum, are becoming more difficult to extract, which will drive the prices still higher. In addition to this, nuclear power, which is used as an energy source in many countries, is extremely dangerous if there is an accident that allows radiation to escape from the power station.

Several alternative energy sources – also referred to as renewable energy – are available, and their use is growing all the time.

A recent example of this was the earthquake in Japan in March 2011, which damaged five nuclear reactors.

- Wind power: "wind farms" are created in areas with high and more constant wind speeds. Such areas are typically found at high altitudes or offshore. The air currents turn wind turbines, creating energy that is converted into electricity.
- Solar power: the sun's rays are collected in solar panels. This technology can also be used for individual buildings and private homes. Solar panels are installed on the roof, and can be used to heat the building.
- Hydropower: the energy in flowing water is used to make electricity. This can be done by building a large hydroelectric dam, although the flow of some rivers can also be used, without the need of a dam.

- Biomass: energy is created by burning plant material. The plants have absorbed the sun's energy while growing, which is released when they are burnt. It is important to ensure that only the amount of biomass needed is grown so that this energy source remains sustainable.
- Biofuel: biofuels come from biomass, and can be solid, liquid or gas. To name one example, bioethanol is a type of alcohol made from sugar and starch crops (such as sugarcane, wheat and corn). It can be used as an alternative to petrol for vehicles.
- Geothermal energy: the heat that comes from beneath the surface of the earth (e.g. the same energy that heats natural hot springs) can be harnessed and used to generate electricity.

The use of renewable energy can make a considerable difference to life in developing countries. Particularly in rural areas, it is not possible for households to be connected to a supply of electricity as we know it. However, small solar panels can be installed in villages, providing lighting and heat for cooking at half the price of kerosene, which was commonly used as the only option in such places. There are also other positive effects. If power is available, it is possible for people to start up a business and earn money. In addition to this, options for education improve, as schools can be provided with electricity.

Food: global versus local

Increasingly, people are thinking more about where their food comes from. In the past, when the economy of all countries was based on agriculture, all food was locally grown, often by each individual family. Nowadays, both exotic and "ordinary" food is available throughout the world and, often, throughout the year. Pineapples and melons are flown in from South America, lamb from New Zealand, grapes from South Africa. Strawberries from Spain are available to buy long before the fruit is ready on local fields in northern Europe. As with consumer goods, people love having such a wide choice of products, all easily available at the local supermarket.

However, the matter of "food miles" also needs to be considered here. The term means the distance that food has to travel from its source, i.e. the place in which it was grown, to the consumer. With regard to the environmental impact of food transportation, the method of transportation also needs to be taken into consideration, in other words, whether the products are being transported a short distance by road or flown in from the other side of the world. These issues are the impulse behind campaigns to encourage consumers to buy locally grown food, seasonal fruit and vegetables, and meat products from local sources. This seems to make good sense, as food is seen as being healthier for being in season when it is eaten, and better for not having travelled hundreds or even thousands of miles, and. This is certainly true of meat, as buying locally means that the animals have not be transported live, under cruel or stressful conditions. Shopping locally also helps to support local businesses and maintain local jobs rather than supporting large, anonymous companies.

The situation is not, however, as clear-cut as it may seem. Although, as discussed above, air and road transportation adds to greenhouse emissions, in the case of food the largest part of these emissions are caused by the actual food production itself. For example, farm animals – for meat and dairy products – cause up to 30 % of the greenhouse gas emissions throughout the world. In general, more greenhouse gases are released into the atmosphere during food cultivation and production than during transportation. Certain types of fertilizers, for example, give off a considerable amount of greenhouse gas. It also depends on the conditions in which animals are kept. Those that can eat fresh grass straight from the field all year round can be kept in a more energy-efficient way than those that have to be fed on additional food brought in from elsewhere.

6.6 Globalisation and local character

Talking about: World issues

aerosol – *die Sprühdose*
anxiety – *das Angstgefühl*
brain drain – *die Abwanderung hochqualifizierter Arbeitskräfte*
to bully someone – *jemanden schikanieren, einschüchtern, mobben*
carbon footprint – *der CO_2-Fußabdruck*
catalytic converter – *der Katalysator*
child labour – *die Kinderarbeit*
competition – *die Konkurrenz*
consumer – *der Verbraucher*
controversial – *umstritten*
culprit – *der Übeltäter*
CV [= curriculum vitae (BE); resume (AE)] – *der Lebenslauf*
cyberbullying – *das Cyber-Mobbing*
downturn – *die Konjunkturabschwächung*
exhaust fumes – *die Abgase*
exploitation – *die Ausbeutung*
fossil fuels – *fossile Brennstoffe*
freight – *die Fracht*
greenhouse gases – *die Treibhausgase*
incentive – *der Anreiz*
industrial tribunal – *das Arbeitsgericht*
long-haul flight – *der Langstreckenflug*
national – *(hier) Staatsangehörige/r*
to offset – *etwas ausgleichen*
to pick on someone – *jemanden hänseln*
plate tectonics – *die Plattentektonik*
purchase decision – *die Kaufentscheidung*
to rig something (e. g. an election) – *manipulieren*
to be on sick leave – *krankgeschrieben sein*
sustainable – *nachhaltig*
sweat shop – *der Ausbeuterbetrieb*
trade route – *der Handelsweg*
trade union – *die Gewerkschaft*
ventilation – *die Belüftung*
violation – *der Missbrauch*

6.6 Globalisation and local character

An additional effect of globalisation is that it can take away some of the local character of a city, because of the wider availability of all kinds of goods and because several shops and restaurants now have branches throughout the world. To name just one example, it used to be the case that, if you travelled around Europe and went to supermarkets in different places, the chocolate and other confectionery on offer was different in each country. It was interesting to be able to try something new, or to take back something unusual as a gift. Today you are likely to find the same products wherever you go, with perhaps a few local specialities.

However, even more obvious than this is the fact that certain fast-food and coffee chains can be found everywhere you go. In most major cities, there is no need to try something local and unfamiliar; you can simply eat in the same restaurant as you are used to at home. Some cities, for example in former Eastern Bloc countries, see the arrival of such international chains as a confirmation that they have international appeal. They were also regarded as a chance to sample a western lifestyle: in fact, the McDonald's restaurant in Pushkin Square, Moscow, is the busiest in the world.

Restaurants like McDonald's are now a symbol of globalisation. They are instantly recognisable and customers know what to expect. The price of a Big Mac is even used by some economists to demonstrate the relative cost of living in different parts of the world. A comparison like this is possible because almost everyone knows what a Big Mac is, and has an approximate idea of what it costs.

> Die Globalisierung beziehungsweise deren Folgen sind so allgegenwärtig und alltäglich, dass man über deren „Manifestationen" gar nicht mehr nachdenkt. Beispielsweise benutzt ein hoher Anteil der Bevölkerung das Internet, ohne sich bewusst zu machen, dass diese Form der Kommunikation und Informationsverbreitung ein globales Phänomen ist. Die Weltwirtschaft ist durch internationalen Handel verbunden, was sowohl positive als auch negative Konsequenzen hat. Im Ganzen betrachtet sieht es so aus, als würden die Industriestaaten mehr durch Globalisierung profitieren als die Entwicklungsländer. „Globalisierte" Kommunikation bedeutet aber auch, dass man über viele Vorgänge auf dem Globus besser Bescheid weiß. So können Menschen sich Informationen beschaffen, um Entscheidungen zu treffen, die andere unterstützen, zum Beispiel, indem sie fair gehandelten Produkte den Vorzug geben. Globalisierung birgt die Chance zu globaler Solidariät.

7 Kurze Literaturgeschichte: Großbritannien und USA

Literatur entsteht stets aus einem Kontext heraus.
Bei der Lektüre hilft deswegen eine solide Kenntnis derjenigen Umstände, welche die Autoren bei der Schreibarbeit umgeben haben.
Dieses Kapitel soll Ihnen ein Überblick über die Entwicklung der englischen Literatur im Laufe der letzten 1400 Jahre ermöglichen.

Zum **literarischen Kontext** gehören ganz unterschiedliche Bereiche: Sprache, Kultur, Genre-Traditionen, Buchmarkt, politisches Klima, ethnische Zugehörigkeit, Religion oder Geschlechterrollen. All diese Bereiche unterliegen einem historischen Wandel, der sowohl das einzelne Werk betrifft als auch, unter Umständen, von diesem selbst aktiv beeinflusst werden kann. So hat sicherlich für die Frauenrechts- oder Bürgerrechtsbewegung die entsprechende Literatur mit dazu beigetragen, ein Bewusstsein in der Bevölkerung zu schaffen, das den jeweilgen Reformbewegungen zusätzliche Dynamik verlieh.

Auch für die Gegenwart gilt, dass die Bereiche Literatur und Realität keineswegs getrennt voneinander existieren. So zeigt sich beispielsweise in der literarischen Beschäftigung mit der politischen Vergangenheit Deutschlands, dem kolonialen Erbe Englands oder der Rassenpolitik in den USA, dass der historische und der literarische Prozess sich gegenseitig bedingen.

Im Einzelfall kann von literarischen Texten sogar ein Impuls für gesellschaftlichen Wandel ausgehen: So hat Upton Sinclair mit *The Jungle* (1906) zur Veränderung der Lebensverhältnisse der Bevölkerung von Chicago direkt beigetragen. Während die sprachlichen und landeskundlichen Gegebenheiten der Britischen Inseln und der Vereinigten Staaten auf den Seiten 38 bis 112 behandelt werden, soll dieser Teil in die literarischen Traditionen einführen. Kapitel 8 liefert darauf aufbauend einige grundsätzliche Hilfestellungen zur Kunst der literarischen Interpretation. Den Anfang macht jedoch hier ein knapper Überblick über die Entwicklung der englischen Literatur im Laufe der letzten 1400 Jahre.

7.1 Tabellarischer Überblick

Epoche	Zeitraum	Beispiele	Kontext
Altenglisch (Old English)	450 n. Chr. – 11. JHdt.	Beowulf	Einfluss der Angelsachsen
Mittelenglisch (Middle English)	11. Jhdt. – 14. Jhdt.	Canterbury Tales	französischer Einfluss durch Normannen
Utopie	Renaissance	Utopia (Thomas Morus)	Humanisten betonen und verbreiten die antike Bildung und Gelehrsamkeit.
Englisches Sonett	14. Jhdt.	William Shakespeare, Henry Howard	Schwerpunkt Liebesthematik
Elisabethanisches Drama	16. Jhdt.	William Shakespeare, Christopher Marlowe, Ben Johnson	Theater für alle Bevölkerungsschichten
Restaurationskomödie	17. Jhdt.	– The Country Wife (William Wycherly) – The Rover (Aphra Behn – erste weibliche Literatin)	Reaktion auf puritanisches England; unter Einfluss Karl II (Restaurationszeit)
Metaphysische Lyrik (metaphysical poetry)	17. Jhdt.	John Donne	hohe Komplexität und Dichte durch Metaphern (conceit)
Höfische Dichtung (cavalier poetry)	17. Jhdt.	Paradise Lost (John Milton)	von klassischen Formen geprägt, repräsentiert aber weltliche, fast hedonistische Lebensauffassung
Prosa-Allegorie	17. Jhdt.	The Pilgrim's Progress (John Bunyan)	Meilenstein in der Entwicklung des Romans
Romances	17. Jhdt.	Oroonoko (Aphra Behn)	fantastische Romanzen um die höfische Liebe
Englischer Roman (novel) Briefroman Bildungsroman Abenteuerroman Gesellschaftskritischer Roman Metafiktionaler Roman	18. Jhdt	– Robinson Crusoe (Daniel Defoe) – Pamela or Virtue Rewarded (Samuel Richardson) – Joseph Andrews (Henry Fielding) – Gulliver's Travel (Jonathan Swift) – Tristram Shandy (Laurence Stern)	Sprache lehnt sich an das gesprochene Englisch an; bürgerliches Interesse an realistischen Themen aus eigenem Lebensumfeld.
Romantik	18. Jhdt.	– The Rape of the Lock (Alexander Pope) – Seasons (Alexander Thomas) – Lyrical Ballads (William Woodsworth & Samuel Coleridge)	Neue lyrische Form, in der die strenge Metrik aufgegeben wird und ein anderes Medium für dichterische Sprache entdeckt wird.
Amerikanische Literatur	18. Jhdt.	– Common Sense (Thomas Paine) – Autobiography (Benjamin Franklin) – Letters from an American Farmer (J. Hector St Jean de Crevecoeur)	Formung des amerikanischen Bewusstseins durch Literatur
Amerikanischer Roman	18. Jhdt.	– The Power of Sympathy (William Hill Browns)	Gilt als erster amerikanischer Roman.

7.1 Tabellarischer Überblick

Epoche	Zeitraum	Beispiele	Kontext
Spätromantik	19. Jhdt.	– *Ode on an Grecian Urn* (John Keats) – *Child Harold's Pilgrimage* (Lord Byron) – *Ode to the West, The cloud* (Percey Shelley)	
Schauerroman (gothic novel)		– *The Castle Otranto* (Horace Walpole) – *Frankenstein* (Mary Shelley)	Als Gegentendenz zur Aufklärung widmet sich der Schauerroman dem Unerklärlichen und dem Verbotenen.
Der weibliche Roman		– *Pride and Prejudice* (Jane Austen) – *The Mill on the Floss* (George Elliot) – *Jane Eyre* (Charlotte Bronte) – *Wuthering Heights* (Emily Bronte) – *Agnes Grey* (Anne Bronte)	zunehmende Thematisierung der Situation der Frau
Realismus	19. Jhdt. (2. Hälfte)	– *Oliver Twist* (Charles Dickens) – *Mary Barton* (Elizabeth Gaskell)	Gegenreaktion zur Romantik und literarische Verdeutlichung der Lebensumstände des Industrieproletariats
Utopische und dystopische Romane	Spätes 19. Jhdt bis ins 20. Jhdt.	– *News from Nowhere* (William Morris) – *Time Machine* (H. G. Wells) – *Brave New World* (Aldrous Huxley) – *1984* (George Orwell)	fiktive Auswege aus der Lebenskrise aber auch kritische Hinterfragung der technisch orientierten Lösungen in Science-Fiction-Werken
Nonsense-Dichtung	19. Jhdt.	– *Alice's Adventures in Wonderland* (Lewis Carrol)	Abkehr von der Realität, diese Form der Dichtung etabliert sich zur britischen Spezialität.
Gesellschaftskritische Romane	19. Jhdt.	– *Tess of the d'Urbervilles* (Thomas Hardy) – *Heart of Darkness* (Joseph Conrad)	Auseinandersetzung mit dem Wandel der Geschlechterrollen und dem Verhältnis des Empire zu seinen Kolonien
Ästhetizismus	19. Jhdt.	– *The Picture of Dorian Grey* (Oscar Wilde)	Suche nach dem Sinn der Kunst in der Schönheit, Symbolcharakter der Sprache, Endzeitstimmung
Historischer Roman (Amerika)	19. Jhdt.	– *Lederstrumpf*-Romane (Fenimore Cooper) – *Uncle Tom's Cabin* (Harriet Beecher Stowe) – *The Adventures of Huckleberry Finn* (Mark Twain)	Rassismus der Europäer und Entrechtung der Ureinwohner wird thematisiert.
Hochphase der amerikanischen Literatur	19. Jhdt. (Mitte)	– *Leaves of Grass*, Lyric (Walt Whitman) – *Moby Dick* (Hermann Melville) – *The Scarlett Letter* (Nathaniel Hawthorne) – *Walden*, Prosa (Henry David Thoreau)	literarische Behandlung der Naturlandschaften Amerikas sowie des intuitiven und individuellen Erlebens der Natur Konflikt mit den Naturgewalten
Transzendentalismus		– Ralph Waldo Emerson – Emily Dickinson – Henry James	erste Andeutungen der Moderne

Epoche	Zeitraum	Beispiele	Kontext
Moderne (High Modernism)	20. Jhdt.	– *Ulysses* (James Joyce) – *Mrs. Dalloway* (Virgina Woolf)	stärkere Fokussierung auf die Innenwelt der Romanfiguren durch Bewusstseinsströme und innere Monologe
Feministische afro-amerikanische Erzählung		– *Her Eyes Were Watching* (Zora Neal Hurston)	
Irische Literatur		– *At Swim-Two-Birds* (Flann O'Briens)	
Englisches Drama		– *Mrs Warren's Profession* (G. B. Shaw)	neue Impulse für das Englische Drama z. B. durch deutliche politische Stellungnahme
Amerikanisches Drama		– *Death of a Salesman* (Arthur Miller)	Probleme der amerikanischen Mittelschicht werden thematisiert.
Lyrik der Moderne		– *The Second Coming* (William Butler Yeats) – *The Love Song of J. Alfred Prufrock* (T.S.Eliot) – *In a Station of the Metro* (Ezra Pound)	Urbane Anonymität, der innere Zerfall als moderne Befindlichkeit werden thematisiert.
Postmoderne Der englischsprachige Nachkriegsroman	20. Jhdt.	– *The Golden Notebook* (Doris Lessing) – *Bloody Chamber* (Angela Carter) – *The House of Doctor Dee* (Peter Ackroyd)	Verlust des Glaubens an sinnstiftende (Lebens-)Einheit als zentrales Element; neue Auseinandersetzung mit der (Literatur-)Geschichte; spielerisch-ironische Einstellung zu Literatur und Wirklichkeit
Ironisierung des Viktorianischen Romans		– *The French Lieutenant's Woman* (John Fowle) – *White Noise* (Don DeLillo) – *Life after God* (Douglas Coupland)	Thematisieren den inneren Zerfall der (amerikanischen) postmodernen Gesellschaft
Nordamerikanische englische Literatur		– *Desert Solitaire* (Edward Abbey) – *Pilgrim at Tinker Creek* (Annie Dillard) – *The Handmaid's Tale* (Margaret Atwood)	inspiriert durch die Naturlandschaft Nordamerikas
Postmodernes Drama		– *Amadeus* (Peter Shaffer) – *Rosencrantz and Guildenstern are dead* (Tom Stoppard)	befasst sich mit der Frage, wie eine historische Erinnerung entsteht; Selbst- und Fremdbestimmung
Postkoloniale Literatur	20. Jhdt.	– *Midnight's Children* (Salman Rushdie) – *The God of Small Things* (Arundhati Roy) – *Omeros* (Derek Walcott)	Autoren aus den ehemaligen Kolonien und Migraten werden zu zentralen Autoren, „The Empire writes back" als Ausdruck für ehemals unterworfene Kulturen, die nun ihre literarische Stimme erheben.
Anglophone afrikanische Literatur		– *Things Fall Apart* (Chinua Achebe) – *The Whale Rider* (Witi Ihimaera) – *My Beautiful Laundrette* (Hanif Kureishi)	Tendenz, die Heterogenität einer Gesellschaft auszudrücken, steht im Vordergrund
Englische Gesellschaftsstudien in Romanform		– *The Remains of the Day* (Kazuo Ishiguro) – *Brick Lane* (Monika Ali) – *The Color Purple* (Alice Walker)	Portraits von Menschen in Großstädten, die aufgrund ihrer Abstammung, Klassenzugehörigkeit oder sexuellen Orientierung am Rande der Gesellschaft leben müssen.
Amerikanische Gesellschaftsstudien in Romanform		– *Beloved* (Toni Morrison) – *The Woman Warrior* (Maxine Hong Kingston) – *Love Medicine* (Louise Erdrich) – *Green Grass, Running Water* (Thomas King)	Fragen nach persönlichen, ethnischen aber auch nationalen Identitäten stehen im Vordergrund. Thematisierung der Problematik der Integration von Menschen mit Migrationshintergrund.

7.2 Alt- und Mittelenglisch

Nach dem Abzug der Römer um das Jahr 400 n. Chr. können sich die keltisch sprechenden Einwohner der britischen Inseln nur kurz ihrer politischen (und linguistischen) Freiheit erfreuen. Schon sehr bald, um 450, müssen sie sich mit den verstärkt anlandenden Angeln, Sachsen und Jüten auseinandersetzen. Deren Zuwanderung bringt germanische Dialekte in das spätere England; bis ins 11. Jahrhundert bleiben die Angelsachsen linguistisch betrachtet die vorherrschende Volksgruppe. Ihre Sprache bezeichnet man als **Altenglisch** (Old English). Einer der wichtigsten überlieferten Texte aus dieser Zeit ist das Heldenepos *Beowulf*, das zwischen dem 6. und 8. Jahrhundert entsteht. Ursprünglich wohl mündlich überliefert, findet das Werk um das Jahr 1000 eine schriftliche Form.

Das sprachliche Umfeld der „Engländer" ändert sich grundlegend mit der Ankunft des Normannenkönigs Wilhelm (*William the Conqueror*), der aus Nordfrankreich kommend ab 1066 England zu einem **französisch sprechenden** Herrschaftsgebiet macht. Da Englisch für offizielle Anlässe keine Verwendung mehr findet, sondern „nur" noch von der allgemeinen Bevölkerung gesprochen wird, verwandelt es sich in relativ kurzer Zeit in sehr starker Weise: Ist das Altenglische noch eine typische germanische Sprache, mit all den dazugehörigen Flexionsformen, Höflichkeitspronomina und Syntaxvorgaben, so entsteht nun eine neue Sprachform, die man **Mittelenglisch** (Middle English) nennt. Sie zeichnet sich außer durch die stark vereinfachten Endungen auch durch einen hohen Zuwachs an französischen Lehnwörtern aus. Diese Bereitschaft, fremde Wörter in die eigene Sprache aufzunehmen, trägt noch heute dazu bei, dass das Englische einen sehr großen Wortschatz hat.

Trotz der historischen Distanz lässt sich die mittelenglische Literatur relativ gut lesen. Einer der berühmtesten Texte aus dieser Zeit, die sonst vor allem Rittererzählungen hervorbringt, ist *The Canterbury Tales* (ca. 1386). Der Autor, Geoffrey Chaucer, schreibt bis zu seinem Tod im Jahre 1400 an dem Werk, das sich aus einem Prolog und 24 Erzählungen der unterschiedlichen Pilger zusammensetzt, die auf dem Weg zur Wallfahrtsstätte Canterbury sind.

7.3 Renaissance und 16. Jahrhundert

Der Epochenbegriff der Renaissance, die das lange „dunkle" Mittelalter (Dark Age) ablöst, bezeichnet die Wiedergeburt oder Rückbesinnung auf die griechisch-römische Antike. Die technischen Entwicklungen in der europäischen Waffen- und Navigationstechnik, die „Entdeckung" Amerikas ab dem Jahre 1492 sowie die revolutionäre Erfindung des Buchdrucks durch Gutenberg, der die Technik 1448 in Mainz demonstriert, und dessen Verbreitung in England (1476/77) durch William Caxton verändern die Lebensumstände in ganz Europa grundsätzlich. Martin Luthers Reformation, seine Bibelübersetzung und die sich daran anschließenden verheerenden Konfessionskriege tun ein Übriges.

Die antike Bildung und Gelehrsamkeit betonen und verbreiten in der Renaissance die Humanisten.

Es ändern sich jedoch auch die Kunstformen, oft ebenfalls in Anlehnung an klassische Vorbilder: eine Entwicklung, die auch auf die neue Verbreitung des Altgriechischen zurückgeht.

Eine bedeutende lyrische Form der Renaissance ist das Sonett, das von Petrarca im 14. Jahrhundert in Italien etabliert wird und bald in ganz Europa begeisterte Nachahmer findet. Das englische Sonett unterscheidet sich in seinem Reimschema und der Stropheneinteilung von der italienischen Vorgabe. Beide vereint die Liebesthematik.

In England verhilft die Unterstützung von Königin Elisabeth I (1558–1603), der letzten Monarchin der Tudor-Dynastie, dem **Theater** zu einer neuen Blüte, die den Namen Elisabethanisches Drama zu Recht trägt.

Der bedeutendste Autor dieser Zeit ist jedoch **William Shakespeare**, dessen Werk wie kaum ein anderes die englische Literatur dominiert. Viele seiner knapp 40 Dramen stehen noch heute in den wichtigsten Theatern der Welt regelmäßig auf dem Programm: *Macbeth, Hamlet, Othello, The Tempest, Romeo and Juliet, Julius Caesar, A Midsummer Night's Dream*. Die Spanne reicht von Historien über Tragödien zu Komödien und Romanzen, in denen übernatürliche Kräfte walten. Gerade in den Tragödien zeigt sich die Zeitlosigkeit von Shakespeare, dessen Protagonisten stets mit ihren Leidenschaften ringen, sei es die Eifersucht in *Othello* oder der Ehrgeiz in *Macbeth*. Zu Shakespeares Genialität gehört neben seiner Sicherheit in der Figurenentwicklung und sprachlichen Ausführung auch die Bereitschaft, bereits bestehende Stoffe, wie in *Hamlet* oder *Romeo and Juliet*, neu zu interpretieren. Diese Tradition setzt sich nach Shakespeare fort. Auch im 21. Jahrhundert entstehen regelmäßig Verfilmungen sowie Neufassungen von Shakespeares Dramen, sei es in Romanform oder als Musical.

7.4 Das 17. Jahrhundert

Die politische Entwicklung des 17. Jahrhunderts hat weitläufige Konsequenzen für das literarische Schaffen der Zeit. Während das Theater unter Elisabeth eine Hochzeit erlebt, muss es unter den Puritanern, die nach der Hinrichtung von Karl I (1625–1649) unter Oliver Cromwell eine Militärherrschaft einführen, erst einmal vollständig im Untergrund verschwinden. Nach einem Parlamentsbeschluss werden 1642 alle Theateraufführungen verboten, da sie den religiös konservativen Puritanern als frivol gelten. Erst 1660 kommt es mit der Restauration, der Wiedereinsetzung der Monarchie, auch zu einer Wiedereröffnung der Theater, zuerst allerdings nur auf zwei Londoner Bühnen. Der frisch gekrönte Karl II (1660–1685) hatte in seinem französischen Exil neue Theatertraditionen zu schätzen gelernt, was nun auch zu veränderten Räumlichkeiten führt: nämlich zur Verbreitung der Guckkastenbühne, die abgesehen von dem noch eher bescheidenen Bühnenhaus schon an die heutigen Theatergebäude erinnert. Die Kulissen und Beleuchtung versuchen, die Wirklichkeit durch Illusion nachzubilden. Das Publikum muss nun weniger eigene Vorstellungsarbeit aufbringen.

Diese Tendenz hin zu einer weniger anspruchsvollen Bühnenkunst zeigt sich auch darin, dass als wichtigste Untergattung die Komödie große Bedeutung gewinnt. Stücke wie William Wycherlys *The Country Wife* (1675) oder George Etheregs *The Man of Mode* (1676) erfreuen sich noch heute großer Beliebtheit.

Dramatik

Mit Aphra Behn weist die Restaurationszeit auch die erste weibliche Literatin auf, die das Schreiben zu ihrem Beruf macht: Neben Dramen wie *The Rover* (1677) schrieb sie mit *Oroonoko* (1688) auch einen frühen Roman.

Viele der Dramen-Charaktere dieser Zeit stellen eher Typen als Individuen dar: den Einfaltspinsel, den unmoralischen Schurken oder den Heiratsschwindler. Sie greifen damit auch mittelalterliche Traditionen auf, die sich oft allegorischer Figuren bedienten. Ihre Aktualität können die Stücke aufgrund dieser zeitlosen und allgemeinmenschlichen Ansprüche gut erhalten. Anders als die damals ebenfalls populären klassizistischen Heldendramen wie John Drydens *All for Love* (1678) oder die eher seltenen Tragödien wie Thomas Otways *Venice Preserved* (1682) überlebt die Restaurationskomödie ihre Zeit.

Allerdings wird gegen die oft freizügigen Stücke schon im späten 17. Jahrhundert der Vorwurf der Amoralität vorgebracht. Die Tatsache, dass nun erstmals auch weibliche Schauspielerinnen auf der Bühne zu sehen sind, tut ihr Übriges, dem Theater einen moralisch zwielichtigen Ruf zu verschaffen. Die bald öffentlich geführte Debatte über den moralischen Anspruch des Theaters leitet den zwischenzeitlichen Niedergang der englischen Theatertradition ein: Zwischen dem frühen 18. Jahrhundert und dem späten 19. Jahrhundert entwickelt sich die Dramentradition in Großbritannien dann auch kaum weiter.

Zwar bleiben die Schauspielhäuser gut gefüllt, jedoch stehen auf dem Programm vornehmlich leichte Melodramen und Musikstücke, die vor allem ein Massenpublikum zu unterhalten suchen. Sowohl der ästhetische als auch der politische Anspruch der meisten dieser Stücke reicht nicht an ihre Vorgänger oder Nachfolger heran.

Lyrik   Die lyrische Tradition weist im 17. Jahrhundert ebenfalls neue Tendenzen auf. Am Hofe kommt es zu Anfang des Jahrhunderts zu einer Glanzphase der Poesie, die sich etwa in den Werken der *metaphysical poets* ausdrückt. Ihre komplexe, bildreiche Sprache bedient sich oft ausgedehnter Metaphern. Eine gegenläufige Tendenz, die sich weniger okkult und elitär gibt, wird als *cavalier poetry* bezeichnet, also als **höfische Dichtung**. Unter dem Einfluss von Ben Johnson schreiben diese Dichter stärker von klassischen Formen geprägte Werke, die jedoch in ganz weltlicher Manier eine nahezu hedonistische Lebensauffassung vertreten. John Milton dichtet in *Paradise Lost* (1667) den biblischen Sündenfall und die darauf folgende Heilsgeschichte in epischer Breite nach: Das Werk zählt zu den literarischen Höhepunkten des Jahrhunderts.

Epik   Dass nicht alle Erzählwerke dieser Epoche sich so komplexer Themen widmen, zeigt einer der größten Bucherfolge aller Zeiten: Izaak Waltons *The Compleat Angler* (1653), der als philosophische Anleitung zum Angeln verstanden werden kann und seit über 350 Jahren beständig Leser findet.

Die Kolonien   Obwohl durch die Landung der Puritaner mit der Mayflower 1620 die Besiedelung von Nordamerika neuen Aufschwung erfährt, läuft das literarische Schaffen in der Kolonie noch sehr zögerlich an. Bedeutsame Texte aus dem 17. Jahrhundert beschäftigen sich oft mit religiösen und politischen Themen, die aus dem Prozess der geographischen und später nationalen Selbstfindung entstehen.

7.5 Das 18. Jahrhundert

Das 18. Jahrhundert liefert gerade englischen Literaturhistorikern in verschiedenen Bereichen spannende Entwicklungen: In den Anfang des Jahrhunderts fällt die Entstehung des englischen Romans; am Ende des Jahrhunderts entwickelt sich mit der Romantik ein grundsätzlich neues Kunstverständnis.

In den seit 1776 unabhängigen Vereinigten Staaten entsteht zudem eine eigene literarische Tradition, die mit dazu beiträgt, dem neu geborenen Staat eine eigene Identität zu verschaffen.

Roman

Mit zunehmender Alphabetisierung der Bevölkerung und wachsendem Wohlstand der aufstrebenden Mittelklasse, die in ihrem Freizeitverhalten auch die Kunstgepflogenheiten der Oberschicht nachzuahmen sucht, ist ein Umfeld geschaffen, das für die Lektüre von längeren Erzähltexten ideal geeignet ist. Das gesteigerte Bedürfnis nach realistischen Darstellungen der Welt befriedigt sich an einer veränderten Darstellungsform: Der Roman ist geboren.

Bis zum 17. Jahrhundert sind die beliebtesten Prosatexte vor allem fantastische Romanzen *(romances)*, in denen ritterliche Männer im Kampf mit Fabelwesen die Herzen reiner Damen für sich gewinnen. Diese höfische Liebe wird in platonisch reiner Distanz genossen und eben nicht ausgelebt. Aphra Behns bereits erwähnter Proto-Roman *Oroonoko* (1688) liefert dafür ein gutes Beispiel; der Erfolg von Elizabeth Haywoods *Love in Excess* (1719) zeigt dagegen, dass es durchaus auch ein Lesepublikum für Geschichten gibt, die es mit der vorherrschenden Sexualmoral weniger ernst nehmen.

Rein formal liefert dann ein neu aufkommender Texttyp (das englische Wort für **Roman**, „novel", bedeutet Neuheit) den Lesern andere Muster. Daniel Defoe stellt mit *Robinson Crusoe* (1719) eine Vorlage bereit, die zugleich als die Geburtsstunde des englischen Romans gilt. Sein Held ist kein Königssohn, seine Erlebnisse sind alle vorstellbar und die erzählte Geschichte ist nicht mehr dem altbekannten Fundus der mythischen Erzählungen entnommen. Zudem lehnt sich die Sprache stark an das tatsächlich gesprochene Englisch an; der Protagonist tritt als Individuum hervor.

„Das Muster": Robinson Crusoe

Romantik

Ähnlich wie der Roman mit den tradierten Erzählformen bricht, ändert sich auch der Ton der Lyrik. Hatte im 17. Jahrhundert der Klassizismus noch eine an antike Muster angelehnte formale Strenge propagiert, so bereiten die satirischen Lyriker des 18. Jahrhunderts, eine neue Einstellung zur Lyrik vor.

Der neue Künstlertypus

In der zweiten Hälfte des Jahrhunderts entwickelt sich mit dem empfindenden, genial-schaffenden Dichter der Romantiker ein neuer Typus des Künstlers. Hatte sich diese Entwicklung bei William Blake erst angedeutet, so wird schließlich mit der Veröffentlichung des von William Wordsworth und Samuel Coleridge gemeinsam verfassten Gedichtbandes *Lyrical Ballads* (1798) eine neue Epoche in England eingeläutet. Inspiriert von Entwicklungen in Deutschland und Frankreich vertreten die beiden Autoren eine neue lyrische Form. Sie schreiben Gedichte, die sich in oft alltäglicher Sprache mit dem englischen Leben und der englischen Natur befassen.

Amerika

Die kontinentalen Entwicklungen haben im 18. Jahrhundert auch direkte Auswirkungen auf die literarische Situation in Nordamerika, vor allem bis zu dessen Abspaltung vom Mutterland am 4. Juli 1776, der als Unabhängigkeitstag bis heute begangen wird.

In dieser Phase kommt auch die amerikanische Literatur zu einer ersten Blüte. Werke wie Thomas Paines *Common Sense* (1776) liefern ein philosophisches Fundament für die sich entwickelnden Unabhängigkeitsbestrebungen des jungen Landes.

Benjamin Franklins *Autobiography* (1791) gehört ebenso zu den wichtigen Texten, die ein amerikanisches Bewusstsein formen, wie die umfassenden Berichte von J. Hector St Jean de Crèvecœur über das ländliche Leben in der neuen Welt, veröffentlicht als *Letters from an American Farmer* (1782).

Die europäische Strömung der Romantik produziert in Nordamerika als Transzendentalismus ähnliche Tendenzen, allerdings zeitlich verschoben erst ab dem frühen 19. Jahrhundert.

7.6 Das 19. Jahrhundert

Spätromantik und Schauerroman

Die Romantik wirkt in das neue Jahrhundert noch mit hinein. Als Gegentendenz zu der alles rational auflösenden **Aufklärung**, der zunehmenden Wissenschaftlichkeit und Entmystifizierung der Welt, widmet sich der Schauerroman den unerklärlichen Vorgängen in Spukschlössern, den verbotenen, diabolischen Begierden der menschlichen Psyche und der streng tabuisierten Sexualität.

Der weibliche Roman

Die sprichwörtliche Prüderie der Viktorianer, die selbst Stuhlbeine züchtig verhüllen, geht meist mit einer scheinheiligen Doppelmoral einher, die Männern Freizügigkeiten erlaubt, die sie Frauen vorwirft. Überhaupt wird im 19. Jahrhundert die Situation der Frau zunehmend thematisiert, was auch an der wachsenden weiblichen Leserschaft liegt.

In den Romanen von Jane Austen, bei den Brontë-Schwestern und in den Werken von George Eliot wird die Situation der Frau im 19. Jahrhundert, die sich stets in Abhängigkeit von der Männerwelt befindet, durchweg kritisch dargestellt. Dabei kommen jedoch, etwa in Jane Austens *Pride and Prejudice* (1813), nach wie vor Rollenbilder der Frau zur Geltung, die vor allem in der Ehe die weibliche Lebensaufgabe erfüllt sehen.

Realismus und Naturalismus

In der zweiten Jahrhunderthälfte entwickeln sich zwei gegenläufige Tendenzen. Auf der einen Seite propagieren Realismus und Naturalismus eine größere Nähe zur tatsächlichen Lebenswelt; auf der anderen Seite zelebriert der Ästhetizismus die Abkehr von der Welt.

Der Realismus entsteht als Gegenreaktion zu der als zu idealistisch und verklärt empfundenen Romantik.

Die oft schrecklichen Lebensumstände des neuen Industrieproletariats verhelfen nicht nur den Ideen von Karl Marx, der mit Friedrich Engels 1848 *Das kommunistische Manifest* veröffentlicht, zu großer Bekanntheit, sie tragen auch dazu bei, dass sich die Literatur in einer neuen Welle von utopischen und dystopischen Romanen fiktive Auswege aus der Lebenskrise sucht.

Die großen sozialen und weltpolitischen Veränderungen am Jahrhundertende treten dann ebenfalls in literarischen Werken zu Tage. Der Wandel der Geschlechterrollen und das Verhältnis des britischen Weltreichs zu seinen Kolonien tritt verstärkt in den Vordergrund.

Ästhetizismus

Die Freude an der Künstlichkeit der Sprache drückt sich auch in Wildes Aphorismen und paradoxen Wortspielen aus.

Anders als Realisten und Utopisten suchen die Anhänger des Ästhetizismus, allen voran Oscar Wilde, in der reinen Schönheit den Sinn der Kunst. Die Lyrik des Fin-de-Siècle ist während der 1880er- und 90er-Jahre von einer Endzeitstimmung bestimmt, die sich dadurch auszeichnet, dass man in dekadenten Eskapaden einen neuen Reichtum der lyrischen Erfahrung zu finden hofft. Zugleich versucht man, in Metaphern des Untergangs, Abends oder Herbstes das nahende Ende auszudrücken. Die Antwort des Ästhetizismus auf Tod und Untergang ist stets die Schönheit und das Artifizielle.

In der Hinwendung zum Symbolcharakter der Sprache, die nun immer stärker als von der Wirklichkeit getrennt existierend begriffen wird, deutet sich schon die starke Auflösung des Sprachlichen während Moderne und Postmoderne an. Sowohl die philosophischen Arbeiten von Friedrich Nietzsche, der wie Oscar Wilde 1900 stirbt, als auch die linguistischen Erkenntnisse von Ferdinand de Saussure bereiten in unterschiedlichen europäischen Ländern den großen sprachlichen Wandel *(linguistic turn)* in den literarischen Formen des 20. Jahrhunderts vor.

Amerika

Die Phase um die Jahrhundertmitte, von 1830–1870, gilt als die erste Hochphase der amerikanischen Literatur. Sie entwickelt sich aus der europäischen Romantik, nimmt jedoch eigene Züge an. Neben dem literarischen Vorbild aus Europa fordert auch die beeindruckende Naturlandschaft des neuen Kontinents eine ästhetische Behandlung. Thoreau und Emerson begründen den Transzendentalismus, der für ein individuelles und intuitives Erleben der gottgegebenen Natur eintritt. Die Gründung des weltweit ersten Nationalparks, des Yellowstone Parks im Jahre 1872, fällt ebenfalls in diese Zeit.

7.7 Das 20. Jahrhundert

Im 20. Jahrhundert lassen sich vor allem die Moderne und die Postmoderne unterscheiden.

Moderne

Die Moderne (im Englischen auch als „High Modernism" bezeichnet) beginnt am Anfang des 20. Jahrhunderts und findet ihren Höhepunkt in den Jahren zwischen den beiden Weltkriegen. Zwei der wichtigsten Autoren sind James Joyce und Virginia Woolf.

Beide Autoren entwickeln den Roman durch eine stärkere Fokussierung auf die Innenwelt der Figuren weiter. Bewusstseinsstrom und innerer Monolog verschaffen die Möglichkeit, das meist zerrissene Innenleben der Figuren direkt darzustellen.

Das englische Drama erhält neue Impulse und erwacht aus den Jahrzehnten seiner relativen Unbedeutsamkeit. In der Tat tritt die Moderne stärker als die meisten früheren Epochen als eine europäische, wenn nicht sogar globale Erscheinung auf, die mit dem Zweiten Weltkrieg ihren Schlusspunkt erhält.

Postmoderne

Der englischsprachige Nachkriegsroman steht unter dem Zeichen der Postmoderne. Vor allem amerikanische Autoren lassen sich neue experimentelle Erzählformen einfallen, die oft das Erzählen selbst thematisieren. Der Verlust des Glaubens an große sinnstiftende (Lebens-)Einheiten – ein zentrales Merkmale der postmodernen Befindlichkeit – findet somit auch direkt Eingang in die Struktur der Literatur. Zugleich entdeckt die Postmoderne die Allgegenwart des Erzählens und stellt die Geschichte als ein textliches Konstrukt dar.

Postkoloniale Literaturen

In der Literatur der Gegenwart nehmen vor allem auch Autoren aus den ehemaligen Kolonien sowie Migranten eine zentrale Position ein. Ehemals unterworfene Kulturen erheben nun selbst ihre literarische Stimme und setzen sich gegen den Vormachtsanspruch der ehemaligen (europäischen) Kolonialherren zur Wehr. Dabei kommt es, in postmoderner Manier, auch zur Nach- und Umdichtung kanonischer Texte.

Die Tendenz, in der Literatur die Heterogenität einer Gesellschaft auszudrücken, tritt generell stärker in den Vordergrund.

Innerhalb Englands haben Kazuo Ishiguro, Hanif Kureishi und Monika Ali große Bedeutung gewonnen. Ihre Texte porträtieren das Großstadtleben von Menschen, die aufgrund ihrer Abstammung, Klassenzugehörigkeit oder auch sexuellen Orientierung am Rande der Gesellschaft leben (müssen).

> Die nach wie vor nicht problemfreie Integration von Menschen mit Migrationshintergrund schlägt damit auch in der Literatur direkt zu Buche.

Eine ähnliche Funktion übernehmen in den USA die Afroamerikanerinnen Alice Walker, Toni Morrison, die asiatisch-amerikanische Schriftstellerin Maxine Hong Kingston, der kubanisch-amerikanische Autor Oscar Hijuelos, oder indianische Autoren wie Louise Erdrich. In diesen Werken stehen oft Fragen nach der persönlichen, ethnischen aber auch nationalen Identität im Vordergrund.

Mit dieser neuerlichen Betonung der Bedeutung des historisch-gesellschaftlich-politischen Hintergrundes des Literatursystems, zu dem außer den Autoren natürlich Verleger, Buchhändler und Käufer mit all ihren politischen und ideologischen Erwartungen gehören, kehrt dieser Überblick zur englisch-amerikanischen Literaturgeschichte wieder zu seinem Ausgangspunkt zurück.

Literatur ist immer ein Spiegel der gesellschaftlichen Gepflogenheiten, aber auch ihrer Unzulänglichkeiten und ihrer Umbrüche und Entwicklungen. Um literarische Texte inhaltlich sinnvoll begreifen und einordnen zu können, ist es unerlässlich sich mit literaturgeschichtlichen Besonderheiten vertraut zum machen. Literatur will und muss im Kontext verstanden werden und die Erläuterungen in diesem Kapitel sollten Ihnen dabei dienlich sein. Es ist empfehlenswert, als nachfolgenden Schritt Ihre prüfungsrelevante Literatur nun in den literaturgeschichtlichen Kontext zu stellen.

Die Interpretation literarischer Texte 8

Literatur verrät bei näherer Analyse nicht nur etwas zur Auseinandersetzung mit „ewigen" Themen (Liebe, Rache, Krieg, Verzweiflung ...), sondern auch zu Eigenheiten der Entstehungszeit. Verknüpft man dieses Wissen nun mit eigenen Gedanken, Assoziationen und Stellungnahmen, kann eine vertiefte Auseinandersetzung mit verschiedensten Themen stattfinden. Um die Interpretation literarischer Text meistern zu können, sollten Sie sich mit dem Inhalt dieses Kapitels vertraut machen und versuchen, so viele eigene Texte wie möglich zu erarbeiten.

8.1 Vorbemerkung

Anders als bei Gebrauchstexten, die in den meisten Fällen fast ausschließlich der Inhaltsvermittlung dienen, haben literarische Texte eine weitere Dimension, eben die literarische. Das **Wesen des Literarischen** genau zu bestimmen, ist allerdings ein schwieriges Unterfangen.

Die Aufteilung der Literatur in drei **Großgattungen** – Lyrik, Drama und Erzähltexte – vermittelt in doppelter Hinsicht einen falschen Eindruck. Zum einen suggeriert eine solche Gliederung, dass es nur drei Möglichkeiten gibt, sich literarisch zu äußern. Formen wie etwa der Essay kommen in einer solchen Aufteilung meist zu kurz. Man müsste also eigentlich eine weit größere Anzahl an Schreibarten beachten. Zum anderen kann der Eindruck entstehen, als ob die jeweilige Definition der drei Gattungen problemfrei sei. Die Frage, was überhaupt eine Gattung ausmacht, wird sehr unterschiedlich beantwortet. Einen großen Anteil an der Festlegung der Zugehörigkeit eines Textes zu einer bestimmten Gattung hat sicherlich der Leser.

Anwendung
Jeder der folgenden Unterabschnitte zu den drei Gattungen Lyrik, Drama und Prosa endet mit Modellanalysen in englischer Sprache. Sie sollen als Beispiele für die Verbindung der unterschiedlichen Aspekte gattungsspezifischer Textanalyse dienen und zugleich eine Hilfestellung für die englischsprachige Interpretationsarbeit liefern. Wichtig für eine knappe literarische Interpretation ist die Konzentration auf entscheidende Aspekte eines Textes. Dafür sollen die folgenden Kategorien und Begriffe eine erste Anleitung geben.

8.2 Lyrik

Entwicklung der Lyrik

Lyrische Texte haben eine lange Tradition. Der Name leitet sich vom griechischen Wort für die Leier *(lyra)* ab und deutet darauf hin, dass es sich bei lyrischen Texten ursprünglich um mit musikalischer Begleitung vorgetragene Lieder handelte. In der Tat ist die Sangbarkeit der Lyrik eines ihrer zentralen Merkmale, das sich auch in der rhythmischen Struktur der Sprache zeigt.

Viele der frühen Gedichte wurden vor ihrer schriftlichen Fixierung mündlich überliefert. Die strenge Ordnung der lautlichen Struktur lyrischer Texte deutet somit ebenfalls das Alter dieses Genres an: Die Aufteilung eines Gedichts in Strophen, Verse und Versfüße sowie die Gliederung durch Reimschemata unterstützen das Auswendiglernen lyrischer Texte.

Es dauert schließlich bis zum Anfang des 20. Jahrhunderts, ehe sich die Lyrik fast vollkommen von Traditionen wie Reim oder Metrum befreit. Die Moderne Lyrik ist auf den ersten Blick oft nur noch daran zu erkennen, wie der Text auf der Seite arrangiert ist. Neben den kurzen Zeilen fallen dann jedoch meist auch die starke Bildhaftigkeit und die nach wie vor feststellbare lautliche Struktur von Gedichten auf.

Neben ihrer starken Strukturiertheit fällt bei der lyrischen Sprache auf, dass sie meist von der Alltagssprache abweicht. Die Tendenz zum sorgfältig gewählten Ausdruck und zum hohen Stil ist jedoch ebenfalls keine absolute Notwendigkeit. Spätestens seit der Romantik findet auch ein stärker alltäglich gefärbter Sprachduktus Eingang in die Lyrik. Viele Dichter des 20. Jahrhunderts verzichteten vollends darauf, in ihrer Sprache an den hohen Stil traditioneller Lyrik anzuschließen. Sogar bewusst umgangssprachliche Dichtung behauptet heute ihren Platz neben traditionelleren Formen.

Lyrische Formen

Ein wichtiges Merkmal lyrischer Texte ist die relative Kürze von Gedichten. Während japanische Haikus oder der in Großbritannien beliebte Limerick mit wenigen Versen auskommen, gibt es daneben allerdings auch Langformen. Lyrische Texte lassen sich somit außer nach Thema und Struktur auch nach ihrer Länge in unterschiedliche Gruppen einteilen.

Lyrische Form	Beispiel	Kriterien
Epos	*Paradise lost* (John Milton)	– sehr lange lyrische Form (kann Romanlänge erreichen) – lässt sich als Loblied auf das Leben und die Taten eines Helden beschreiben – meist übernatürliche Fähigkeiten des Helden – meist Musenanruf zu Beginn – feierlicher Ton – hoher Stil – geht oft auf mündliche Überlieferungen tatsächlicher Ereignisse zurück
Ballade	*The Highwayman* (Alfred Noyes)	– längere lyrische Form – stark erzählerische *(engl. narrative)* Struktur (deutlicher Unterschied zu anderen lyrischen Formen)
Limerick	→ „Beispiel: Limerick" siehe unten	– sehr beliebt – als Nonsens-Dichtung fester Platz in der englischen literarischen Tradition – Anapästisches Metrum (→ Glossar S. 235) – verwendet Reime, die aufgrund von Doppeldeutigkeit, Betonungsverschiebungen, Wortwitz komisch sind
Petrarkistisches Sonett	Texte von Petrarcas (14. Jhdt., Italien)	– Hauptthema: die Liebe – gliedert sich in zwei Quartette und zwei Terzette – These und Gegenthese
Englisches Sonett Shakespearean Sonnet	Sonnette (William Shakespeare)	– Aufteilung in drei Quartette und abschließendes *heroic couplet* (führt Thematik des Gedichts nochmal zusammen, oder wirft neues Licht auf das Gesamte)
Ode	*Intimations of immortality from recollection of early childhood* (William Wordsworth, Romantik)	– formstreng (in einigen Ausprägungen mit der Hymne verwandt) – feierlich, weihevoll – erhabener Stil – oftmals direkt angesprochenes Gegenüber „Du"
Elegy	*Written in a Country Churchyard* (1751) (Thomas Grey)	– Totenklage oder Lied über den Tod (in England seit dem 16. Jhdt.) auf jeden Fall traurige, klagende Inhalte – in Distichen verfasst

Tab. 8.1: Übersicht der lyrischen Formen

Beispiel: Limerick

There was a young lady from Niger
Who smiled as she rode on the tiger.
They came back from the ride
With the lady inside,
And the smile on the face of the tiger.

Margaret Ferguson et al. (Hrsg.): The Norton Anthology of Poetry: Shorter Fourth Edition. Norton, New York, 1977, Seite 1118

Subjektivität

Eines der Merkmale, das lyrische Werke von den Texten der Großgattungen Dramatik und Erzähltexte unterscheidet, ist die besondere „Stimme" von Gedichten. Die Stimme, die in einem Gedicht spricht, nennt man das **lyrische Ich**. Je nachdem, ob es direkt in Erscheinung tritt oder nicht, unterscheidet man zwischen einem expliziten und einem impliziten lyrischen Ich. Im folgendem Gedicht von W. H. Auden tritt das lyrische Ich explizit auf:

> **Beispiel**
>
> W. H. Auden
> ### Twelve Songs, IX (1936)
>
> Stop all the clocks, cut off the telephone,
> Prevent the dog from barking with a juicy bone,
> Silence the pianos and with muffled drum
> Bring out the coffin, let the mourners come.
>
> 5   Let aeroplanes circle moaning overhead
> Scribbling in the sky the message He Is Dead,
> Put crêpe bows round the white necks of the public doves,
> Let the traffic policemen wear black cotton gloves.
>
> He was my North, my South, my East and West,
> 10 My working week and my Sunday rest,
> My noon, my midnight, my talk, my song;
> I thought that love would last for ever: I was wrong.
>
> The stars are not wanted now: put out every one;
> Pack up the moon and dismantle the sun;
> 15 Pour away the ocean and sweep up the wood;
> For nothing now can ever come to any good.
>
> W. H. Auden: Collected Poems. Faber & Faber, London, 1976, Seite 120

Sowohl das Possessivadjektiv „my" als auch das klare „I" verdeutlichen, dass hier eine Stimme spricht. Dieses lyrische Ich empfindet und drückt eine Reihe von Gefühlen aus: Trauer, Enttäuschung, Verzweiflung. Dabei wird deutlich, dass die Umwelt nur bedingt diese Trauer teilt. Zwar nehmen andere Menschen („mourners") an der Trauerfeier statt; aber der verzweifelte Versuch, selbst Hunde, Flugzeuge und Polizisten in den persönlichen Schmerz einzubeziehen, zeigt zugleich, dass der Tod des geliebten Menschen für das lyrische Ich eine zutiefst persönliche und eigene Erfahrung ist. Gerade dieser

Ausdruck des Persönlichen zeichnet die literarische Gattung der Lyrik aus: Man spricht deswegen auch von der Subjektivität als einem zentralen Merkmal lyrischer Texte.

Nicht alle Gedichte lassen ihre Subjektivität so direkt erkennen wie die Verse von Auden. Oft muss man sich das subjektive Empfinden erst erschließen, dann nämlich, wenn das lyrische Ich nur implizit vorhanden ist, wie im folgenden Beispiel:

> William Blake   Beispiel
>
> **The Tyger (1794)**
>
> Tyger! Tyger! burning bright
> In the forests of the night,
> What immortal hand or eye
> Could frame thy fearful symmetry?
>
> In what distant deeps or skies   5
> Burnt the fire of thine eyes?
> On what wings dare he aspire?
> What the hand, dare seize the fire?
>
> And what shoulder, & what art,
> Could twist the sinews of thy heart?   10
> And when thy heart began to beat,
> What dread hand? & what dread feet?
>
> What the hammer? what the chain?
> In what furnace was thy brain?
> What the anvil? what dread grasp   15
> Dare its deadly terrors clasp?
> When the stars threw down their spears,
> And water'd heaven with their tears,
> Did he smile his work to see?
> Did he who made the Lamb make thee?   20
>
> Tyger! Tyger! burning bright
> In the forests of the night,
> What immortal hand or eye
> Dare frame thy fearful symmetry?
>
> Margaret Ferguson et al. (Hrsg.): The Norton Anthology of Poetry: Shorter Fourth Edition. Norton, New York, 1997, Seite 395

In Blakes Gedicht wird der Konflikt zwischen dem furchteinflößenden mächtigen Tiger und dem gütigen Gott der Bibel thematisiert. Das lyrische Ich, das diese Stimmung empfindet, kann man nur dadurch bestimmen, dass das zentrale Objekt des Gedichts, der Tiger, aus einer persönlichen, subjektiven Warte beschrieben wird.

Jedes lyrische Ich, egal ob explizit oder implizit vorhanden, wendet sich an ein **lyrisches Du**, das ebenfalls wieder explizit oder implizit vorhanden sein kann. In Audens Gedicht ist die Beschreibung des lyrischen Du nicht ganz einfach. Der erste Vers richtet sich mit den Imperativen „Stop all the clocks, cut off the telefone" (Z. 1) an jemanden, der ungenannt bleibt.

Da der Geliebte, wie man bald feststellt, nicht mehr lebt – „He Is Dead" (Z. 6) –, handelt es sich beim lyrischen Du wohl um jemand anderes. Die weite Streuung der angesprochenen Personen macht deutlich, dass weniger ein einzelner Mensch als eher eine Gruppe gemeint ist. In der Tat richtet sich das Gedicht an das Umfeld des Trauernden, an die allgemeine Gesellschaft jenseits der Trauergäste.

In Blakes Gedicht ist das lyrische Du der Tiger. Allerdings wird der Tiger eher angerufen als direkt angesprochen.

Sowohl der Tiger als auch das Lamm sind durch die Großschrift zusätzlich betont. Das Wort „god" steht dagegen ohne Großbuchstaben, wodurch das lyrische Du, der Tiger in seiner Stellvertreterposition für die natürliche Energie, nicht nur als Gegensatz zur göttlichen Macht gesetzt wird, sondern sogar als dieser Macht eventuell überlegen geschildert wird.

Lyrische Syntax

Die starke Künstlichkeit der lyrischen Sprache zeigt sich teilweise auch in der syntaktischen Auflösung ihrer Sätze. Aufgrund metrischer Begebenheiten kann der Satzbau eines Verses von den „normalen" Regeln der Sprache abweichen.

Syntaktische Form	Beispiel	Kriterien
Chiasmus (chiasmus)	Never Let a Fool Kiss You or a Kiss Fool You (Mardy Grothe Viking, 1999)	– die überkreuzte oder umgekehrte Anordnung von Satzelementen in einem Satz oder einer Aussage
Parallelismus (parallelism)	Did he smile his work to see? Did he who made the lamb make thee? (Z. 19–20 aus The Tyger, William Blake)	– die identische Abfolge von Satzgliedern in mehreren Sätzen
Ellipse (ellipis)	The streets were deserted, the doors bolted. (Report to Greco, Nikos Kazantzakis, 1965)	– Auslassung eines Satzteils
Inversion (inversion)	Yet know I how the heather looks, Yet certain am I of the spot. (Chartless, Emily Dickinson)	– Umkehrung des normalen Satzbaus
Asyndeton (asyndeton)	Ah, miserable and unkind, untrue, unknightly, traitor-hearted! Woe is me! (Idylls of the King Lord Alfred Tennyson)	– Aneinanderreihung von Satzteilen ohne Konjunktion

Tab. 8.2: Übersicht zur lyrischen Syntax

Versfuß und Metrum

Die meisten Gedichte vor der Moderne zeichnen sich durch eine sehr stark strukturierte innere Form aus. Liest man ein solches Gedicht, fällt schnell auf, dass die Abfolge der betonten und unbetonten Silben in Mustern auftritt. Man unterscheidet je nach Betonungsmuster unterschiedliche Versfüße. Um den vorherrschenden Versfuß eines Gedichts zu bestimmen, sucht man nach der kleinsten sich wiederholenden Einheit von betonten und unbetonten Silben. Liest man also „xx́xx́xx́", ist es ein jambischer Versfuß. Wiederholen sich, wie in einem Limerick, immer „xxx́xxx́xxx́", liegt ein Anapäst vor.

zur Begrifflichkeit
→ Glossar, S. 234–246

- **Jambus** (iamb): eine unbetonte und eine betonte Silbe
  „A síght so tóuching ín its májestý"
- **Trochäus** (trochee): eine betonte und eine unbetonte Silbe
  „Týger! Týger! búrning brígt"
- **Spondeus** (spondee): zwei betonte Silben
  „Wíld mén who cáught and sáng" (nach dem Spondeus hier Jamben)

- **Daktylus** *(dactyl)*: eine betonte und zwei unbetonte Silben
  „Cánada"
- **Anapäst** *(anapest)*: zwei unbetonte und eine betonte Silbe
  „They came báck from the ríde"
- **Amphibrach** *(amphibrach)*: eine betonte Silbe mit je einer unbetonten Silbe vorher und nachher
  „ambítious"

Je nachdem, wie oft ein Versfuß pro Vers (Zeile) wiederholt wird, spricht man von einem drei-, vier- oder fünfhebigen Versmaß. Die entsprechenden griechischen Begriffe lauten
- Trimeter (3),
- Tetrameter (4),
- Pentameter (5),
- Hexameter (6) etc.

In einem jambischen Pentameter findet man demnach in jedem Vers fünf Gruppen von je zwei Silben, wobei immer die zweite betont ist.

Natürlich halten sich nicht alle Gedichte immer an ihr Versmaß. Vielmehr verwenden manche Dichter Variationen, durch die sie bestimmte Textpassagen hervorheben. Im Gedicht von Auden werden die regelmäßig jambischen Verse der dritten Strophe am Ende durch eine Pause vor dem „I was wrong" unterbrochen. Dadurch bekommt diese Aussage besonderes Gewicht. Eine solche Unterbrechung oder Pause innerhalb eines Verses nennt man **Zäsur** *(caesura)*. Richtig erkannte Zäsuren ermöglichen es, die Aussage eines Gedichtes besser zu verstehen. Oft hilft dabei die Interpunktion, da vor Zäsuren häufig ein Gedankenstrich, Strichpunkt oder Doppelpunkt steht. Das Gegenstück zur Zäsur ist das **Enjambement** *(enjambment)*, der Zeilensprung. Dabei geht eine Sinneinheit über ein Zeilenende hinaus und in den nächsten Vers hinein. In der ersten Strophe von Audens Gedicht läuft der dritte Vers unmittelbar in den vierten weiter. Der Satz „and with muffled drum / Bring out the coffin" bereitet mit seinem Enjambement bereits auf die direkt anschließende Zäsur vor. Ein Enjambement ist in der Wirkung aufmerksamkeitsheischend; es markiert oftmals Textpassagen großer Bedeutung.

Neben der metrischen Struktur sind lyrische Texte auch von der Klangfarbe der einzelnen Wörter, der Länge der jeweiligen Silbe und schließlich dem Betonungsmuster der verwendeten Wörter in der normalen Sprache bestimmt. Erst wenn diesen Aspekten beim (lauten) Lesen eines Gedichtes Rechnung getragen wird, entsteht ein Eindruck vom **Rhythmus** *(rhythm)* eines lyrischen Textes.

Strophe und Reim

Die nächst größere Ordnungseinheit eines Gedichts nach Versfuß und Vers ist die **Strophe** *(stanza)*, die man oft schon durch die Anordnung des Textes auf der Seite erkennen kann: Leerzeilen (oder andere optische Merkmale) trennen meist die Strophen. Je nach Anzahl der in einer Strophe enthaltenen Verse unterscheidet man zwischen

Terzett	tercet	3 Verse pro Strophe
Quartett	quartrain	4 Verse pro Strophe
Sextett	sestet	6 Verse pro Strophe
Oktett	octave	8 Verse pro Strophe

Tab. 8.3: Strophen

Die Strophe ist gleichzeitig auch die Größeneinheit eines Gedichts, innerhalb derer das Reimschema deutlich wird.

Reimschemata

Stabreim *(alliteration)*	*Beowulf*	– reiner Reim *(true rhyme)* – lautlicher Gleichklang am Wortanfang – wurde durch Endreim abgelöst
Endreim *(end-rhyme)*	*Whose woods these are I think I know,* *His house is in the village, though;* *He will not see me stopping here* *To watch his woods fill up with snow."* (*Stopping by Woods on a snowy evening*, Robert Frost)	– reiner Reim *(true rhyme)* – üblichster Reim in englischer Lyrik – lautlicher Gleichklang wird an das Versende verlegt
Männlicher / stumpfer Reim *(masculine rhyme)*	*Stand still, and I will read to thee* *A lecture, love, in Love's philosophy.* *These three hours that we have spent* *Walking here, two shadows went* (*Lecture Upon the Shadow*, John Donne)	– Gleichklang ab dem Vokal der letzten betonten Silbe *(bet/let)*
Weiblicher / klingender Reim *(feminine rhyme)*	*A woman's face with Nature's own hand painted* *Hast thou, the master-mistress of my passion;* *A woman's gentle heart, but not acquainted* *With shifting change, as is false women's fashion;* (Sonnet 20, William Shakespeare)	– Gleichklang ab dem Vokal der vorletzten betonten Silbe *(better/ letter)*
Dreisilbiger Reim *(triple rhyme)*	*Don Juan* (Lord Byron)	– Gleichklang ab dem Vokal der betonten drittletzten Silbe *(bettering/ lettering)*

Reimschemata		
Assonanz (engl. assonance)	Hear the mellow wedding bells – (Edgar Allan Poe)	– Gleichklang nur der Vokale
Konsonanz (consonance)	'T'was later when the summer went Than when the cricket came, And yet we knew that gentle clock Meant nought but going home. 'T'was sooner when the cricket went Than when the winter came, Yet that pathetic pendulum Keeps esoteric time. (Emily Dickinson, 'T'was later when the summer went)	– Gleichklang nur der Konsonanten
Historischer Reim (historical rhyme)	Come live with me and be my Love, And we will all the pleasures prove, That hills and valleys, dale and field, And all the craggy mountains yield. (The passionate Shepherd to his love, Christopher Marlowe)	– Ein Reim aus einem alten Gedicht, bei dem sich der Reim durch die ursprüngliche Aussprache der Wörter ergab, dies aber heute nicht mehr der Fall ist.

Tab. 8.4: Übersicht der Reimschemata

Das Reimschema beschreibt man, indem alle reimenden Verse mit einem identischen Buchstaben markiert werden. Für die häufigsten der daraus entstehenden Gruppierungen von Endreimen existieren die folgenden Begriffe:
- **Paarreim** *(rhyming couplet)*: zwei unmittelbar aufeinander folgende Verse (aa bb cc …)
- **Kreuzreim** *(alternate rhyme)*: je zwei alternierende Reime (abab cdcd efef …)
- **umarmender Reim** *(embracing rhyme)*: ein Paarreim umgeben von zwei reimenden Versen (abba cddc effe …)
- **geschweifter Reim** *(tail rhyme)*: auf wechselnde Paarreime folgt ein sich reimender weiterer Vers (aab ccb ddb …)
- **Kettenreim** *(chain rhyme)*: der von einem Reimpaar umgebene mittlere Vers wird zum Reimpaar der nächsten Dreiergruppe (aba bcb cdc …)

Das folgende Gedicht von William Wordsworth, *Composed Upon Westminster Bridge*, zeigt, wie schon das Reimschema eine deutliche Hilfestellung für die inhaltliche Deutung eines Gedichts geben kann.

> William Wordsworth
>
> **Composed upon Westminster Bridge, September 3, 1802**
>
> Earth has not anything to show more fair:
> Dull would he be of soul who could pass by
> A sight so touching in its majesty:
> This City now doth, like a garment, wear
> The beauty of the morning; silent, bare, 5
> Ships, towers, domes, theatres, and temples lie
> Open unto the fields, and to the sky;
> All bright and glittering in the smokeless air.
> Never did sun more beautifully steep
> In his first splendour, valley, rock, or hill; 10
> Ne'er, saw I, never felt, a calm so deep!
> The river glideth at his own sweet will:
> Dear God! the very houses seem asleep;
> And all that mighty heart is lying still.
>
> William Wordsworth: The Works of William Wordsworth. Wordsworth, Ware, 1994, Seite 269

Beispiel

Das Reimschema tritt zuerst durch den umfassenden Reim des ersten Quartetts in Erscheinung: Die Wörter „*fair*" und „*wear*" umarmen dabei den zweiten und dritten Vers. So entsteht ein typisches „abba" Muster. Das zweite Quartett wiederholt die Reimlaute, folgt also der „abba" Struktur des ersten Quartetts. Man könnte diese erste Großeinheit auch Oktett nennen, und in der Tat bilden die ersten acht Verse eine Sinneinheit: Das lyrische Ich beschreibt, in noch relativ neutralen Tönen, den Anblick der Großstadt London. Es ist wohl noch sehr früh am Morgen, da vor allem die Abwesenheit anderer Menschen und jeglicher Aktivität auffällt. Die starke Personifizierung der Stadt führt dazu, dass ein Eindruck von ihrer Schönheit als Menschenwerk entsteht. Die nächsten Verse führen neue Reime ein: Die Endlautung der Wörter „*steep*" und „*hill*" wiederholt sich in den abschließenden Versen, die im Reimschema „cdc dcd" entweder als zwei Terzette und damit als Kreuzreim, oder als Sextett mit einem alternierenden Reim geordnet werden können. Im Gegensatz zum Oktett am Anfang des Gedichts schildert das abschließende Sextett das persönliche Empfinden des lyrischen Ich, das in Vers 11 auch erstmals explizit in Erscheinung tritt.

Im Oktett wird die bereits in Vers 4 durch den Bezug auf Kleidung personifizierte Stadt nun vollends zu einem komplexen Organismus: Das abschließende Bild des „mächtigen Herzens" („*mighty heart*") betont die zentrale Spannung des Gedichts, die sich aus dem Gegensatz der im Morgengrauen noch schlafenden Stadt London und ihrer tatsächlichen globalen Bedeutung als Zentrum eines Imperiums nährt. Die (wie die typischerweise sublim beschriebene Natur der Romantiker) hier erhaben beschriebene Stadt vermittelt damit ein quasi-religiöses Empfinden. Die Großschreibung der beiden Wörter „*City*" und „*God*" betont dieses innere Verhältnis zwischen den beiden Bereichen. Wordsworth folgt in der Struktur seines Gedichtes, der Gliederung in ein Oktett und ein Sextett, eng der Vorlage von Petrarka. Allerdings weicht sein Sonett von der typischen Liebesthematik dieser lyrischen Form ab. Shakespeare dagegen verwendet in dem folgenden Sonett die englische Variante dieser lyrischen Untergattung:

Beispiel

William Shakespeare

Sonnet 138

When my love swears that she is made of truth,
I do believe her, though I know she lies,
That she might think me some untutor'd youth,
Unlearned in the world's false subtleties.
Thus vainly thinking that she thinks me young   5
Although she knows my days are past the best,
Simply I credit her false-speaking tongue:
On both sides thus is simple truth supprest.
But wherefore says she not she is unjust?
And wherefore say not I that I am old?   10
O! love's best habit is in seeming trust,
And age in love loves not to have years told:
   Therefore I lie with her, and she with me,
   And in our faults by lies we flatter'd be.

William Shakespeare: The Complete Works of William Shakespeare. Pordes, London, 1993, Seite 1218

Das Reimschema in Shakespeares Sonett ist ebenfalls hilfreich für das Verständnis des Gedichts. Das Schema lässt sich mit abab cdcd efef gg einfach darstellen. Anders ausgedrückt: Auf drei Quartette folgt ein Paarreim. Da dieser in der Form eines jambischen Pentameters auftritt, kann man ihn auch direkt als *heroic couplet* benennen. Die Sonderstellung der letzten beiden Verse beruht nicht nur auf dem neuen Reim, sondern bezieht sich auch auf die inhaltliche Seite: Wie in den meisten Sonetten, die dieser Gliederung folgen, liefert das *heroic couplet* eine Art von Synthese oder Zusammenfassung der in den Quartetten vorgestellten Thematik.

In *Sonett 138* zeigt das *heroic couplet*, dass es sich bei der „Liebe" zwischen dem lyrischen Ich und der als „*my love*" bezeichneten Angebeteten (die hier übrigens nicht als lyrisches Du direkt angesprochen wird) bestenfalls um eine Zweckbeziehung handelt. Die Doppeldeutigkeit des Wortspiels um „lie", das sowohl „liegen" als auch „lügen" bedeuten kann, impliziert in den letzten beiden Versen, dass es sich bei der hier beschriebenen Liebe („*lie with her*") eben um eine Lüge handelt, wie es in den ersten beiden Versen des Gedichts bereits indirekt angesprochen wurde.

> Bei der Analyse von formalen Aspekten eines lyrischen Textes (Versfuß, Metrum, Reimschema etc) sollte stets die inhaltliche Deutung des Gedichts im Vordergrund stehen. Die Benennung eines bestimmten Reimschemas liefert auf sich allein gestellt selten etwas Spannendes; erst die Beschreibung der Wirkung einer konkreten Gliederung liefert einen sinnvollen Kommentar.

Tipp: Formale Gedichtanalyse

Stilmittel *(stylistic device)*: Bildhaftigkeit *(imagery)*

Auf der sprachlichen Seite zeichnen sich lyrische Texte durch eine große Dichte von Stilmitteln aus, die zwar auch in der Alltagssprache (und etwa in Drama und Roman) existieren, in der Lyrik aber gedrängt zum Einsatz kommen. Gerade die Verwendung bildhafter Sprache verdeutlicht dies gut.

- **Metapher (*metaphor*):** Statt jemanden mit einem **Vergleich** *(simile)* zu beschreiben („er ist stark wie ein Löwe"), verlangt die **Metapher** *(metaphor)* von ihren Lesern eine höhere Eigenarbeit. Bei einem Ausdruck wie „er ist ein Löwe" müssen die Leser selbst erkennen, welche Eigenschaft des Tieres hier angesprochen ist. Eine Metapher überträgt ein Wort aus einem Bereich in einen sinnverwandten anderen, wobei ein bestimmter Aspekt der ursprünglichen Bedeutung erhalten bleibt, hier also die vermeintliche Stärke eines Löwen.
- **Metonymie (*metonymy*):** Die **Metonymie** *(metonymy)*. Sie kann ebenfalls als uneigentlicher Vergleich bezeichnet werden, unterscheidet sich jedoch im Verhältnis von Bildsender und Bildempfänger. Bei einer Metonymie verwendet man ein Wort für ein anderes, mit dem es in einem engen Sinnzusammenhang steht. Eine Frage wie „Kann ich noch eine Tasse haben?" verwendet „Tasse" metonymisch, da mit der Aussage kaum je eine Bitte um ein Stück Geschirr, sondern (meistens) um ein weiteres Getränk verbunden ist.
- **Synekdote (*synecdoche*):** Die dritte häufig verwendete Form der bildhaften Sprache ist die **Synekdoche** *(synecdoche)*. Bei ihr steht ein Teil für ein Ganzes *(pars pro toto)* oder umgekehrt das Ganze für den Teil *(totum pro parte)*. Wer sich „in den Sattel schwingt" oder „gegen das Leder tritt"

verwendet den Sattel als Synekdoche für das Fahrradfahren beziehungsweise die Lederhülle für das Fußballspiel.
- **Euphemismus** (*euphemism*)**:** Der **Euphemismus** ist die positive und beschönigende Darstellung eines negativen Sachverhalts. In Shakespeares Sonett lässt sich *„my days are past the best"* (Vers 6) so deuten, dass sich das lyrische Ich nicht einmal sich selbst gegenüber das eigene Alter eingestehen will: Die euphemistische Verwendung bestärkt damit die lügnerische Gesamtstimmung des Gedichts.
- **Hyperbel** (*hyperbole*)**:** Die **Hyperbel** ist eine deutliche Über- oder Untertreibung. In Audens Gedicht beinhalten die ersten drei Verse der letzten Strophe stark übertriebene Imperative: Durch diese Betonung oder Emphase wird zum Schluss des Gedichts noch einmal die Tragweite der Trauer verdeutlicht.
- **Hendiadyoin** (*hendiadys*)**:** Der **Hendiadyoin** ist die Verwendung zweier sehr ähnlicher Wörter, meist durch ein „und" verbunden. Bei Wordsworth bereitet der Ausdruck *„bright and glittering"* (Vers 8) auf den Sonnenaufgang im folgenden Vers vor. Das helle Strahlen der Sonne wird durch die Doppelung zusätzlich betont.
- **Oxymoron** (*oxymoron*)**:** Das **Oxymoron** besteht aus zwei gegensätzlichen Worten, etwa „süß-sauer".
- **Paradoxon** (*paradox*)**:** Das **Paradoxon** verbindet Worte oder Gedanken, die zuerst einen Widerspruch ergeben, nach kurzem Nachdenken jedoch auf einen tieferen Sinn hinweisen.

Obwohl die bildhafte Verwendung von Sprache auch im Alltag eine große Rolle spielen kann, ist die Bedeutung dieser Stilmittel in lyrischen Texten ungleich größer, nicht zuletzt weil Dichter wesentlich bewusster mit konkreten Bildern spielen. Allen bildhaften Stilmitteln ist gemein, dass sie einen bestimmten Aspekt einer Situation verdeutlichen wollen, der durch direkte, nicht bildhafte Ausdrucksweise nicht in gleicher Weise zur Geltung käme. Damit können lyrische Texte vermeintlich vertraute Gegenstände und Situationen in einem neuen, verfremdeten Licht erscheinen lassen.

Stilmittel: Wortwiederholung *(repetition)*

Wortwiederholung vom Dichter gewollt eingesetzt. Sie können Situationen und Umstände auf vielfältige Art und Weise betonen und Interpretationsansätze liefern.

Je nachdem, wo im Vers und wie die Wiederholung auftritt, kann man unterschiedliche Typen unterscheiden:

Anapher	Wiederholung am Anfang von Versen oder Sätzen
Epipher	Wiederholung am Ende von Versen oder Sätzen
Epanalepse	unmittelbare oder nur durch ein bis zwei Wörter unterbrochene Wiederholung
Polyptoton	Wiederholung in verschiedenen Flexionsformen
Figura etymologica	Wiederholung in verschiedenen Wortarten

In Wordsworths Gedicht (→ Seite 163) betont die dreifache Wiederholung von „never", die zugleich Anapher und Epanalepse ist, die Einzigartigkeit des Erlebnisses. Erst durch die einzigartigen Umstände dieses besonderen Morgens kommt es zu dem subjektiven Empfinden, das den Anlass für das Gedicht liefert.

Beispielanalysen

Christopher Marlowe (1564–1593)

The Passionate Shepherd to His Love

Beispielanalyse 1

Come live with me, and be my love,
And we will all the pleasures prove
That valleys, groves, hills and fields,
Woods, or steepy mountain yields.

5   And we will sit upon the rocks,
Seeing the shepherds feed their flocks
By shallow rivers, to whose falls
Melodious birds sing madrigals.

And I will make thee beds of roses,
10   And a thousand fragrant posies,
A cap of flowers, and a kirtle,
Embroidered all with leaves of myrtle.

A gown made of the finest wool
Which from our pretty lambs we pull,
15   Fair lined slippers for the cold,
With buckles of the purest gold.

A belt of straw and ivy buds,
With coral clasps and amber studs,
And if these pleasures may thee move,
20   Come live with me, and be my love.

The shepherd swains shall dance and sing
For thy delight each May-morning.
If these delights thy mind may move,
Then live with me, and be my love.

_{Christopher Marlowe: The Collected Poems of Christopher Marlowe. Oxford University Press, New York, 2006, Seiten 157–158}

Christopher Marlowe's poem belongs to the tradition of pastoral poetry: it presents the lives of shepherds in an idealized manner. The lyrical *I* approaches the lyrical *you* with promises of love and devotion. The natural environment appears as a bountiful source of beauty – all, it seems, in the service of the pair of lovers.

The poem follows its metre and rhyme scheme very strictly. An iambic tetrameter is observed throughout; all the quatrains consist of two rhyming couplets. When the poem, in the first verse of the third stanza, switches from the dominant masculine to a feminine rhyme, it keeps this pattern for the whole stanza. For the modern reader, the renaissance text has a few surprises in terms of word stress and also pronunciation: the first and the last couplet are examples of an historical rhyme; the word "lined" in verse 15 has two syllables. If one considers all the historical changes, the poem shows remarkable regularity and a very smooth rhythm.

The tone of the poem is light: not only do the scenes, like the sitting on a rock in verse 5 or the bird song in verse 8, exude an atmosphere of ease and relaxation, there is hardly a moment in the poem where the lyrical *I* seems ruled by passion. The love expressed in the poem in fact concentrates on an almost courtly celebration of romantic love. The second verse, with its mentioning of "pleasure", is about the only reference to sexual love. However, verse 19, which repeats "pleasures", implies that the lyrical I does not think of his beloved as a lover. While metaphorical language in love poetry is often a coded form of describing sexual love, this poem does not follow such a strategy. In fact, the ideal of pastoral love presented in this poem seems to be free of sexual desire.

Instead, the area from which imagery is drawn, namely nature, hints at a different understanding of the role of love. The conspicuous absence of passion and the focus on the detailed description of the shepherds' environment together lend weight to the notion that the poem is not in the strict sense of the word a love poem; or rather, that Marlowe's work is less in praise of passionate (physical) love but instead a celebration of a life-style that, for most of his contemporaries, has been lost. What the poem then expresses is great admiration for the natural environment, the purity of flowers, rivers, lambs, or straw. While many love poems praise the beloved by going over all of her or his beautiful attributes, this poem provides no information about the lyrical *you*: the object of love becomes almost unimportant. It would also be possible to see in this refusal to acknowledge the individuality of the beloved woman a certain unwillingness to see her as anything but "my love". Marlowe's poem thus fits in the idealistic tradition of pastoral poetry. It praises the purity and beauty of nature, while it presents love as untainted by sexual desire. As a result, it celebrates life as a sequence of leisurely amusements in a beautiful natural environment.

The absence of a critical attitude towards questions of love, work, gender identity, or social issues in general hints at the fact that Marlowe's poem was written for an audience that did not feel the need for social change, either out of complacency or out of a feeling that subordination to social inequalities was an unchangeable necessity. It is precisely such an audience that may have appreciated the kind of dreamy utopianism that is one of the trademarks of pastoral poetry.

Dylan Thomas
Do not go gentle into that good night

Beispielanalyse 2

Do not go gentle into that good night,
Old age should burn and rave at close of day;
Rage, rage against the dying of the light.

Though wise men in their end know dark is right,
5   Because their words had forked no lightning they
Do not go gentle into that good night.

Good men, the last wave by, crying how bright
Their frail deeds might have danced in a green bay,
Rage, rage against the dying of the light.

10   Wild men who caught and sang the sun in flight,
And learn, too late, they grieved it on its way,
Do not go gentle into that good night.

Grave men, near death, who see with blinding sight
Blind eyes could blaze like meteors and be gay,
15   Rage, rage against the dying of the light.

> And you, my father, there on the sad height,
> Curse, bless me now with your fierce tears, I pray.
> Do not go gentle into that good night.
> Rage, rage against the dying of the light.

<small>Dylan Thomas: Collected Poems, 1934–1953. Everyman, London, 1993, Seite 148</small>

This poem by Dylan Thomas has a very clear structure. It consists of five tercets rhyming aba followed by one quatrain rhyming abaa. Two lines from the first tercet are repeated in other stanzas of the poem: the first line also ends the second and fourth tercet; the third line ends the third and fifth stanzas. The two lines also reappear as a rhyming couplet at the very end of the poem. Since the metre throughout the poem is an iambic pentameter, the last two verses form a heroic couplet. The repetition of two verses gives the poem the quality of a song with a recurring refrain. The reference to music is not accidental: this poem uses the structure of the villanelle, which derives from a folk song tradition.

At a few moments in the poem, the strict metre forms a contrast with the natural rhythm of the words used. In particular the first syllables of the third verse, "Rage, rage", break with the iambic pattern and instead present a spondaic opening of the line. The dual emphasis on the word "rage" is at the same time a clue to the dominant emotions in the poem: rage, anger, and powerless frustration.

While the rhyme and metre are highly regular, the poem frequently uses enjambments that add easy flow to an otherwise very regular text. Verses 5 and 6 very elegantly tie in the refrain at the end of the stanza with the syntactical structure of the previous verse. The third stanza opens with another enjambment. This frequent use of open line structures can be seen as a refusal to obey and be controlled by the format of the traditional line of a poem. Like the overall refusal to accept death as the absolute limitation of life, Dylan Thomas resorts to enjambments as a means to break up the confines of his strict format.

Since this is a poem about dying, a topic that is traditionally banned from direct discussion by taboo, it is not surprising to find figural language used frequently. The first verse uses a euphemism: the image of "going into the night" that avoids direct mention of death. The second refrain, verse three, also avoids direct reference of human death. Instead, it uses "light," with its lexical relationship to "eye light", as a synecdoche: as the light in the eyes is extinguished, the person dies.

Verse 17, the last verse before the final refrain, includes the image of "fierce tears": this personification implies that even tears, usually devoid of their own emotions, are overcome by wild passions. The anger of the lyrical *I* is projected onto the surrounding objects. They appear to be in a state of heightened emotions, replicating the inner feelings of the speaker.

The lyrical *I* in this poem only appears in the last stanza of the poem. It is also only at this point that the implicit lyrical *you*, which was addressed indirectly in the imperatives of the refrain verses, is stated directly. It now becomes clear that the poem is written by a son whose father is dying. The anger thus becomes more focused on one particular death. At the same time, the universal fact of mortality receives an individual note: each death is presented as both a universal and thereby normal experience and simultaneously an individual and thereby extremely sad moment.

The repetition of "men" at the opening of all but the first and last stanza further emphasizes the omnipresence of death. If one understands "men" as referring, gender-neutrally, to all of humanity, it becomes clear that it does not matter how one lives. "[W]ise men", "Good men", "Wild men", and "Grave men": they all rebel against approaching death; or at least that is the hope that the lyrical *I* expresses in the poem. While the dual refrain of the poem gives voice to the anger of the lyrical *I*, the poem's atmosphere also allows for a more positive reading of death. Rage may not stop death, but it at least offers a response, a verbal reaction to a fact of life that is unalterable. Seen in this way, the poem as a verbal protest becomes an act of rebellion.

8.3 Dramatik

Das Drama – ein Theaterstück

Die Unterscheidung der drei großen Gattungen hilft zwar dabei, literarische Texte in einen ersten Ordnungszusammenhang zu stellen, allerdings sollte man sich dessen bewusst sein, dass die Grenzen zwischen den einzelnen Genres nicht immer eindeutig zu ziehen sind. Die Tatsache, dass Romane dramatische oder lyrische Momente enthalten können, macht dies deutlich.

Es kann bei einer literarischen Interpretation also auch darauf ankommen, die Abweichungen von Genrekonventionen zu beschreiben.

Entscheidend für eine sinnvolle Interpretation von Dramen ist die Einsicht, dass die meisten Dramentexte für die **Aufführung im Theater** geschrieben sind.

Dialog, Figurenkonstellation und die Entwicklung einer Handlung kennzeichnen somit das Drama neben seinen rein theatralischen Seiten. Bei älteren Dramen mit ihren streng metrisch strukturierten und oft gar gereimten Sprechtexten fällt zudem auf, dass die Sprache sich durchgängig einer lyrischen Ausdrucksart bedient. Dabei wird deutlich, wie problematisch die Unterscheidung in die drei Großgattungen ist.

Untergattungen des Dramas

Seit der Antike unterscheidet man zwei große Untergattungen des Dramas: die Tragödie und Komödie.

- **Tragödie** *(tragedy)*: Die Tragödie beschreibt den Sturz eines Helden, der meist der oberen Gesellschaftsschicht entstammt. Eingeleitet wird dieser Fall durch einen Fehltritt oder einen Irrtum, den man **Hamartia** *(hamartia)* nennt. Meist entsteht dieser Fehler aus einer Situation heraus, die der Held nicht vollkommen überblickt. Dennoch kommt es am Ende beim Publikum durch die auf die Hamartia folgende **Katharsis** *(catharsis)*, der reinigenden tragischen Auflösung, zu einem Empfinden der Erleichterung. Mit der Bestrafung des Helden für sein Verbrechen wahrt die Tragödie auch das Prinzip von *poetic justice*, also einer Gerechtigkeit, die stets das Schlechte straft und das Gute belohnt. Das Adjektiv *poetic* betont dabei, dass es sich hier um eine rein poetische oder kunstinterne Gerechtigkeit handelt, die von der Realität leider abweicht: Im wahren Leben wird nicht jede Missetat gesühnt und auch nicht jede gute Tat belohnt.
- **Rachetragödie** *(revenge-tragedy)*: Eine für die englische Literatur wichtige Sonderform der Tragödie ist die **Rachetragödie**. Das Muster dieser Tragödien sieht vor, dass ein Mord zuerst ungerächt bleibt, dann seine Strafe findet, schließlich aber oft auch zum Tod des Rächers führt, der sich mit seiner Umwelt nach der Bluttat nicht mehr arrangieren kann. Shakespeares *Hamlet* folgt dieser Struktur in weiten Teilen.
- **Komödie** *(comedy)*: Die Komödie hat weniger stark ausgeprägte formale Vorgaben. Sie setzt sich das Ziel, ihr Publikum zu unterhalten. Die Figuren der Komödie rekrutieren sich meist aus den niederen Schichten,

womit sich auch die oft einfachere und schlichtere Sprache der Komödie erklärt. Die Themen entstammen in vielen Fällen ebenfalls alltäglichen Situationen: Sie geben das Leben mit all seinen Wechselfällen, Schicksalsschlägen und den so menschlichen Schwächen der Figuren wieder. Während einige Komödien die Verfehlungen von Figuren durch lächerliche Situationen dem Spott des Publikums preisgeben und dadurch die Normen der Gesellschaft implizit unterstützen, verwenden andere Komödien Gelächter, um Würdenträger oder andere wichtige Funktionäre der Gesellschaft zu verlachen.

- **Restaurationskomödie** *(restoration comedy)***:** Die schwierige Frage des Umgangs mit der in einer Gesellschaft gültigen Moral muss fast jede Komödie direkt oder indirekt beantworten. Da die **Restaurationskomödie** im späten 17. Jahrhundert allzu freizügig mit sozial brisanten Themen wie Ehebruch umging, sah sie sich bald einer moralisierenden Kritik ausgesetzt. Ein zentraler Vorwurf war dabei, dass das Prinzip *poetic justice* nicht befolgt wurde: Die Schurken fanden keine Strafe, vielmehr wurden sie wiederholt zu den eigentlichen Helden. Der an die Kunst oft gestellte moralische Anspruch wurde damit nicht erfüllt.

Auftakt und Exposition

Da anders als der Leser von Romanen oder Gedichten der Zuschauer einer Theateraufführung den Anfangsmoment des literarischen Werkes nicht selbst bestimmen kann, kommt dem Einstieg von Dramen, vor allem bei Theateraufführungen, eine besondere Bedeutung zu. Man kann dabei zwischen zwei Funktionen unterscheiden.

Der Auftakt signalisiert den Beginn der Aufführung und stellt einen Kommunikationskanal zwischen Publikum und Schauspielern her.

Auftakt – *opening*

Peter Shaffer
Amadeus

Darkness.
Savage whispers fill the theatre. We can distinguish nothing at first from this snake-like hissing save the word Salieri! repeated here, there and everywhere around the theatre.
Also, the barely distinguishable word Assassin!

Beispiel

Peter Shaffer: Amadeus. In: Landmarks of Modern British Theatre: The Plays of the Seventies. Methuen, London, 1986, Seiten 219–327; hier: 225

Die Formulierung „*everywhere around the theatre*" legt nahe, dass die Figuren nicht nur auf der Bühne angesiedelt sind, sondern ebenfalls im Zuschauerraum flüstern. Durch die Vermengung von Publikum und Schauspielern involviert Shaffer nicht nur seine Zuschauer stark mit dem Dargestellten, er zeigt zudem, dass die Grenze zwischen tatsächlicher und dargestellter Wirklichkeit fließend ist. Diese postmoderne Tendenz seines Dramas wird so bereits im Auftakt etabliert. Während der Auftakt einfach gesagt den Beginn einer Theateraufführung festlegt, hat die **Exposition** *(exposition)* die Funktion, eine inhaltliche Einführung in die Figurenkonstellation und Thematik zu liefern. In *Romeo and Juliet* kommt diese Funktion dem Chor zu, dessen, das Drama eröffnende, Sonett eine Zusammenfassung nicht nur des Liebeskonflikts beinhaltet, sondern darüber hinaus bereits den Ausgang des Dramas vorwegnimmt. Diese Form der Exposition, auch **initiale Exposition** genannt und von der langsamer vorgehenden **sukzessiven Exposition** zu unterscheiden, ist normalerweise eher die Ausnahme. Shakespeare lässt durch diesen Beginn die Funktionen von Auftakt und Exposition verschmelzen. In *Amadeus* wird das Publikum ebenfalls frühzeitig mit dem Konflikt zwischen Salieri und Mozart vertraut gemacht. Allerdings erfährt man erst allmählich von der Tragweite dieses Verhältnisses. Die Exposition hat die Aufgabe dem Publikum eine inhaltliche Einführung in die Thematik und die Figurenkonstellation zu liefern. Der Prolog in "*Romeo and Juliet*" ist ein Beispiel.

Exposition – *exposition*

> **Beispiel**
>
> William Shakespeare
> # Romeo and Juliet
>
> *Enter Chorus*
> Two households, both alike in dignity
> In fair Verona, where we lay our scene,
> From ancient grudge break to new mutiny,
> Where civil blood makes civil hands unclean.
> From forth the fatal loins of these two foes
> A pair of star-cross'd lovers take their life;
> Whose misadventur'd piteous overthrows
> Doth with their death bury their parents' strife.
> The fearful passage of their death-mark'd love
> And the continuance of their parents' rage,
> Which, but their children's end, nought could remove,
> Is now the two hours' traffick of our stage;
> The which if you with patient ears attend,
> What here shall miss, our toil shall strive to mend.
>
> William Shakespeare: The Complete Works of William Shakespeare. Pordes, London, 1993, Seite 826.

Sprache im Drama

Anders als in den meisten Theaterstücken seit der Restauration und in modernen Dramen kommt der Sprache in klassizistischen Dramen oder in den Werken von Shakespeare eine zentrale Unterscheidungsfunktion der einzelnen Figuren zu. Je nachdem, ob sich eine Figur in metrischer oder gar gereimter Sprache ausdrückt oder in mehr oder weniger alltäglichen Wendungen spricht, lässt sich der soziale Stand des Sprechers eindeutig zuordnen. Dabei kann man bei Shakespeare mindestens drei Stufen der Sprachebene allein nach der metrischen Struktur unterscheiden. Für besondere Momente, oder um Figuren aus ihrem Umfeld abzuheben, verwendet Shakespeare gereimte und streng metrisch gefasste Verse. So beschließen oft zwei gereimte jambische Pentameter, genannt *heroic couplet*, eine Szene oder einen Akt, um dem Publikum das Ende einer inhaltlichen Einheit deutlich zu machen. Beispielsweise endet die erste Szene im ersten Akt mit je einem Vers von Romeo und Benvolio, wodurch ein *heroic couplet* entsteht: „Farewell. Thou canst not teach me to forget. / I'll pay that doctrine, or else die in debt." Sehr häufig tritt der ungereimte fünfhebige Jambus auf, auch Blankvers *(blank verse)* genannt, der sich zwischen Renaissance und Moderne größter Beliebtheit erfreute. Diese immerhin metrisch strukturierte Sprache unterscheidet sich stilistisch betrachtet nach oben hin zu gereimten Versen und nach unten hin zur ungereimten und nicht-metrischen Sprache. Diese dritte Art des Ausdrucks nennt man, nicht nur bei Shakespeare, *free verse*.

In modernen Bühnenstücken ist diese freie, beinahe alltägliche Sprache längst Normalität. Spätestens im 19. Jahrhundert setzt sich im Theater eine natürliche und realistische Sprache durch, die sich von Reim und Metrum vollständig befreit zeigt. Allerdings markiert auch hier noch die Sprache soziale Hintergründe: In G. B. Shaws Drama *Pygmalion* (1913), das auch in der Musicalversion unter dem Titel *My Fair Lady* große Erfolge feiert, wird diese sehr englische Angewohnheit, Menschen nach ihrer Sprache zu beurteilen, ironisch thematisiert. Spätestens in den Dramen des 20. Jahrhunderts kommt der Alltagssprache, abgebrochenen Sätzen oder langen Pausen (zum Beispiel bei Harold Pinter) eine große Bedeutung zu.

Sprache kann also durch verschiedene Griffe ...

Was?	Beispiel	Wie?
... das Ende einer Szene oder eines Aktes durch ein *heroic couplet* anzeigen.	*Romeo and Juliet* Romeo: "Farewell. Thou canst teach me to forget." Benvolio: "I'll pay that doctrine or else die in debt."	durch unterschiedliche metrische Strukturen. Der erste Akt endet durch je einen Vers von Romeo und einen Vers von Benvolio = *heroic couplet* (zwei gereimte jambische Pentameter).
... Figuren hervorheben und ihren gesellschaftlichen Stand oder ihre Position anzeigen.	*Romeo and Juliet* → „Beispiel" siehe unten	Zu Beginn der Szene sprechen einfache Bedienstete, die Sprache wandelt sich zu metrischer Form als Benvolio als Mitglied der Oberschicht auftritt.
... Kontraste auf inhaltlicher Seite vorführen.	*Romeo and Juliet* Chor zu Begin Szene 1, Act 1 Gespräch zwischen Sam, Gregory, Sampson und Abram)	Der Chor spricht in metrischer Sprache von der Liebe zweier Menschen und dem tragischen Verlauf der Geschichte. Die derbe, umgangssprachliche Ebene der Bediensteten dagegen verstärkt die aggressiven und sexuellen Anspielungen.

> **Beispiel**
>
> William Shakespeare
>
> ## Romeo and Juliet
>
> **Gre.** *[Aside to Sampson.]* Say 'better'; here comes one of my master's kinsmen.
> **Sam.** Yes, better, sir.
> **Ab.** You lie.
> **Sam.** Draw, if you be men. Gregory, remember thy swashing blow.
>   *[They fight. Enter Benvolio].*
> **Ben.** Part, fools!
>   Put up your swords; you know not what you do.
>
> William Shakespeare: The Complete Works of William Shakespeare. Pordes, London, 1993, Seite 827

Figuren und Sprecher

aside – Beiseitesprechen

Auf der Bühne agieren die Figuren in Gruppen oder alleine. Je nachdem, wer zu wem spricht, unterscheidet man zwischen Dialogen und Monologen. Wie das Beiseitesprechen hat der Monolog vor allem die Funktion, Einblicke in die innere Verfassung einer Figur zu liefern. Das Fehlen eines Erzählers wie im Roman, der meistens Informationen über das Innenleben von zumindest einer Figur liefern kann, führt dazu, dass das Drama seine eigenen Techniken entwickelt hat, wie dem Leser oder dem Publikum die innere, psychische Entwicklung der Figuren offenbart werden können. Während in Dialogen nicht unbedingt alle Figuren ihre tatsächliche Meinung an den Tag legen, liefert der Monolog die Möglichkeit, das eigentliche Befinden einer Figur deutlich zu machen. Oft befindet sich eine Figur für ihren Monolog allein auf der Bühne, führt also ein Selbstgespräch. Im Englischen nennt man einen solchen Monolog *soliloquy*. Daneben gibt es natürlich auch längere Reden, die sich direkt an andere Figuren richten. Diese Solorede *(monologue)* tritt meist an einer zentralen Stelle des Dramas auf. Sie verdeutlicht eine wichtige innere Entwicklung einer der Hauptfiguren.

Solorede – monologue

Die Figuren eines Dramas lassen sich auch nach ihrer jeweiligen Bedeutung für die Kernhandlung des Stückes unterscheiden. Während die Bedeutung der Hauptfiguren unschwer erkannt werden kann, ist die Funktion der Nebenfiguren nicht immer auf den ersten Blick erkenntlich. Diese durch komische Elemente erreichte Aufheiterung einer tragischen Handlung *(comic relief)* wird im klassischen Drama oft durch eine Figur niederen Standes wahrgenommen. Da nicht alle Begebenheiten einer dramatischen Handlung auf der Bühne dargestellt werden können, beispielsweise große kriegerische Auseinandersetzungen oder die Landung eines Flugzeugs, gibt es für solche Momente wie bei der Wortkulisse eine verbale Lösung. Anstatt mit großem Aufwand einen Kriegsschauplatz darzustellen, verwendet man oft einen Boten, der von den Entwicklungen jenseits des auf der Bühne dargestellten Raums berichtet. Verwandt mit diesem **Botenbericht** ist die **Mauerschau**, bei der Figuren auf der Bühne kommentierend berichten, was auf der anderen Seite einer Mauer und damit unsichtbar für das Publikum geschieht. Beide Techniken helfen ebenfalls, grausame Szenen von der Bühne fernzuhalten.

Der Bote – messenger

Dramatische Ironie

Der Spannungsaufbau vieler Dramen lebt davon, dass das Publikum bereits den Ausgang der Handlung kennt, während die Figuren ihrem Schicksal noch ahnungslos gegenüber stehen. Es braucht für diesen Spannungsaufbau einen unterschiedlichen Kenntnisstand zwischen Zuschauer und Figur: Die Zuschauer wissen etwas, was die Figur nicht weiß; eine Figur ist sich der Bedeutung ihrer Aussage nicht bewusst, dem Publikum hingegen ist die Bedeutung und Tragweite klar.

Für die Informationsvergabe an das Publikum sind das **Beiseitesprechen** *(aside)* und Monologe von zentraler Bedeutung. In beiden Fällen kommt es zur Informationsvergabe von einer Figur an das Publikum, ohne dass die anderen Figuren den Inhalt erfahren. Durch das Beiseitesprechen tritt auch das Empfinden der Figuren deutlicher hervor, da in solchen Momenten meist die Gedanken, Ängste oder Wünsche der Figuren zum Ausdruck kommen. Die gleiche Funktion haben Monologe.

In *Romeo and Juliet* besteht somit vom ersten Moment an diskrepante Informiertheit zwischen Figuren und Publikum, da der Chor bereits das Ergebnis der Liebesbeziehung vorweggenommen hat.

In *Romeo and Juliet* geht der Wissensvorsprung auf den Anfang des Dramas zurück. Noch vor dem ersten Akt betritt der Chor die Bühne und liefert eine vollständige Zusammenfassung der Handlung, die nicht nur den Familienzwist und die vom Schicksal verdammte Liebe der Hauptfiguren ankündigt, sondern auch deren letztendlichen Tod.

In *Amadeus* weiß das Publikum ebenfalls von Salieris üblen Plänen, befindet sich also Mozart gegenüber, der sich von Salieri Hilfe erhofft, in einem Wissensvorsprung. Aussagen von Mozart zu oder über Salieri, sofern diese das Verhältnis der beiden angehen, bekommen dadurch eine ironische Note.

Diskrepante Informiertheit kann jedoch auch zwischen den einzelnen Figuren entstehen. Die berühmte erste Balkonszene in *Romeo and Juliet* zeigt, wie das Beiseitesprechen Romeos von Julia nicht wahrgenommen wird, ihre Liebeserklärung von Romeo jedoch gehört wird, wodurch für ihn ein Wissensvorsprung entsteht.

Beispiel

William Shakespeare

Romeo and Juliet

Jul. O Romeo, Romeo! – wherefore art thou Romeo?
     Deny thy father and refuse thy name;
     Or, if thou wilt not, be but sworn my love,
     And I'll no longer be a Capulet.
Rom. [*Aside.*] Shall I hear more, or shall I speak at this?
Jul. 'Tis but thy name that is my enemy;
     Thou art thyself though, not a Montague

William Shakespeare: The Complete Works of William Shakespeare. Pordes, London, 1993, Seite 826.

Romeo weiß ab diesem Moment von Julias Gefühlen, wodurch sich der Prozess des Sich-Näherkommens deutlich beschleunigt. Wenn sich später in *Romeo and Juliet* die Ereignisse überstürzen, dann wird diese große Geschwindigkeit auch dadurch ermöglicht, dass die beiden Liebenden schon hier von ihrer Liebe Kenntnis bekommen. Die Szene birgt noch einen weiteren Moment der dramatischen Ironie, wenn nämlich Julia davon spricht, dass sie nicht mehr lange eine Capulet sein werde: Darin deutet sich ihr baldiger Tod bereits an.

Beispielanalysen

Tom Stoppard (1937–)

Rosencrantz and Guildenstern Are Dead (1966) ACT TWO

Beispielinterpretation 1

Hamlet, Ros[encrantz] and Guil[denstern] talking, the continuation of the previous scene. Their conversation, on the move, is indecipherable at first. The first intelligible line is Hamlet's, coming at the end of a short speech – see Shakespeare Act II, scene ii.

Hamlet: S'blood, there is something in this more than natural, if philosophy could find it out. *[A flourish from the Tragedians' band.]*

Guil: There are the players.

Hamlet: Gentlemen, you are welcome to Elsinore. Your hands, come then. *[He takes their hands.]* The appurtenance of welcome is fashion and ceremony. Let me comply with you in this garb, lest my extent to the players (which I tell you must show fairly outwards) should more appear like entertainment than yours. You are welcome. *[About to leave]* But my uncle-father and aunt-mother are deceived.

Guil: In what, my dear lord?

Hamlet: I am but mad north north-west; when the wind is southerly I know a hawk from a handsaw.

[Polonius enters as Guil turns away.]

Polonius: Well be with you gentlemen.

Hamlet: *[To Ros]* Mark you, Guildenstern *[Uncertainly to Guil]* and you too; at each ear a hearer. That great baby you see there is not yet out of his swaddling clouts ... *[He takes Ros upstage with him, talking together.]*

Polonius: My Lord! I have news to tell you.

Hamlet: *[Releasing Ros and mimicking]* My lord, I have news to tell you ... When Roscius was an actor in Rome ...

[Ros comes downstage to re-join Guil.]

Polonius: *[As he follows Hamlet out]* The actors are come hither my lord.

Hamlet: Buzz, buzz.

[Exeunt Hamlet and Polonius.]

[Ros and Guil ponder. Each reluctant to speak first.]

Guil: Hm?

Ros: Yes?

Guil: What?

Ros: I thought you ...

Guil:	No.
Ros:	Ah.
[Pause.]	
Guil:	I think we can say we made some headway.
Ros:	You think so?
Guil:	I think we can say that.
Ros:	I think we can say he made us look ridiculous.
Guil:	We played it close to the chest of course.
Ros:	*[Derisively]* 'Questions and answers. Old ways are the best ways'!
	He was scoring off us all down the line.
Guil:	He caught us on the wrong foot once or twice, perhaps, but I thought we gained some ground.
Ros:	*[Simply.]* He murdered us.
Guil:	He might have had the edge.
Ros:	*[Roused]* Twenty-seven-three, and you think he might have had the edge? He murdered us.

Tom Stoppard: Rosencrantz and Guildenstern Are Dead. Faber & Faber, London, 1967, Seiten 40–41

Stoppard's play takes place inside the world of Shakespeare's *Hamlet*. It uses two minor characters from the play both to celebrate the original play from the perspective of (post)modern art and to ask questions about the nature of theatre, language, and history.

The first half of the excerpt above comes directly from Shakespeare's play. However, whereas in the original, Rosencrantz and Guildenstern simply disappear from the rest of the scene only to reappear later in the play, the action in Stoppard's re-invention of Hamlet stays with the two hapless characters. Through subverting a canonical text, Stoppard's play also questions the system of literature and the formation of a canon.

While Shakespeare's Hamlet already plays with the power of language by pretending to have gone mad, Stoppard's play takes this critical attitude towards the power of language a step further. The fact that none of the other characters ever seems to be quite clear how to tell Hamlet's two friends apart (he himself is revealed in the stage directions to turn „Uncertainly to Guil", having just addressed Rosencrantz by his friend's name) already points to the fact that language does not always clearly refer to particular referents.

The second half of the excerpt above takes this playful notion of language one step further. As in other moments of the play, Rosencrantz and Guildenstern are shown to use language simply as a game. They turn their conversation with Hamlet into a sort of word-tennis, where they are losing badly to their royal friend. However, the ultimate (dramatic) irony at the end of the passage above is reached when they argue that Hamlet „murdered us". The remark emphasizes that there is a reality beyond words: after all, both characters are killed at the end of the play, and it is Hamlet's scheming that leads to their death. So, ultimately, Hamlet's skilled use of language leads to the death of Rosencrantz and Guildenstern.

Looked at from this perspective, their conversation with Hamlet does have a deadly meaning. Other than what the rest of the play may imply, language is then, after all, shown to create facts, to have an effect on reality. The play, in many ways, presents the complex case of both making an argument and at the same time presenting evidence against it. The relationship of *Rosencrantz and Guildenstern Are Dead* to Shakespeare's *Hamlet* repeats this dual attitude. By writing a satirical comment on the earlier play, Stoppard both subverts his source and, through his text, contributes to the lasting importance of Shakespeare's work.

Arthur Miller (1915–2005)

Death of a Salesman (1949)

Beispielinterpretation 2

Willy *[stops short, looking at Biff]:* Glad to hear it, boy.
Happy: He wanted to say good night to you, sport.
Willy: *[to Biff]* Yeah. Knock him dead, boy. What'd you want to tell me?
Biff: Just take it easy, Pop. Good night. *[He turns to go.]*
Willy: *[unable to resist]:* And if anything falls off the desk while you're talking to him – like a package or something – don't you pick it up. They have office boys for that.
Linda: I'll make a big breakfast –
Willy: Will you let me finish? *[To Biff.]* Tell him you were in the business in the West. Not farm work.
Biff: All right, Dad.
Linda: I think everything –
Willy: *[going right through her speech]:* And don't undersell yourself. No less than fifteen thousand dollars.
Biff: *[unable to bear him]:* Okay. Good night, Mom. *[He starts moving.]*
Willy: Because you got greatness in you, Biff, remember that. You got all kinds of greatness ... *[He lies back, exhausted. Biff walks out.]*
Linda: *[calling after Biff]:* Sleep well, darling!

Happy: I'm gonna get married, Mom. I wanted to tell you.
Linda: Go to sleep, dear.
Happy: *[going]:* I just wanted to tell you.
Willy: Keep up the good work. *[Happy exits.]* God … remember that Ebbets Field game? The championship of the city?

From DEATH OF A SALESMAN by Arthur Miller, copyright 1949, renewed copyright 1977 by Arthur Miller. Used by permission of Viking Penguin, a division of Penguin Group (USA) Inc. – New York, 1949, S. 67–68.

Arthur Miller's *Death of a Salesman* is considered to be one of the most American plays ever written. First produced in 1949, it is an open condemnation of the underside of the American dream: dishonesty, superficiality, and appearances are shown to contribute to the suicide of a father and the spoiling of his sons. Willy, the eponymous salesman, lives in a world of pretense, reminiscing about the past, day-dreaming about his professional success, imagining brilliant futures for his sons. Secretly, however, he has been plotting his own death so as to leave his family the insurance money that will provide them with the financial security he has been never able to achieve.

The excerpt above, taken from the end of the first act, shows how Willy is prone to withdraw into his inner world of happiness and promise, ignoring all evidence from around him that would contradict him. While Biff is obviously unwilling to dream along in this scene, his father imagines a very positive outcome from the planned meeting next morning. His social pretensions become clear when he tells his son not to be too subservient: "They have office boys for that." Even though his son has hardly any qualifications that would justify the kind of treatment Willy expects, the simple promise "you got greatness in you" is supposed to make up for all shortcomings.

The relationship between Willy and his wife, Linda, highlights the fragile psychic state of the husband. While his outer world is falling apart, he compensates by ruling over his wife, talking over her, telling her to be quiet and insisting on her showing him respect. At this stage in their relationship, Linda has also become affected by her husband's tendency to block out reality by withdrawing into an inner world. The announcement of Happy that he will get married is met with silence. While his statement would surely warrant some kind of response, she simply tells him: "Go to sleep, dear." By protecting her feeble husband, whose suicidal tendencies she had already started to notice, she herself has also begun to withdraw from reality. She does not want to face the facts and instead choses to ignore aspects of the life around her that may upset the equilibrium.

The stage directions in this scene, beyond pointing out characters' coming and going, contribute to the understanding of the relationship between the characters. Willy's dismissive tone towards his wife is emphasized by the stage directions, making it clear to the reader (and the director) how Miller had envisioned the balance of power on stage. Biff's view of his father, whose shallowness he has seen through when still a child, is also frequently expressed non-verbally, through the stage directions that indicate his thoughts and feelings. Biff also does not voice his opinion so as not to shatter the imaginary realm of Willy's view of life.

Lastly, the language marks the characters throughout as inauthentic and struggling for a personal sense of belonging. The repeated use of clichéd expressions paired with words that hardly describe clearly what is being meant, add to the feeling that Willy (and his family) is unable to use thinking and speaking as a means to represent reality. Willy's phrase "You got all kinds of greatness" provides a good example: while "you got greatness" is highly unspecific and in the case of Biff at best wishful thinking (as Biff himself points out at the end of the play), the addition of "all kinds" hardly makes Willy's statement any clearer. In fact, nearly every single sentence in the scene above (like "Glad to hear it" or "Knock him dead") is an empty phrase. Language, as a whole, has turned into an empty vessel.

The banalities that the characters in *Death of a Salesman* exchange on stage point to one of the central themes of the play, namely the emptiness that is at the centre of Willy, the protagonist. His suicide at the end of the play represents the climax of the process of self-annihilation that has been going on for most of his life. The absence of meaning that marks most sentences thus mirrors the absence of meaning from his life; and the play's superficial dialogue echoes the superficiality of Willy's view of life. The play thus presents some clear, if indirect, criticism of the vacuity at the heart of the American way of life during the post-war years.

8.4 Prosa

Der Begriff der Prosa geht auf das lateinische Wort für „schlichte Rede" zurück, beschreibt also vor allem eine Art der Sprachverwendung. Definiert man Prosatexte negativ, durch ihre Unterschiede zu den anderen beiden Hauptgattungen, bleiben die nicht-lyrische Sprache und das nicht-szenische Darstellen als Ausscheidungskriterien bestehen. Die verbleibenden Texte schließen bei einer solchen Beschreibung eine Großzahl an Gebrauchstexten, wissenschaftlichen Abhandlungen und anderen Veröffentlichungen ein, die nicht notwendigerweise alle in den Bereich der Literatur fallen. Von besonderem Interesse ist dagegen die „schlichte Rede", wenn sie künstlerischen Charakter hat. Eng verwandt mit dem Begriff der Prosa, aber nicht mit ihr identisch, ist die Bezeichnung Erzähltexte. Sie beschreibt deutlicher (und positiv) das zentrale Erkennungsmerkmal der dritten Hauptgattung, nämlich die Anwesenheit einer erzählenden Instanz, die zwischen Leser und Figurenrealität vermittelt.

> Der früher häufig verwendete Begriff Epik für die dritte Hauptgattung ist aufgrund seiner Bezüge zum Epos, dem aus der Antike bekannten Heldengedicht, wenig hilfreich.

Untergattungen von Prosatexten

Die Untergattungen der Prosa unterscheiden sich vor allem durch ihre jeweilige Länge und den damit verbundenen Einschränkungen. Kann ein Roman das Leben seiner Hauptfigur über viele Jahrzehnte und große Räume hinweg begleiten, etwa in Daniel Defoes *Robinson Crusoe* (1719) oder in Virgina Woolfs *Orlando* (1928), so verhindert die Knappheit der Kurzgeschichte das Entstehen solch epischer Breite.

Prosaformen	Beispiele	Kriterien
Kurzgeschichte (short story)	*An Occurrence at Owl Creek Bridge* (Ambrose Bierce)	– die Kurzgeschichte will ein konkretes Gefühl oder eine bestimmt Stimmung erzeugen – unmittelbarer Einstieg in die Handlung – fehlende Entwicklung der wenigen Charaktere – Beschränkung auf ein einziges, oft schicksalhaftes Ereignis
Roman (novel) Kurzroman (short novel)	*Ulysses*, *Finnegan's Wake* (James Joyce) *Heart of darkness* (George Orwell)	– der Roman will eine Gesamtdarstellung des Lebens liefern – zeichnet sich durch seine Länge aus – Zeitspanne umfasst oft mehrere Jahre oder gar Generationen – viele, detaillierte Charaktere – detaillierte Beschreibung des geografischen, politischen und sozialen Umfeldes

Tab. 8.5: Untergattungen von Prosa

Mimesis/Poiesis

Grundsätzlich unterscheidet man zwischen fantastischer und realistischer Literatur. Die realistische Literatur folgt dem Prinzip Nachahmung oder Mimesis, wohingegen die fantastische Literatur eher auf eine ästhetische Neuschaffung der Welt oder Poiesis abzielt.

Tatsächlich findet man deswegen in Romanen eine je nach Text individuelle Gewichtung von realistischen und fantastischen Elementen. Während Tolkiens *The Lord of the Rings* oder die *Harry-Potter*-Romane viele fantastische Elemente beinhalten, findet man in Nick Hornbys *About a Boy* oder in J. D. Salingers *The Catcher in the Rye* vor allem eine genau beobachtete Wirklichkeit, die sich natürlich auch fiktiver Elemente wie erfundener Personen, Orte, Namen oder Ereignisse bedient.

Eine erfolgreiche Mischform der beiden Grundtendenzen liegt in *Science-Fiction*-Werken vor. Während der Bezug auf die Naturwissenschaften *(Science)* natürlich die Realitätsnähe solcher Texte betont, führt der Als-Ob-Charakter *(Fiction)* dieser Texte in eine imaginäre Welt ein. So verbindet sich auch in Mary Shelleys *Frankenstein* (1818) das Wunschdenken der Menschen, durch die Wissenschaft die Probleme des Lebens zu meistern, mit der irrealen Option, Leben neu zu schaffen.

Grundelemente von Erzählungen

Wohl die wichtigste Erkenntnis in der Beschreibung von Erzähltexten bezieht sich auf die Unterscheidung von *story* und *discourse*. Mit diesen beiden oder ähnlichen Begriffen bezeichnet man auf der einen Seite das *Was* einer Erzählung *(story)* und auf der anderen das *Wie* ihrer Darstellung *(discourse)*.

> Bei der Analyse von Erzähltexten ist es wichtig, sich darüber im Klaren zu sein, dass jede Erzählung immer zugleich über *story* und *discourse* verfügt. Es ist zudem unmöglich, *story* in quasi reiner Form, ohne Verwendung von *discourse*, zu vermitteln. Selbst eine denkbar knappe Wiedergabe eines Romans (Mann baut Monster aus Leichenteilen; Monster tötet alle Freunde und Verwandten seines Schöpfers; beide sterben im ewigen Eis) kommt nicht ohne *discourse*-Elemente aus: hier im Beispiel die gewählte Formulierung der wichtigsten Romanmomente aus *Frankenstein* im Telegrammstil.

Tipp
Bausteine des Erzählens

Bei der Beschreibung einer Erzählung kann man auch nach anderen Begriffen Unterscheidungen treffen. Der Romanautor und Essayist E.M. Forster hat in *Aspects of the Novel* (1927) mit dem Begriffspaar *story* und *plot* Teilaspekte von Erzählungen unterschieden, wobei seine Vorstellung von *story* nicht gleichzusetzen ist mit dem *story*-Begriff aus dem Gegensatzpaar *discourse/story*. Forster bezeichnet mit *story* den **chronologischen Ablauf** einer Erzählung und mit *plot* die **logisch-kausale Verknüpfung** der einzelnen Elemente, also den logischen Verlauf der Ereignisse.

story/plot
story/discourse

Die Betonung von logisch-kausalen Inhaltsmomenten führt dazu, dass man Teile einer Erzählung danach unterscheiden kann, ob sie das Geschehen weiterführen oder nicht. Dementsprechend nennt man einen entscheidenden oder handlungstragenden Aspekt einer Erzählung *kernel* und eher digressive, vom Thema abschweifende Teile *satellites*. **Textbausteine** aus dem Bereich *kernel* für eine Kriminalgeschichte zu definieren, ist vergleichsweise einfach: Der Ablauf des Mordes, das genaue Tatmotiv und das den Täter überführende Beweismaterial gehören sicher dazu. In den meisten Kurzgeschichten kann man dagegen fast keine Textpassagen als *satellites* beschreiben.

Erzählsituation

Während man bei einem Drama den Fortgang der Ereignisse direkt dargestellt bekommt und bei einem Gedicht das persönlich-subjektive Empfinden eines lyrischen Ichs nacherlebt, bieten Erzähltexte eine grundsätzlich andere Art der Inhaltsvermittlung. Diese kann nach unterschiedlichen Aspekten genauer definiert werden. Eben dies steht oft am Anfang einer Interpretation narrativer Texte.

Die Form des Erzählens, die Erzählsituation, tritt in drei Grundtypen in Erscheinung: als **auktoriale, personale oder Ich-Erzählsituation**. Selbstverständlich gibt es darüber hinaus weitere Erzählsituationen, z.B. eine Du-Erzählsituation, bei der sich der Text direkt an einen Leser wendet, oder den Briefroman, der streng genommen keinen Erzähler hat. Ebenso findet man regelmäßig Mischformen der drei Grundtypen. Die drei Grundtypen des Erzählens kann man anhand zentraler Merkmale unterscheiden:

- Die **auktoriale Erzählsituation** *(authorial narrative situation)* hat einen allwissenden Erzähler, der außerhalb der Welt der Romanhandlung angesiedelt ist. Dieser Erzähler hat Einblick in die Psyche der Figuren, kann also über die Motivation, die Ängste oder Wünsche einzelner Charaktere Auskunft geben. Ebenso ist diesem Erzähler die Vorgeschichte sowie der Ausgang der Handlung bekannt.

- Die **Ich-Erzählsituation** *(first-person narrative situation)* hat einen Erzähler, der in der ersten Person erzählt. Der Erzähler gehört der gleichen Welt an wie die anderen Charaktere der Handlung. Oft ist der Erzähler zugleich der Protagonist. Da der Erzähler keinen Zugang zu den Gedanken und Gefühlen der anderen Personen hat, ist die Ich-Erzählsituation in ihren Darstellungsmöglichkeiten stark eingeschränkt. Allerdings kann der Erzähler Kenntnis vom Ausgang des Geschehens haben, vor allem dann, wenn das erzählende Ich *(narrating I)* von einem deutlich späteren Zeitpunkt aus die früheren Abenteuer des erlebenden Ich *(experiencing I)* schildert.
- Die **personale Erzählsituation** *(figural narrative situation)* ist gekennzeichnet von einem Erzählen, das nicht einer bestimmten Figur zugerechnet werden kann. Anders als bei den anderen beiden Grundtypen gibt es hier keinen eigentlichen Erzähler; vielmehr *wird* erzählt. Diese passive Distanz entwickelt sich aus dem wechselnden Fokus auf einzelne Personen der Erzählung, aus deren Perspektive berichtet wird. Eine solche Reflektorfigur *(focaliser)* ist jedoch für sich kein Erzähler: Sie fungiert lediglich als Spiegel, der den Fortgang der Handlung wiedergibt.

Die folgenden drei Romananfänge sind Beispiele für die Grundtypen des Erzählens.

Beispiel 1 auktoriale Erzählsituation

It is a truth universally acknowledged, that a single man in possession of a good fortune, must be in want of a wife.
However little known the feelings or views of such a man may be on his first entering the neighbourhood, this truth is so well fixed in the minds of the surrounding families, that he is considered as the rightful property of some one or other of their daughters.
"My dear Mr. Bennet," said his lady to him one day, "have you heard that Netherfield Park is let at last?"
Mr. Bennet replied that he had not.

Jane Austen: Pride and Prejudice. Penguin, London, 2003, Seite 5

Im ersten Beispiel eines Romananfangs klingt die ironisch-zynische Stimme des Erzählers von außerhalb und jenseits der Figuren. Die Wünsche und Hoffnungen der beteiligten Personen werden jedoch nicht nur dargestellt, sind dem auktorialen Erzähler also offensichtlich einsehbar, sie werden zugleich kommentiert. Die Tatsache, dass die Nachbarn keine Einsicht in die Psyche anderer haben, ausgedrückt in der dritten Zeile des zweiten Absatzes, lässt vermuten, dass die Erzählstimme in Austens *Pride and Prejudice* sehr wohl Kenntnis des Innenlebens der Figuren hat.

> **Beispiel 2**
> **Ich-Erzählsituation**
>
> In my younger and more vulnerable years my father gave me some advice that I've been turning over in my mind ever since.
> "Whenever you feel like criticizing any one," he told me, "just remember that all the people in the world haven't had the advantages that you've had."
> He didn't say any more but we've always been unusually communicative in a reserved way and I understood that he meant a great deal more than that.
>
> F. Scott Fitzgerald: The Great Gatsby. Scribner, New York, 2003, Seite 5

Das zweite Beispiel verwendet eine Ich-Erzählsituation. Der Erzähler, Nick Carraway, ist zwar nicht der Protagonist, er ist aber die Figur, die uns von Gatsbys Erlebnissen berichtet. Der fehlende Einblick in die Motivation der anderen Figuren wird bereits in diesen ersten Zeilen des Romans deutlich. Nick zitiert seinen Vater, ist sich aber nicht ganz sicher, ob er dessen Aussage richtig verstanden hat. Diese fehlende Einsicht in die Innenwelt der anderen Figuren, die sich aus der Ich-Erzählsituation von Nick zwangsweise ergibt, hat jedoch den Vorteil, dass Gatsby den Lesern bis zum Schluss als eine mysteriöse Figur erscheint. Die Erzählsituation trägt zu der Stimmung des Romans entscheidend bei.

> **Beispiel 3**
> **personale Erzählsituation**
>
> Mrs Dalloway said she would buy the flowers herself.
> For Lucy had her work cut out for her. The doors would be taken off their hinges; Rumpelmayer's men were coming. And then, thought Clarissa Dalloway, what a morning – fresh as if issued to children on a beach. What a lark! What a plunge! For so it had always seemed to her when, with a little squeak of the hinges, which she could hear now, she had burst open the French windows and plunged at Bourton into the open air.
>
> Virginia Woolf: Mrs Dalloway. Wordsworth, Ware, 2003, Seite 3

Das dritte Beispiel zeigt, wie eine personale Erzählsituation zwischen verschiedenen Reflektorfiguren oszilliert. Virginia Woolfs *Mrs Dalloway* verzichtet fast vollständig auf eine erzählende Stimme, die man als Person fassen könnte. Vielmehr liefert der Text verschiedene Einblicke in das Innenleben der wichtigsten Figuren, vor allem Clarissa Dalloway und Septimus Warren Smith. Deren innere Zustände werden mehr oder weniger unvermittelt dargestellt. Sie liefern dabei einen stark idiosynkratischen Blick auf die Situation. Die Handlung, bzw. *story*, von *Mrs Dalloway* müssen sich die Leser aus den einzelnen Eindrücken selbst konstruieren.

Einblick in das Bewusstsein der Figuren

Romanfiguren können in Texten auf verschiedene Art und Weisen vorgestellt werden. E. M. Forster benennt die beiden Möglichkeiten *showing* und *telling*. Danach werden Figuren entweder durch ihre Handlungen charakterisiert (also vorgeführt – *showing*) oder direkt beschrieben (*telling*). Es existieren jedoch noch differenziertere Möglichkeiten, Einblick in die Psyche der einzelnen Figuren zu liefern. Dabei unterscheidet man zwischen drei Typen:

Gedankenbericht (engl. *psycho narration*)	*Mr Bennet replied that he had not.* → Seite 187	– tritt häufig in der autokorialen Erzählsituation *(authorial narrative situation)* auf – Verwendung der 3. Person und des Präteritums *(past tense)* bei der Darstellung des Bewusstseins einer Figur – Gegensatz zu innerer Monolog
Innerer Monolog (*interior monologue*)	*What a lark! What a plunge!* → unteres Beispiel Seite 188	– Sprache gibt formal den assoziativen Gedankenfluss einer Person wieder – oftmals Verwendung der 1. Person und des Präsens *(present tense)* – oft abgebrochene Sätze (Anakoluth, *anacoluthon*) – fehlende Interpunktion *(punctuation)* – umgangssprachliche Ausdrücke *(colloquial expressions)* – unzensierte Gedankengänge *(uncensored train of thought)*
Erlebte Rede (*free indirect discourse*)	*The Dead, Ulysses* (James Joyce) *Mrs Dalloway, To the Lighthouse* (Virginia Woolf)	– Stimme der Figur und Stimme des Erzählers überlagern sich – das Fehlen von „er sagte…" oder „sie dachte…." – Raumadverbien, die sich auf den Figurenstandpunkt beziehen (wie morgen, hier, nun). – affektive und argumentative Interjektionen (gewiss, jedoch) – emphatische Ausrufe (Ach!) – rhetorische Fragen

Tab. 8.6: Typen der Einsichtnahme in die Psyche

Raum und Zeit

So wie man grundsätzlich zwischen *discourse* und *story* unterscheidet, differenziert man auch zwischen **Erzählzeit** *(discourse time)* und **erzählter Zeit** *(story time)*, also zum einen der Zeit, die man benötigt, um ein Ereignis zu erzählen (Erzählzeit), und zum anderen der Zeit, die innerhalb der erzählten Welt vergeht. In *House Mother Normal* (1971) schildert B. S. Johnson, einer der wichtigsten Vertreter des experimentellen postmodernen englischen Romans, einen Abend in einer psychiatrischen Anstalt aus der inneren Sicht der neun anwesenden Personen. Die Erzählzeit ist dabei genau neun Mal länger als die erzählte Zeit, da alle Figuren etwa in realer Geschwindigkeit berichten.

<small>Generell kann man drei Grundtypen der relativen Geschwindigkeit *(pace)* eines Erzählverhaltens unterscheiden, die sich in ihrem Verhältnis von erzählter Zeit zur Erzählzeit grundsätzlich unterscheiden.</small>

In den meisten Erzähltexten fluktuiert das Zeitverhalten: Manchmal überschlagen sich die *story*-Ereignisse innerhalb einer kurzen *discourse*-Zeit, dann wird wieder ausgedehnt über eine lange ereignislose Phase berichtet. Ein Unterschied in der relativen Erzählzeit hat meist auch inhaltliche Gründe, die es zu erkennen und darzustellen gilt.

Virginia Woolfs *Mrs Dalloway* ist gerade in Hinsicht auf die Zeitstruktur sehr sorgfältig durchorganisiert: Nicht umsonst hatte der Roman den Arbeitstitel „The Hours". Die Erlebnisse der Hauptfiguren werden immer wieder vom stündlichen Läuten der Glocken von Big Ben unterbrochen. Die Mitte des Romans ist konsequenterweise vom 12-Uhr-Läuten unterbrochen.

- **Einheit zwischen den Erzählzeiten**: Erzählzeit = erzählte Zeit (narrated time) = (narrative time)
- **Zeitraffung**: Erzählzeit kleiner als erzählte Zeit (narrated time) < (narrative time)
- **Zeitdehnun**g: Erzählzeit größer als erzählte Zeit (narrated time) > (narrative time)

Neben der Zeit kommt auch dem Raum einer Erzählung große Bedeutung zu. Viele Romanautoren beschreiben detailliert die Örtlichkeiten ihrer Handlung. Im Idealfall trägt die Lokalität einer Begebenheit zu ihrem Verständnis bei, wobei die räumliche Situiertheit einer Szene oft in einem metaphorischen Verhältnis zur Handlung steht. Im Schauerroman etwa kommt den gruseligen Kellergewölben von verwunschenen Schlössern ebenso große Bedeutung zu wie der mystischen Macht der Natur.

In *Mrs Dalloway* führt die Großstadt in ihrem hektischen Treiben die zunehmende Isolation des Individuums vor. Die Trennung in Innen- und Außenräume betont zudem das psychologische Interesse von Woolf an den Geisteszuständen ihrer Protagonisten. In fast schon impressionistischer Manier wirkt die Stadt um die beiden Hauptpersonen als eine Ansammlung von Eindrücken: Geräusche, Gerüche, Menschen, Autos, Flugzeuge. Der physische Raum, in dem die Figuren agieren, wird somit zu einem psychischen Raum, was das Grundinteresse von *Mrs Dalloway* deutlich unterstützt.

Gerade in amerikanischen Romanen spielt der Raum oft eine besondere Rolle. Die Vorstellung einer Abgrenzung, oder *frontier*, von kultiviertem Land im Osten und „wildem" Westen diente nicht nur als Entschuldigung für die

Besitznahme des Kontinents (bzw. die gewaltsame Vertreibung der indianischen Bevölkerung), sondern spiegelt auch die Auseinandersetzung mit der immensen Weite des Landes und seiner beeindruckenden Natur wider.

Beispielanalysen
Mary Shelley (1797–1822)
Frankenstein (1818)

Beispielanalyse 1

[…] These motives urged me to comply with his demand. We crossed the ice, therefore, and ascended the opposite rock. The air was cold, and the rain again began to descend: we entered the hut, the fiend with an air of exultation, I with a heavy heart and depressed spirits. But I consented to listen; and, seating myself by the fire which my odious companion had lighted, he thus began his tale.

Chapter 11
'It is with considerable difficulty that I remember the original era of my being: all the events of that period appear confused and indistinct. A strange multiplicity of sensations seized me, and I saw, felt, heard, and smelt, at the same time; and it was, indeed, a long time before I learned to distinguish between the operations of my various senses. […]

Mary Shelley: Frankenstein, or, The Modern Prometheus. Wordsworth, Ware, 1993, Seite 71

Shelley's novel is presented in a highly complex and densely structured fashion. Most of the novel appears to be told in the first person by Victor Frankenstein, who is the first person narrator at the end of chapter 10. Chapter 11, however, begins the tale of his creature. The novel uses various layers of embedded narratives. In fact, the first narrative frame has a young scientist, R. Walton, travel to the North pole. He is writing letters to his sister, telling her, at one point, about having met Victor Frankenstein, who then takes over as (embedded) first person narrator.

The layering of the narrative frames makes it easier for the readers to move from the scientific Walton, whom one may take to be reliable, to the fantastic creature. The novel thus incorporates a number of narrative modes that cover both realistic and fantastic ground. In fact, Shelley's novel has been called one of the earliest science fiction texts since it mixes some realistic portrayals of scientific, or rather medical, advances with highly imaginary (and somewhat Gothic) inventions that are clearly not derived from a mimetic approach to reality.

The insistence on keeping to first person narratives hightens the novel's atmosphere of being a genuine report of events that truly happened. The continued use of opening quotation marks throughout chapters 11 to 16 not only reminds readers of a change of speaker, it also emphasizes the fact that somebody is speaking, that a person is recounting his personal memories. Through relying on eyewitnesses, the text claims greater veracity. By situating the various episodes of the novel in easily identifiable parts of Europe, Shelley further heightens the mimetic quality of her narrative. She also brings the natural environment directly into her text, which is filled with the Romantic view of nature as a powerful place that confronts humanity with its own insignificancy vis-à-vis the divine creation.

The scene quoted above takes place in a typical location for *Frankenstein*, namely in a sublime natural environment. The inhospitability is emphasized by words like "ice", "rock", and "fire." Surrounded by the elements, Victor appears fragile and at risk. His creature, on the other hand, seems remarkably at ease on the glacier. Victor's scientific rationality is in direct opposition to the creature's physical presence. While Victor is all scheming intellect, the creature turns out to be driven by desires and emotions; it (or rather, he) almost seems to be the better human being. The opening words of Chapter 11 show that the creature is by no means a brute: on the contrary, both the eloquent tone of voice and the keen perceptions that mark the first moments of his life present him as a sensitive being. When he claims that he "saw, felt, heard, and smelt," he proves to be connected to his environment, in touch with the natural world around him. The fact that later on he "learned" proves him to have intelligence, so that he can be said to fulfil at least the second half of the *homo sapiens* description.

In contrast to the creature's harmonious relationship with the powerful natural environment, Victor's distance from his physical surroundings is highly noticeable. His arrogant hubris raises moral questions. The novel as a whole has been described as a critique of the scientific world view. The need to question the responsibility of science can easily be transferred to a contemporary setting. Shelley's novel can thus even be read as a commentary on such questions as whether cloning has to be discussed from a moral point of view.

J.M. Coetzee (1940–)

Foe (1986)

Beispielanalyse 2

"'I must go, Friday. You thought that carrying stones was the hardest of labours. But when you see me at Mr Foe's desk making marks with the quill, think of each mark as a stone, and think of the paper as the island, and imagine that I must disperse the stones over the face of the island, and when that is done and the taskmaster is not satisfied (was Cruso ever satisfied with your labours?) must pick them up again (which, in the figure, is scoring out the marks) and dispose them according to another scheme, and so forth, day after day; all of this because Mr Foe has run away from his debts. Sometimes I believe it is I who have become the slave. No doubt you would smile, if you could understand.'"

From FOE by J. M. Coetzee, copyright 1986 by J. M. Coetzee. Used by permission of Viking Penguin, a division of Penguin Group (USA) Inc. – London, 1987, Seite 87

Coetzee's novel is a postmodern rewriting of Daniel Defoe's *Robinson Crusoe* (1719), which has been called the first English novel. In truly postmodern fashion, Coetzee openly plays with conventions of writing, of authorship, and of narrating. His whole novel is based on the idea that the small Caribbean island was inhabited not just by Cruso [sic!] and Friday, but also by a woman called Susan Barton, who is the ostensible narrator of *Foe*. However, as the section above shows, her words are for the most part put in quotation marks. Everything she says, from the moment the novel begins, is presented as something mediated. The topic of representation, and in particular of writing, is one of the key themes of the book.

In the excerpt above, Susan Barton discusses the pains of writing with Friday, who has been mute since his tongue was cut out. Barton's comparison of writing to physical labour introduces the body, pain, and desires into the process of writing stories. For Barton, the story she tells is not so much a representation of reality and thus a realistic portrayal of life, but rather a text: on the surface, it consists of marks on a piece of paper. She says she produces "marks with a quill". However, as the novel progresses, it becomes clear that Barton's version is being written for a specific purpose, namely to please somebody, in this case the future author, (De)Foe. Through making obvious the various fields of motivation that drive authors, Coetzee comments on the system that his own text is part of. This metafictional aspect of his work marks him as a postmodern writer.

The focus on the text as a material object also marks the naming of the text. The novel's title changes Defoe's name to Foe, playing with the fact that a writer is not necessarily a friend but may well be a foe. The reader has to confront this enemy with caution, not taking what is written as truthful representation of reality, but rather as trickery and deceit. The mentioning of the fact that "Mr Foe has run away from his debts" also makes it more than clear that writing, and thus the lofty field of literature, are determined by capitalistic and materialistic interests. The way Susan Barton changes her story while writing confirms this: at first she complains that nothing ever happened on the island but insists that the book reflect this truthfully. Later she is willing to invent as she goes along, in effect creating a fiction and abandoning the idea of truthfully representing reality. In the image of Friday's labour that the excerpt uses, Barton keeps moving her stones until the result is satisfactory, as if she were playing on a game board. The importance of power for the process of writing becomes obvious in this subordination to external rules.

Power also determines the relationship between the various characters. In addressing Friday as if he were a child, Susan Barton becomes involved in the process of colonization. She, in fact, controls Friday's every move. In presenting her writing as equivalent to his slavery, Coetzee implicitly addresses the distance between literature and reality. While writing may be strenuous, it does not compare to forced physical labour or slavery. Thus, the text shows to what extent Barton is unable to put herself in Friday's place. Her inability to show empathy is a portrayal of the arrogance that often lies behind a colonial system of exploitation. In the same way that Friday's voice has been made inaudible, his thoughts and feelings have been rendered unimportant.

Since Coetzee wrote *Foe* from within the context of South Africa's system of apartheid, a system he has variously criticised, the novel can also be read as an allegorical comment on the political situation in South Africa; with this focus on the question of the nation the text follows a frequent pattern of postcolonial writing. The suppression of Friday, whose racial background is clearly marked in the text as non-white, can also be read as a critical comment on any form of racism.

Überblick

Sie haben nun einen Überblick über die verschiedenen Literaturgattungen und deren Besonderheiten bekommen. Gleichzeitig wurden Ihnen anhand von Beispielen Vorgehensweisen vorgestellt. Je mehr Texte Sie nunmehr selbst verfassen, desto klarer werden Zusammenhänge und umso sicherer wird ihr persönlicher Schreibstil werden.

Analyse und Interpretation von Sachtexten

9

Wenden wir uns den nüchtern erscheinenden Sachtexten zu. Im Folgenden werden Sie erfahren, welche Textsorten in diese Gruppierung gehören. Der Umgang mit Sachtexten in Vorbereitung auf das Abitur erfordert Ihre Kenntnisse der Operatoren sowie Kenntnisse verschiedener Stil- und Sprachmittel. Unsicher? Schlagen Sie Operatoren und Stilmittel ruhig nochmals in den Kapiteln 1 und 8 nach. In diesem Kapitel werden Sie Redemittel als Anregung und Hilfestellung finden, um die Anforderungen der Aufgaben in diesem Bereich erfolgreich lösen zu können.

9.1 Verschiedene Texttypen

Im Bereich der Sachtexte gibt es verschiedene Gattungen, die sich durch Besonderheiten im Stil oder in der Form auszeichnen. Im Folgenden finden Sie die Auflistung einiger Gattungen.

Gattungen *genre*	Besonderheiten	Beispiel
Speech	Eine vorbereitete Rede, die sich inhaltlich mit einem bestimmten Sachverhalt oder einer Situation auseinandersetzt	– *The Spanish Armada Speech* Queen Elizabeth 1st of England – 1588 – *Quit India* Mahatma Gandhi – August 8th 1942 – *I Have a Dream* Martin Luther King Jnr – August 28th 1963
Editorial	Ein Artikel, der die Ansichten und Meinung des Redakteurs oder des Verlages wiedergibt.	– 2011 Joseph Rago of The Wall Street Journal (Gewinner des Pulitzer-Preises)
Feature Story	Ein Leitartikel, der sich mit einem wesentlichen Ereignis auseinandersetzt.	*Mystery of the dying bees* 7 March 2007 by Benjamin Lester (Cosmos magazine)
Autobiography	Der Autor beschreibt erzählend wichtige Ereignisse seines Lebens in chronologischer Reihenfolge.	18 Jhdt. Edward Gibbon, Benjamin Franklin,

Gattungen *genre*	Besonderheiten	Beispiel
Biography	Ein Autor beschreibt ausführlich das Leben einer anderen Person.	20. Jhdt. Nancy Millford *Zelda*
Essay	Das Essay ist meist der Ausdruck der persönlichen Ansichten und Meinungen des Autoren zu einem bestimmten Thema, beispielsweise: politische Manifeste, Literaturkritiken, Beobachtungen des täglichen Lebens.	19. Jhdt. William Hazlitt, Charles Lamb, Leigh Hunt und Thomas de Quincey *(essays on diverse subjects)* 20. Jhdt. T. S. Eliot, Robert Louis Stevenson, Willa Cather *(lighter essays)* Virginia Woolf, Edmund Wilson und Charles du Bos *(literary criticism essays)*

Je nach Aufgabenstellung können Sie mit einem oder mehreren Texten konfrontiert werden. Sie werden aufgefordert, Fragen zu diesen Texten zu beantworten (siehe, Kapitel 1 Prüfungen Aufgabentyp I) und sollten dazu die am Anfang dieses Buches behandelten Methoden anwenden (siehe Kapitel 2, Methoden und Arbeitstechniken).

Üblicherweise werden Sie drei Hauptaspekte bearbeiten:
1. Womit befasst sich der vorliegende Text? *(content* – Inhalt)
2. Was ist die Funktion des vorliegenden Textes? *(text analysis)*
3. Was bringt der Text zum Ausdruck? *(interpretation)*

9.2 Womit befasst sich der Text?

Um diesen Aufgabenbereich zu bearbeiten werden Sie häufig aufgefordert eine kurze Zusammenfassung (*summary*) zu schreiben. In dieser fassen Sie die wichtigsten Aspekte des vorliegenden Textes in eigenen Worten zusammen.

Die sieben Regeln zum Schreiben einer Zusammenfassung:
1. Lesen Sie den vorliegenden Text sorgfältig durch.
2. Markieren Sie wichtige Information (z.B. den Satz, in dem das Hauptthema genannt wird).
3. Formulieren Sie einen einleitenden Satz, der
   – Textsorte,
   – Titel
   – Autor
   – Erscheinungsjahr- und Datum
   sowie das Hauptthema beinhalten sollte.
   The newspaper article "Developing nations leaving rich ones behind" written by Edward J. Blakely and published on September 28, 2010 in The Sydney Morning Herald deals with the consequences of globalization.
4) Schreiben Sie objektiv, worum es geht, und vermeiden Sie Interpretationen sowie Kommentare.
5) Konzentrieren Sie sich auf die wichtigen Informationen (Fakten, Ereignisse, Aspekte) und klammern Sie Details (Zahlen, Statistiken, Zitate) aus.
6) Schreiben Sie im Präsens.
7) Fassen Sie sich kurz!

globalisation (BE) – globalization (AE)

Hier finden Sie einige hilfreiche Redemittel:

Formulierungen, um die Intention des Autors darzulegen	– The author starts his article with … a quote/figures from/facts about – He/she points out that … – He/she suggests that … – He/she emphasizes … – He/she concludes …
Formulierungen, um das Kernthema des Textes vorzustellen	–The author discusses the question of whether… –The general theme/topic/subject of the text is….

9.3 Was ist die Funktion des vorliegenden Textes?

Um eine vollständige Analyse zu erarbeiten, stellen Sie zunächst fest, welcher Art der vorliegende Text ist.

expository (erklärend)	The given text is mainly expository since it is based on the objective analysis of complex facts/ because its main purpose is to inform us about/ as it explains… – He/she points out that …
argumentative (erörternd)	From the focus on the subjective evaluation of the problem we can conclude that this text is argumentative. / The text is argumentative because it intends to convince the reader of…
descriptive (beschreibend)	The given passage from … is descriptive since it illustrates…./ because it describes…
narrative (erzählend)	The concentration on perceptions shows us that the given text is narrative./ The given text is narrative because it tells the story of…

> Gerade in Englands „Yellow Press", der Regenbogenpresse, kommt den Überschriften eine große Bedeutung zu, da diese den eigentlichen Kauf- bzw. Leseanreiz darstellen.

Die Überschrift (*heading*) oder die Schlagzeile (*headline*) sollten ebenfalls Gegenstand Ihrer Betrachtung sein.

Wortwahl/ Sprachgebrauch der Überschrift/Schlagzeile	The heading is worded in a … – *dramatic* – *ambiguous* (unklar, mehrdeutig, doppeldeutig) – *baffling* (verwirrend, verblüffend) … *manner*. The author's intention is to shock/ to baffle/ to interest his reader by means of the headline.

> Unter www.historyplace.com/speeches finden Sie viele der berühmtesten Reden der Geschichte. Untersuchen und vergleichen Sie diese anhand der hier genannten Kriterien.

Versuchen Sie herauszufinden, ob der Text eine der folgenden Absichten verfolgt:

a) informieren *(to inform)*
b) überzeugen *(to persuade)*
c) instruieren *(to instruct)*
d) beschreiben *(to describe)*
e) erörtern *(to discuss)*

Desweiteren untersuchen Sie, wie der Autor seinen Text aufgebaut hat, welche Sprache verwendet wird, etc. – und welche Effekte verwendet werden, um letztendlich die entsprechende Absicht zu erzielen.

9.3 Was ist die Funktion des vorliegenden Textes?

Beginnen Sie mit der Struktur und dem Aufbau des Textes: Wie viele Abschnitte (*paragraphs*) gibt es und was ist deren Inhalt?

Sie können die Untersuchung der Struktur und der angewendeten Mittel gut an Artikeln aus der englischsprachigen Tagespresse versuchen. Unter www.guardian.co.uk oder dem Suchbegriff: *current newspaper articles* werden Sie fündig.

Formulierungen, um die Struktur zu beschreiben	– *The text is divided into....paragraphs.* – Der Text ist in … Abschnitte unterteilt. – *The given passage of the speech consists of/can be categorized into... parts.* – Der Ausschnitt der Rede besteht aus … Teilen/ Kategorien. – *The first paragraph forms a contrast to the ... paragraph since it is ...* – Der erste Abschnitt stellt einen Kontrast zum … Abschnitt dar, weil er … – *In the last two paragraphs the author compares/ contrasts/ deals with ...*

Benennen Sie nun die verwendeten Mittel und verknüpfen Sie diese mit der Wirkung, die sie auf den Leser haben.

Mittel – *typical means*	*effect they have*
use of numbers and data	*gives the reader a sense of reliability* (Glaubwürdigkeit) – Die Verwendung von Zahlen und numerischen Fakten vermitteln dem Leser Glaubwürdigkeit.
quotes from experts	*create reliability and lend authenticity* – Die Verwendung von (Experten) Zitaten vermitteln Glaubwürdigkeit und verleihen Authentizität (Echtheit).
rhetorical questions	*make readers think or be more attentive, flatter the reader, increase interest* – Rhetorische Fragen regen den Leser zum Nachdenken an, steigern seine Aufmerksamkeit, schmeicheln dem Leser, erhöhen das Interesse.
Use of pronouns we, our, you	*gives the reader the feeling of being included* – Der Gebrauch von „wir, uns, du" geben dem Leser das Gefühl, eingebunden zu sein.
repetition	*the intentional message is being emphasized, "hammered in"* – Durch Wiederholungen wird die beabsichtige Botschaft betont, „eingebläut".
figurative language (metaphor, simile, symbol, etc)	*creates a picture in the reader's mind, evokes a clear image* – Bildhafte Sprache vermittelt dem Leser ein Bild, eine klare Vorstellung.
irony, pun	*helps the reader to understand the criticism* – Ironie oder Wortspiele helfen dem Leser, die Kritik zu begreifen.

9.4 Was bringt der Text zum Ausdruck?

In diesem Aufgabenbereich werden Sie aufgefordert, den Text und seine Absicht zu interpretieren. Sie müssen indirekt vermittelte Bedeutungen oder direkt geäußerte Absichten erkennen – das heißt Sie betrachten auch das, was „zwischen den Zeilen" steht. Beachten Sie die vorgegebenen Operatoren in „Ihrer" Aufgabe und die angemessenen Arbeitsweisen.

Die folgenden Redemittel können Ihnen im Bereich der Interpretation weiterhelfen:

Formulierungen, um die Haltung des Autors zu beschreiben	The author ... – *claims* (behauptet) ... – *implies* (deutet an) ... – *rejects* (lehnt ab) ... – *agrees* with (stimmt zu) ... – *is certain about* (ist sicher) ... – *doubts wether* (zweifelt ob) ... The author adopts a(n) ... (Der Autor vertritt eine ... Sichtweise ...) – *pessimistic/optimistic* – *middle class* – *humaritarian* ... *point of view* He shows/displays a(n) ...(Der Autor zeigt/präsentiert eine ... Haltung ...) – *objective/subjective* – *open minded/biased* – *humaritarian* ... *attitude*

Tipp

Erstellen Sie sich eine eigene Schritt-für-Schritt Anleitung für eine vollständige Textanalyse. So überprüfen Sie nicht nur, ob Sie den Aufbau verstanden haben, sondern können sich gleich noch eigene Formulierungen und passende Redewendungen zurechtlegen.

Überblick

Sachtexte können Ihnen in unterschiedlichster Form begegnen. Um diese Texte analysieren und interpretieren zu können, müssen Sie nicht nur mit der inhaltlichen Thematik des Textes vertraut sein, sondern Sie sollten auch sprachlich in der Lage sein, die Absicht des Autors, die verwendeten Stilmittel sowie die Wirkung des Textes zum Ausdruck zu bringen.
Der in diesem Kapitel dargestellte Aufbau einer solchen Analyse und Interpretation hilft Ihnen klar und strukturiert vorzugehen.

Bildbeschreibung und Bildanalyse

10

Bilder oder Illustrationen können zur Unterstützung und Verdeutlichung eines Textes, aber auch als Kontrapunkt eingesetzt werden. Um ein Bild zu analysieren, müssen Sie dieses Bild optisch und inhaltlich so genau wie möglich erfassen. Hierzu sind eine systematische Vorgehensweise und die Verwendung des entsprechenden Vokabulars unabdingbar. Wir unterscheiden zwischen der Bildbeschreibung und der Bildanalyse.

10.1 Bildbeschreibung

Das Ziel der Bildbeschreibung ist es, die Gesamtheit des Bildes so detailliert wie möglich zu erfassen, ohne dabei bereits zu interpretieren oder zu werten. Sie finden im Folgenden thematisch zusammengefasste Redemittel, welche den einzelnen Arbeitsschritten zugeordnet sind. Achten Sie auch bei Verwendung von „Formulierungsblöcken" auf einen natürlichen und authentischen Sprachfluss. Sie sollten Formulierungen wählen, die zu Ihrem persönlichen Schreibstil passen und sich harmonisch einfügen.

Schritt 1 Erster Eindruck

- Beschreiben Sie zunächst die Bildart, die sie sehen.
  The picture is a photograph ...
- Beschreiben Sie kurz, welche Situation das Bild zeigt.
  The picture is a photograph showing a group of monks who are surrounded by armed officers.
- Nennen Sie (wenn angegeben) die Quellen des Bildes. (Titel des Bildes, Künstler oder Fotograf, Entstehungsdatum, Veröffentlichungsort, Veröffentlichungsdatum ...)
  It was taken by an unknown artist and published by National Geographic on the 21st of May, 2010.
  Möglicherweise gibt es auch einen Hinweis bezüglich des Grundes bzw. des Anlasses der Veröffentlichung (z. B.: Olympische Spiele, Wahlen, aktuelle Diskussionen, ...)
  The photograph was published in connection with uprisings in China.

Phrases for describing illustrations and photographs

Formulierungen und Redemittel

Beschreibung der Bildart	The picture is a(n) … – … photograph. – … painting. – … electronic image. – … collage. – … still (from a film). – … illustration.
Beschreibung des ersten Eindrucks	– When I first saw the photograph I thought … – Als ich … zum ersten Mal sah, dachte ich … – The collage reminds me of … – … erinnert mich an … – When I see the painting my first association is … – Meine erste Assoziation bei der Betrachtung des Gemäldes ist … – The picture gives the impression that … – Das Bild vermittelt den Eindruck, …
Beschreibung der gezeigten Situation	– The photograph shows … – … zeigt … – This is a painting showing a typical scene … – … welches … zeigt … – This electronic image illustrates … – … zeigt … – This is a still (from the film …) showing the situation in which … – … welches zeigt … – In this illustration you can see that … – … kann man sehen, dass …

Schritt 2 Beschreibung des Bildes

Bedenken Sie bei der Beschreibung eines Bildes die grammatikalische Zeit, das Tempus. Wenn sie beschreiben, wen oder was Sie auf einem Bild sehen, verwenden Sie das *Simple Present*.
*In the foreground there **is** a young girl.*

Wenn Sie aber beschreiben, was die Person im Bild gerade tut, verwenden Sie *Present Progressive/Present Continuous*.
*She **is holding** a baby in her arms.*

- Betrachten Sie das Bild genau und wählen Sie je nach Art des Bildes eine der beiden, im nachfolgenden beschriebenen Methoden zur Beschreibung. Beantworten Sie möglichst die W-Fragen „wer?" „wo?", „was?".
- Beschreiben Sie die Körpersprache der dargestellten Menschen, also Gestik *(gestures)*, Mimik *(facial expression)*, Körperhaltung *(posture)*, Ausdruck *(expression)*.

Zeigt das Bild eine dominante Situation wie zum Beispiel eine Person in einem Raum, ein Gebäude in einer Landschaft, etc., dann beginnen Sie mit der detaillierten Beschreibung eben dieses Hauptaspekts, der im Vordergrund steht. Danach befassen Sie sich mit der Beschreibung des Hintergrundes.

10.1 Bildbeschreibung

> **Beispiel Bildanalyse Johannes Vermeer, The Milkmaid (circa 1658)**
>
>
>
> Suchen Sie sich dieses Bild im Internet (Suchbegriffe: Vermeer/ the Milkmaid) um es in Farbe und vergrößert betrachten zu können.
>
> *In the centre a young woman, the maid mentioned in the title of the painting, is pouring milk from an earthenware jug. Her dress is that of her time with a simple, narrow cut ochre coloured blouse or bodice and a long skirt in crimson red. There is a white collar showing and she is wearing a white bonnet. A long dark blue apron is draped around her and seems to be tucked into the skirt at the waistline. Her sleeves are rolled up and reveal her strong arms which are slightly reddened from below the elbow towards her hands. Her high forehead is accentuated due to the fact that she is looking downward, fully concentrating on pouring the milk. She has a straight yet natural posture. In front of her is a table covered with a blue tablecloth on which another earthenware jug, a basket with different loaves of bread and bread rolls in various shapes are displayed. There is a taller jug coloured in blue and white and closed with a lid. Beneath the basket a cloth of the same colour as the apron is visible. On the left hand side there is a lattice window and in the left corner of the room in which the scene is set there is a basket hung up on the wall and some kind of lantern next to it. Above the basket there seems to be a picture, but due to the angle and light it is difficult to make out. The wall behind the young woman is white-washed, above her and slightly to the left a nail is visible. At the bottom a row of white and blue tiles form a border and the floor is either wood or flagstone.*

Besteht keine ersichtliche Dominanz einer Person oder eines Gegenstandes, dann empfiehlt es sich mit einer Beschreibungsrichtung zu arbeiten, das heißt, Sie arbeiten beispielsweise von links nach rechts oder von oben nach unten.

Bild und Text
Nennen Sie die Techniken, die der Künstler verwendet. Beschreiben Sie den Einsatz von Licht und Schatten. Gibt es verschwommene, unscharfe Zonen, wie wird Farbe eingesetzt?

Beschreiben, wo sich etwas im Bild befindet	– In the foreground/In the centre you can find … – Im Vordergrund/im Zentrum … – At the top there is … – Oben befindet sich … – At the bottom there is … – Unten befindet sich …
	– In the upper right hand corner you can see … – In der oberen rechten Ecke … – On the left hand side …can be found … – Auf der linken Seite … – In the lower left hand corner the viewer finds … – In der unteren linken Ecke entdeckt der Betrachter … – In the background … can be seen … – Im Hintergrund …
Beschreibung der künstlerischen Techniken	The colours are … – … bright, dark, soft, intensive. – … black and white. The photograph is … – … clear. – … blurred. – … not in focus. – … not well lit. – … full of contrasts. The artist used… – …oils/water colours/crayons. The technique of using… creates … – …light brush strokes/only outlines/a mix of material The photographer used … – a close up/a soft focus/a sharp focus … to stress
Beschreibung der Atmosphäre	This creates a/an … atmosphere. – cosy, friendly, warm, lively, peaceful, … The atmosphere is … – dark, depressing, scary, serious, terrifying, … These factors contribute to the atmosphere being … – exotic, hectic, mysterious, confusing … The … (siehe künstlerische Techniken) in the photo conveys an atmosphere of great … – happiness, sadness, confusion, …
Beschreibung der Mimik, Gestik, Körpersprache	The person's body language shows that he/she is … – … in pain, self confident, scared, insecure, helpless, joyful … From his/her facial expression you can conclude that … – … he/she is … amazed, frightened, annoyed, calm, happy, questioning …

Schritt 3 Die Beschriftung

Beachten Sie Unterschriften *(caption)*, Überschriften *(heading)* oder Titel *(title)* und bringen Sie diese in klaren Bezug zum Dargestellten.

10.2 Bildanalyse/Bildinterpretation

Bei der Bildanalyse und der Bildinterpretation greifen Sie die Informationen auf, die Sie durch die Bildbeschreibung gewonnen haben, und verwerten diese. Das heißt, Sie ziehen Schlussfolgerungen aus dem Beschriebenen bezüglich der Intention *(intention)* des Künstlers und bilden sich abschließend eine persönliche Meinung über das Bild, die Sie hinreichend begründen. Die Bildbeschreibung ist immer der Ausgangspunkt der Bildanalyse.

Schritt 4 Analyse, Interpretation und Intention

Schließen Sie an Ihre vorangegangenen Betrachtungen die Schlussfolgerungen an. Folgende Fragen können hierbei richtungsweisend sein:

- In welcher Beziehung stehen die Menschen auf dem Bild zueinander? Welche Interpretationen lassen die Körperhaltung, Mimik und Gestik der Personen zu und was ist die Botschaft dahinter? Werden die Personen positiv, negativ oder neutral dargestellt?
- Bezieht sich das Bild auf etwas Bestimmtes? (Historisches Ereignis, soziale Fragestellung, politische Entwicklung...)
- Welchen Eindruck versucht das Bild zu vermitteln? Was soll dem Betrachter suggeriert werden?
- Was ist die Absicht des Künstlers? Welche Botschaft möchte er/sie vermitteln und was soll dadurch bewirkt oder erreicht werden?
- Gibt es eine Zielgruppe *(target group)* und wenn ja welche?

Formulierungen und Redemittel

Phrases for analysing and interpreting illustrations and photographs

Analyse	The photograph has to do with ... (e.g. the recent discussion about stem cell research). – The painting deals with ... (e.g. relationships today). – The illustration refers to ... (e.g. the text "..."). – The collage represents ... (e.g. society's fear of Islamic terror). – The electronic image is meant to criticize ... (e.g. Britain's latest regulation regarding...).
Interpretation	– The collage suggests ... – ... deutet an... – The painting gives you the impression that ... – ... erweckt den Eindruck, dass ... – The photograph arouses feeling of ... – ... erzeugt/erweckt ... Gefühle .../lässt den Betrachter fühlen, ... – Considering the facial expression you could conclude that ... – Dem Gesichtsausdruck nach zu urteilen, kann man darauf schließen, dass ... – From the look of the woman, you can assume that ... – Aufgrund des Aussehens der Frau kann man annehmen, dass ...

Intention	– The artist wants to express his/her approval/disapproval of … – …will seine Zustimmung/Ablehung gegenüber … zum Ausdruck bringen. – The artist wants to illustrate the problem of … – … will das Problem der … darstellen. – Perhaps his/her intention is to show … – Vielleicht ist seine/ihre Absicht … – The illustration is aimed at … – … zielt ab auf … – The photograph targets mainly … – …. spricht vor allem … an … – … are the target group. – … sind die Zielgruppe.

Schritt 5 Wirkung und persönliche Meinung

Im abschließenden Teil der Bildanalyse zeigen Sie die Wirkung des Bildes auf Sie auf, stellen ihre persönliche Meinung dazu dar und begründen diese.

Wirkung und persönliche Meinung	In my opinion the painting is meant to … The impression I get from this illustration is that … The painting makes me feel … The collage is … – … shocking/brilliant/terrifying/impressive/depressing/amusing … To my mind it would be better/clearer/more impressive … if the artist had used more/less … It touches/moves me. It does not appeal to me. It leaves me cold. I like/dislike it because … In conclusion I can say …

Beispiel Bildanalyse

Aufgabenstellung: Analyze the photograph dated from the turn of the last century, set in India.

The black and white photograph immediately reminds the viewer of stories about British India. Various books and movies have dealt with this topic portraying the life of British colonizers in India, some more and some less idealistic.
It shows a tea party scene, in which a group of probably British people is seated in a garden surrounded by Indian servants.
A rather white and seemingly large building is visible in the background, located behind bushes and trees. The background is blurred which makes

it hard to say whether that building is a residence or an official building of some sort. The focus is on the group of people in the middle of the picture. They are grouped into two rows. In the back row the Indian servants wait to receive orders. On the left hand side there is an elderly man with a beard, dressed in a dark traditional uniform in military attire. His upright posture and the light coloured, decorated headgear mark him as a personal guard or personal head servant. Next two him, standing a little further to the right, two more servants are visible. These are dressed in white, wearing the traditional wound turban. They are standing very close to each other. The left man is balancing a round, silver tray on one hand and appears to be looking straight into the camera. His companion to the right is staring straight ahead and standing slightly askew. Both men are noticeably younger than the "guard" to the left. Even further to the right there is another servant, glancing downwards to the English man seated directly in front him. This servant is also dressed traditionally, with a dark, long-sleeved shirt belted with some patterned fabric. His headgear resembles that of the "guard" but is not decorated as much and not as noticeable. The last person in that second row is a British gentleman dressed in a dark suit with a white collar and a light top hat. His right hand is on his hip and his left hand seems to be resting on the back of the chair of the lady seated in front of him, although that is not visible due to the angle. He is also looking straight into the camera.

There are six people in the front row, and they seem to be grouped into pairs. Starting from the right, there is an elderly, half-bald and heavily built gentlemen dressed in a dark suit and a dark haired woman who is wearing a white blouse beneath a fitted light-coloured jacket and matching long skirt. While the gentleman is comfortably leaning back in his chair, holding his hat in one hand, her posture is more erect and she is leaning forward. She is holding something on her lap, one object in every hand but due to the slightly blurred quality of the photograph it is almost impossible to make out and could be a cricket bat or a rifle. Moving to the left the viewer finds the next couple who appear to be the centre of the group. First the dark-haired, slim gentleman dressed in a dark suit with a white collar. He is looking straight at the camera and both the gesture of his left hand and his mock stern expression imply that he is communicating with someone. He is actually sitting at the table in front of him. To his right the viewer finds a dark-haired lady dressed in a white fitted dress with a matching white hat leaning forward. She is holding a tea-cup and the saucer in her hands and is looking at someone who seems to be left of the photographer. Her facial expression is rather stern but a hint of amusement can be detected. The last couple on the right hand side of the picture are again a lady and a

>> Beispiel Bildanalyse

>>

>> Beispiel Bildanalyse

gentleman. The lady is comfortably leaning backward and laughing while looking at the couple in the centre. She is wearing a white blouse beneath a fitted jacket and a slim skirt. Her hat is rounded and she appears to be younger than the rest of the group. Next to her on the right there is an elderly gentleman in a dark, striped suit with an open jacket and a waist coat underneath. He has a walking stick in one hand and is looking straight into the camera.

Due to body language and facial expressions of the tea party members the photograph does not convey the atmosphere of a relaxed social get-together but instead reveals undercurrents in regard to the relationship between the members of the tea party as well as the role of the photographer and the servants and guards. Only the young lady who is laughing seems to be relaxed and at ease, while all the other guests appear more or less strained and the lady on the right hand side seems distinctively uncomfortable judging by her facial expression and the fact that she is leaning forward and away from the gentleman's hand resting on the back of her chair. Considering her facial expression and that of the gentleman to her right, one could conclude that there has been or still is reason for embarrassment, possibly caused by the host and his mock stern expression and gesture as he seems to be reprimanding someone. This mock reprimand could be the source of amusement for the youngest lady of the group. Monitoring the servants more closely, the viewer can also detect differences in manner and thus possibly attitude. While the "guard" on the left hand side conveys an air of dignity and professional concentration the other "guard's" body language suggests some kind of suppressed aggression hid behind a mask of humility and resignation into his fate of being the white man's servant. The gentleman seated on the left hand end of the first row appears to be the one who has the most actual power, suggested through is relaxed but dignified composure and his guard's body language, dress and composure whereas the "host" couple in the centre seem to be very full of themselves hence the lack of air of real power surrounding them.

The impression I get from this photograph is that there is an interesting story behind it on the one hand and on the other hand it makes me think about the British rule in India and what that rule implied to both – colonizers and natives alike – with all its consequences.

10.3 *Cartoons* beschreiben und analysieren

Eine besondere Form des Bildes *(visual)* ist die Karikatur *(cartoon)*. Zumeist besteht eine Karikatur aus einem Bild oder einer Skizze und einem kurzen Text. Dieser kann entweder in Form von Sprechblasen *(speech bubble)* oder Beschilderungen *(label)* im Bild integriert sein oder als Bildunterschrift *(caption)* auftreten.

Karikaturen sind satirische Darstellungen von Personen oder Situation. Sie haben zum Ziel, durch Übertreibung und Verformung gesellschaftliche Zustände, Institutionen oder Persönlichkeiten kritisch darzustellen, und bedienen sich dabei verschiedener Stilmittel.

> Sie finden ein Vielzahl an Karikaturen wenn Sie den Suchbegriff: *cartoons* eingeben. Spezifizieren Sie diesen mit entsprechenden politischen, landeskundlichen oder gesellschaftlichen Schlagwörtern und Sie finden die entsprechenden Karikaturen. Auch hier gilt: Je häufiger Sie sich mit diesen befassen und üben, desto sicherer werden Sie im Ernstfall – der Prüfung – sein.

Eigenschaften werden überzogen und überspitzt dargestellt.	– *exaggeration* – Übertreibung – e.g.: *The artist chose to reduce President Sarkozy's actual height to that of a mere child whereas President Obama's height is drastically increased thus stressing the difference in strength by exaggerating their physical appearance.*
Das Gegenteil des Gesagten ist gemeint.	– *irony* – Ironie – e.g.: *The political spokesman is saying that his country would never dream of faking evidence when it comes to mass destruction weapons. The second panel shows a number of faceless employees who are cutting paper and blotting sentences out of reports while President Bush is dictating the following:" …"*
Verdrehung von Wörtern und Doppel- oder Mehrdeutigkeiten	– *pun* – Wortspiel – e.g.: *The young ladies are asking for their salads to be served naked, meaning here without dressing.*
Der direkte Vergleich zwischen zwei Dingen, indem „*like*" oder „*as*" verwendet werden, um sie in Beziehung zu setzen	– *simile* – Vergleich – *She was as light as a feather.*
Der Verweis auf etwas Abstraktes durch etwas Konkretes	– *symbol* – Symbol – e.g.: *The young man is holding a globe, used as a symbol of globalisation, in his hand.*

Grundsätzlich ist die Analyse eines Cartoons ähnlich aufgebaut wie die Bildbeschreibung/Bildanalyse, denn sie gliedert sich ebenfalls in vier Schritte. Redemittel aus dem Bereiche der Bildbeschreibung und Analyse können für diese Analyse übernommen und entsprechend adaptiert werden. Im Folgenden sind zusätzliche und spezifische Redemittel aufgelistet.

Schritt 1 Karikatur beschreiben

Es gibt verschiedene Arten von Karikaturen: Karikaturen, die aus einem Bild und einer entsprechenden Unterschrift unter dem Bild bestehen, werden *single-panel cartoon* genannt.

Karikaturen, die ähnlich einem Comic aus einer inhaltlichen verbundenen Serie von Illustrationen bestehen, werden **comic strip** genannt.

Karikaturen, die im Zusammenhang mit einem (Leit)Artikel stehen, werden *editorial cartoon* genannt und sind häufig ernster in Ton und Thematik. Es werden Metaphern *(metaphors)* und Ironie *(irony)* eingesetzt, um soziale oder politische Situationen oder Zustände satirisch darzustellen *(to satirise)*.

Beschreibung der Karikatur	The cartoon consists of … – … an illustration showing … – … a single panel showing … – … two panels which show … The comic strip shows … There is a caption/speech bubble containing quotation marks enclosing the following: … The caption below the cartoon says: "…" There is a caption which reads: "…" In the first speech bubble it says: "…" The text in the speech bubble is spoken by …
Die Aussagen in den Sprechblasen können auch in indirekter Rede wiedergegeben werden.	In the first speech bubble it says. "Could I perhaps borrow that buggy? I'd look so multi-taskable!" The younger woman is asking if she could perhaps borrow the buggy to appear more "multi-taskable" meaning more attractive due to her multi-tasking abilities. The speechbubble above the man's head reads:" I still like to call it Independence day!" hile the man is trying to hold his balance with a gasoline hose wrapped around his leg he is saying that he still likes to call it Independence day.

Schritt 2 Die Karikatur interpretieren/analysieren

Der Aufbau einer Cartoonanalyse unterscheidet sich kaum vom Aufbau einer Bildanalyse. Zuerst beschreiben Sie um welche Art von Karikatur es sich handelt und welche Situation dargestellt ist (siehe Schritt 1). Im folgenden ist es hilfreich bei der Analyse der Karikatur folgende Fragen in Betracht zu ziehen:

Setting – Zusammenhang	– In welchen räumlichen und zeitlichen Kontext ist die Karikatur zu setzen? – In welchem Zusammenhang steht die Karikatur thematisch?
Characters – Personen	– Welche Aktionen und Gefühle werden durch die Körpersprache *(to communicate through body language)* der Personen zum Ausdruck gebracht? – Welche Gefühle werden durch Mimik *(facial expression)* zum Ausdruck gebracht? – Was wird anhand der Körpersprache bezüglich der Beziehung zwischen den Personen angedeutet oder suggeriert?
Action – Ereignisse	– Was geschieht gerade? – Wie wird das Geschehen dargestellt?
Language – Sprache	– Welches Sprachregister wird verwendet? Was wird tatsächlich gesagt? – Inwiefern wird Interpunktion verwendet, um Emotionen zu suggerieren?
Stereotypes and Symbols – Klischees und Symbole	– Verwendet der Karikaturist/der Künstler Klischees *(stereotypes)*? – Verwendet der Karikaturist/der Künstler Symbole, um auf eine andere Bedeutungsebene zu verweisen?

Ordnen Sie die Informationen bezüglich setting, language, characters, action, etc auf Konzeptpapier mit Hilfe der entsprechenden Methoden (siehe Kapitel 2) und versuchen Sie die ihrem persönlichen Stil entsprechenden Redemittel und Formulierungen einzusetzen.

Formulierungen und Redemittel

Phrases for interpreting and analysing cartoons

Interpretation und Analyse	– The cartoon refers to/deals with … the situation of … – The topic of the cartoon is … (the lack of true environmental awareness). – The figure bears a likeness to … (the current British Prime Minister). – The figure is a caricature of … (the President of the United States of America). – The cartoonist exaggerates character traits by … (means of clothing and body language). – The person's body language conveys that/shows that … – The person's formal language hints at … – From his/her facial expression you can conclude that … – … symbolizes/stands for/is a symbol of …

Schritt 3 Botschaft und persönliche Meinung

In diesem Schritt ist es ratsam, sich nochmals auf die politischen und sozialen Umstände zu besinnen, in deren Kontext die Karikatur zu verstehen ist. In Bezug auf diesen Kontext versuchen Sie nun die Botschaft und die Absicht des Karikaturisten *(cartoonist)* darzulegen. Abschließend bewerten Sie die Karikatur nach Wirkung und Effekt.

Botschaft der Karikatur	The cartoonist is making a sarcastic comment on … He/she is making fun of … He/she wants to ridicule (lächerlich machen) … The artist is criticizing the behaviour of … Perhaps the intention of the cartoonist is to show that … The artists point seems to be … Probably he/she wants to reveal what is behind … He/she wants to make the reader aware of … The real point the cartoon is making seems to be …
Darlegung der persönlichen Meinung	In my opinion, the cartoonist is successful/not successful in … – … his/her portrayal of … because … – … his/her portrait of … because … – … his/her presentation of … because … – … his/her intention of … because … The cartoon is effective/not effective in its presentation/intention/portrayal of … because … In conclusion I do feel touched/don't feel touched by the cartoon because … From my point of view the cartoon is not easy to understand because …

Beispiel Bildanalyse

Cartoon/Karikatur

Analyse this cartoon. (Einstieg und beschreibender Teil sind aufgebaut wie in einer Bildanalyse. Im Folgenden finden Sie den Interpretationsteil und die Botschaft)

The topic of the cartoon is the dynamic of globalization. The person in the foreground, who has been run over by the globe symbolizes mankind as the victim of the globalization process. The big globe is obviously a symbol of globalization and the dark road on which it is rolling ahead the path society paved for it. The fact that there are still people trying to flee by racing ahead of the globe demonstrates that the process is still

>> Beispiel-Bildanalyse
Cartoon/Karikatur

in full swing and we have not reached the end. Due to the sheer size of the globe, and the fact that the path is curving downwards towards the fleeing it seems unlikely that they will be spared the fate which has already struck the victims in the foreground. We can find different layers of interpretation if we look closely. The first vitim seems to be wearing some kind of business suit, so perhaps the cartoonist wants to hint towards the staunch defenders and so called masters of globalization as being run over by their protégée in the end.

The cartoonist is making a sarcastic comment on the process of globalization and those who claim that they control that process and from my point of view the cartoon is very effective in conveying that message because it is kept simple and uses exaggerated elements, such as the huge globe, to manifest its message.

Die Beschreibung, Analyse und Interpretation von Bildern erfordern Kenntnisse der dargestellten Umstände und das Vermögen, sich sprachlich klar und angemessen auszudrücken. Dieses Kapitel hat Ihnen eine Hilfestellung zum Aufbau und Inhalt solcher Beschreibungen/ Analysen/ Interpretationen geliefert und Ihnen einen Fundus an konkreten Redemitteln dargeboten. Beginnen Sie schon bei Ihrem nächsten Text diese Redemittel anzuwenden (Nachschlagen ist nicht verboten), je häufiger Sie das tun, umso selbstverständlicher und stressfreier wird Ihnen das auch in der Prüfung gelingen.

11 Idioms and sayings

Englisch ist eine bildhafte Sprache, in der viele idiomatische Redewendungen zum Einsatz kommen. Da manche dieser Redewendungen sehr offensichtlich sind, andere hingegen aber verwirrend erscheinen, bietet Ihnen dieses Kapitel einen Überblick über die gebräuchlichsten idiomatischen Redewendungen mit Beispielen. Ein sicheres Verständnis dieser Ausdrucksweisen hilft Ihnen, Texte besser zu verstehen, und verleiht Ihren eigenen Texten Authentizität und sprachliche Vielseitigkeit.

11.1 Colour idioms

- out of the blue → suddenly, unexpectedly
  We were sitting around, just chatting, when **out of the blue** Susanne announced that she was moving to Hong Kong for a year. That certainly took us by surprise!
- once in a blue moon → very seldom
  Mrs Matthews is very lonely. She lives in an old people's home and her daughter only visits her **once in a blue moon**.
- to be green with envy → to be very envious of something or somebody
  I was **green with envy** when I heard Chris had got a summer job in New York – I wish I could do something like that!
- to get/be given the green light → to be given permission to go ahead with something
  Opponents to the new airport runway are still hoping that the project will not **get the green light**.
- the grass is always greener on the other side (of the fence) → different circumstances from your own often seem better
  Anthony wishes he had a better paid job, like Dan's, whereas Dan wishes he had more free time, like Anthony. Oh well, **the grass is always greener on the other side**.
- to see red → to become very angry
  It really makes me **see red** when I read about animals being mistreated.
- to catch someone red-handed → to discover someone doing something they shouldn't be doing
  The teacher walked into the room and **caught** the pupils **red-handed** downloading a game onto a school computer.

- to be in the red → to be in debt, to have an overdraft
  The company is badly **in the red**, and the employees are afraid it will go bankrupt.
- in black and white → to have written proof of something
  This job offer seems too good to be true. In fact, I won't believe it until I see it **in black and white**.
- the black sheep (of the family) → someone whose behaviour is very different from the rest of his/her family's, or who goes against other people's values
  Charlie Wood is **the black sheep** of his family: all the others are doctors, but he decided to become a jazz musician.
- a white lie → to tell a lie so as not to hurt someone's feelings
  I knew that Emma had put a lot of work into her talk, so although I found it boring, I told **a white lie** and said I'd enjoyed it.
- as white as a sheet → to become very pale in the face due to fear
  I had no idea Harry was so scared of spiders! He turned **as white as a sheet** when he saw the big black one that had fallen into the bath.
- every cloud has a silver lining → there is a positive side to every bad situation
  Dave's car was stolen and he couldn't afford a new one, so he started cycling everywhere. He's a lot fitter now, though, so it just goes to show that **every cloud has a silver lining**!

11.2 Idioms connected to time

- to have the time of one's life → to really enjoy oneself
  Our holiday in Australia was an unforgettable experience: we **had the time of our lives**!
- to stand the test of time → to be something that is still considered useful or valuable, even after many years have passed
  Nobody thought they'd stay together, but their love has **stood the test of time**: they've been married for nearly 30 years.
- a race against time → something that must be finished very quickly or within a certain time
  The girl was desperately ill, and the doctors were involved in a **race against time** to save her life.
- in the nick of time → at the last moment, when it is almost too late
  We arrived at the station **in the nick of time**, just as the train was about to leave.

- better late than never → it is better to do something late than not do it at all
  *Steve finally paid me back the money he owed me, three months after I lent it to him. Well, **better late than never,** I guess!*
- to lose track of time → to be concentrating so hard on something that you don't realise what time it is
  *Sorry I'm so late. The book I'm reading at the moment is so fascinating that I just **lost all track of time.***

11.3 Idioms with food

- to be the apple of someone's eye → to be very special to someone
  *She always spoilt her son: he was **the apple of her eye** and, as far as she was concerned, could do no wrong.*
- to have one's cake and eat it → to want to have the advantages of two different situations at the same time, even though only one option is possible
  *If you want to save up enough money to buy a car, you can't go on expensive holidays all the time. Sorry, but you can't **have your cake and eat it.***
- a piece of cake → very easy
  *If you study really hard, the test should be **a piece of cake.***
- food for thought → something that makes you think very hard
  *"Did you know that millions of people in the world don't have a supply of clean water?" "Wow. Well, that's certainly **food for thought**."*
- to go pear-shaped → when something that is going well then goes wrong
  *The team was playing really well, but then the other team scored unexpectedly and **it all went pear-shaped** – they lost 5-0 in the end.*
- to take something with a pinch/grain of salt → to not believe something until you have checked all the facts
  *If Andy tells you he's a TV star, you should **take it with a pinch of salt**. He was once in a crowd scene in a soap opera – that's all!*
- to egg someone on → to encourage someone to do something
  *Bill knew it was dangerous to dive off the bridge, but he did it because all the others were **egging him on**.*
- there's no use crying over spilt milk → there is no point in getting upset about something that has happened and cannot be changed
  *So you didn't study at all and then failed the test? Well, **there's no use crying over spilt milk** – you'll just have to do work harder next time!*

- not someone's cup of tea → you don't like something; you are not interested in it
  *I went to a jazz club for the first time with some friends last weekend, but discovered that jazz music really **isn't my cup of tea.***
- a couch potato → someone who sits around most of the time watching TV or DVDs
  *"We are raising a generation of **couch potatoes**", said the sports minister. "We need more programmes to encourage young people to get active."*

11.4 Idioms connected to parts of the body

- to cost an arm and a leg → to be very expensive
  *Have you seen Angie's new designer jacket? That must have **cost an arm and a leg**!*
- to keep someone at arm's length → to be distant rather than friendly towards others
  *Kate tends to **keep people at arm's length** at first, so she comes across as rather unfriendly. But you'll like her once you get to know her!*
- to keep a straight face → to look serious when you want to laugh at something
  *When she got married, my cousin read out a poem she'd written that was so ridiculous I could hardly **keep a straight face**.*
- to face something → to accept the facts in a particular situation
  *Let's **face it**: Manchester United are unlikely to win the championship this year.*
- a no-brainer → when the best option is very obvious
  *Spend the afternoon by the lake or go back to the library for a few hours – well, that's **a no-brainer** on a hot day like today!*
- to keep a level head → to keep calm, even in a stressful or difficult situation
  *When the fire alarm went off, the teacher **kept a level head**: she calmly asked the children to put down their pens and follow her outside.*
- can't make head or tail of something → to be unable to understand something because it is confusing
  *No wonder I **couldn't make head or tail** of Georgia's message: it turns out that the first part was missing, which is why it didn't make any sense!*
- to tear one's hair out → to be very upset or distressed about something

*One evening, my sister didn't come home and we had no idea what had happened to her. My mum was **tearing her hair out** by the time she finally called.*

- to put one's foot in one's mouth → to say something embarrassing or upsetting to somebody, often unintentionally
  *Well, I certainly managed to **put my foot in my mouth** when I asked Toby if his girlfriend was coming out with us tomorrow! Nobody told me they'd split up!*
- to stand on one's own two feet → to do something independently
  *When you go away to university, your mum won't be around to do everything for you any more. You'll have to learn to **stand on your own two feet**.*
- to foot the bill → to pay for something, often unwillingly
  *When the children broke their neighbour's window playing football, their parents had to **foot the bill**.*
- to see eye to eye with someone → to agree with someone
  *Jenny and I used to be close friends, but we lead very different lives now and we just don't **see eye to eye** any more.*
- In one ear and out the other → when something is said to another person but that person does not listen
  *I told him he'd need to put petrol in the car before he set off, but of course it was **in one ear and out the other**, and he didn't do it. Sure enough, the car broke down.*
- to get out of hand → when a situation gets out of control
  *A lot of people at the football match had been drinking, so extra police officers were sent to the ground to make sure things didn't **get out of hand**.*
- to have a change of heart → to change one's mind about something, especially a change from a negative to a positive attitude
  *At first they refused to help us, but they **had a change of heart** when they saw how much time and effort we had put into the project.*
- to look down one's nose → to be snobbish towards someone, to think someone or something is inferior
  *Tina's father came from a rich family, and they always **looked down their noses** at her mother because of her working class background.*
- to stab someone in the back → to betray someone who trusted you
  *I thought Clare was my friend, but then she **stabbed me in the back** by telling my parents what happened on the night of the party.*

11.5 Animal idioms

- to kill two birds with one stone → to do two things at the same time
  Since I had to go into town anyway, I thought I might as well **kill two birds with one stone** and get my hair cut while I was there.
- to be like a bear with a sore head → to be in a bad temper
  Frank **is like a bear with a sore head** when he hasn't slept well: he spends all day shouting at people.
- you can't teach an old dog new tricks → it can be hard for people to change if they are used to doing something in a certain way
  I've shown my granddad how to send e-mails but he still prefers to use the phone. Well, I guess **you can't teach an old dog new tricks.**
- to sound fishy → to seem suspicious, as if there is something wrong
  Hmm, their plan **sounds very fishy** to me. Don't give them any money until you've checked all the facts!
- a wild goose chase → when you waste a lot of time trying to find something that is more or less impossible to find
  We went all over the city looking for my grandma's favourite perfume, but it was **a wild goose chase.** Later we found out that it isn't sold any more.
- to be a guinea pig → to be used to test something out
  I've never cooked this dish before, so all of you are my **guinea pigs** this evening – please give me your honest opinion!
- to have a whale of a time → to really enjoy oneself
  The children **had a whale of a time** at the lake – they didn't want to go home!
- to make a pig's ear of something → to do something badly, to make a mess of it
  Jim completely misunderstood the text and so he **made a real pig's ear of** the translation: it made no sense at all.
- mutton dressed as lamb → when an older person wears clothes intended for younger people
  Those jeans really don't suit Mrs Reilly. She looks like **mutton dressed as lamb** when she wears them.
- a one-horse town → a boring place where nothing much happens
  I come from a real **one-horse town**. That's why I moved to New York as soon as I could – I wanted to live somewhere where there's a bit of action!

11.6 Idioms with clothes

- to tighten one's belt → to spend less money
  *When Mark lost his job, the family had to **tighten their belt**s until he found a new one.*
- to get too big for your boots → to think you are more important than you really are
  *Ever since Ryan got through to the third round of that casting show, he hasn't stopped talking about how talented he is. He's **getting far too big for his boots** if you ask me!*
- to take one's hat off to someone → to show that you admire what someone has done
  *Well, I **take my hat off to you**. I didn't believe you'd be able to fix my computer!*
- to pull one's socks up → to work harder in order to do something better
  *She did very badly on her last test – she'll have to **pull her socks up** if she really wants to graduate well.*
- to put yourself in someone else's shoes → to see things from another person's point of view
  *I know that homeless man stole your wallet, but **put yourself in his shoes** – he was desperate.*

11.7 Miscellaneous idioms

- to cut someone slack → to be less hard on someone, to make allowances
  *Cathy didn't manage to finish her essay on time, but the teacher **cut her some slack** because her grandmother had just died.*
- the penny drops → someone finally understands something
  *My parents told me they'd sold their house and were going to travel around in a caravan for a couple of years. I thought they'd gone mad, till **the penny finally dropped** and I realised it was April 1st!*
- not rocket science → something that is not difficult to do or understand
  *All you have to do is click on this button, and then you can copy and paste the information. Come on, **it's not rocket science**!*
- by no stretch of the imagination → no matter how hard you might try to imagine or believe something, it isn't true
  ***By no stretch of the imagination** could he be called a good goalkeeper: he's let in at least 20 goals in the last two months!*

11.7 Miscellaneous idioms

- to jump to conclusions → to make a judgement of something before you have all the facts
  Don't **jump to conclusions**. Just because English isn't his first language, it doesn't mean he can't understand what you're saying.
- if it ain't broke, don't fix it → don't change something that works well the way it is
  The library system we have now is fine – it'll only lead to confusion if they change it. **If it ain't broke, don't fix it**!
- for love nor money → used to talk about something that is impossible to get, no matter how hard one tries
  I wanted to get a similar jacket to the one I bought a couple of years ago, but they just don't sell them any more. I looked everywhere, but couldn't get one **for love nor money.**
- to make a mountain out of a molehill → to make something unimportant seem far more serious than it really is
  It isn't broken – it just needs new batteries. There's no need to **make a mountain out of a molehill!**

Wenn man Englisch als Fremdsprache erlernt, ist es nur zu natürlich, dass man nicht jede Redewendung des Englischen kennen kann – dazu sind es zu viele. Gelegentlich begegnet man aber Formulierungen, die in ihrer Bildlichkeit etwa Spaß machen. Spätestens dann lohnt es sich, sich mit dieser besonderen Redewendung zu beschäftigen. So erweitert man seinen Vorrat an *idiomatic phrases*. Mitunter kann man sie wortwörtlich übersetzen ("to get the green light" = „grünes Licht bekommen"), andere verwenden eine ganz andere Bildlichkeit ("to kill two birds with one stone" = „zwei Fliegen mit einer Klatsche schlagen") und wieder andere sind nicht in die andere Sprache zu bringen ("a piece of cake" = „sehr einfach"). Man kann also nicht einfach drauflos übersetzen, andernfalls ist die Gefahr zu groß, beim „Filser-Englisch" zu landen: „To race like a monkey-tooth" ist ein viel zitiertes abschreckendes, wenn auch belustigendes Beispiel.

12 Eine „*composition*" schreiben

Wenn es darum geht, einen eigenen längeren Text zu einem bestimmten Thema in einer bestimmten Form zu verfassen, sind verschiedene Dinge gleichzeitig vonnöten. Sie sollten sich einerseits mit der zu bearbeitenden Thematik auskennen (beispielsweise Landeskunde: The melting pot – oder Literatur: Romeo and Juliet) und andererseits wissen, welche Art von Text Sie produzieren sollen. Welche Stilmittel sind erlaubt? Welches Sprachregister ist gewünscht? Wie sollte der Text überhaupt strukturiert sein? All diesen Fragen versuchen wir in diesem Kapitel Rechnung zu tragen.

12.1 Welche Art von Text soll ich schreiben?

In Klausuren und Prüfungen begegnen Ihnen verschiedene Texttypen in der Aufgabenstellung des Bereichs *composition*.

Art des Textes	Zweck	Inhalt und Aufbau	Sprache
Comment	– detaillierte Stellungnahme zu einer Thematik – These/ Argument (Beweis)/ Beispiel – abschließendes Urteil	– Einleitung: Thema umreißen – Hauptteil: Betrachtung verschiedener Aspekte (klar strukturiert: These/ Argument, Beweis/Beispiel) – Schluss: Urteilsfindung und eigene Meinung	formal/ neutral
Essay	– umfängliche Betrachtung einer Thematik, Abwägung positiver und negativer Aspekte – Gründe für und gegen auflisten	– Einleitung: Thema umreißen, erläutern, illustrieren – Hauptteil: variable Anordnung der Argumentationsweise (*pro/con, con/pro* etc.), klare Struktur – Schluss: Betonung des eigenen Standpunkts	formal/ neutral
Interpretation	– Bedeutung eines literarischen oder sach-orientierten Texts oder Bildes – Aufschlüsselung von Symbolen und Bildhaftem – übergeordnete Bezüge herstellen – eigene Meinung zum Dargestellten	– Einleitung: Fakten bezgl. des Textes/ Bildes, erste Eindrücke – Hauptteil: detaillierte Betrachtung und daraus resultierende Schlussfolgerungen und Vermutungen in größeren Kontext stellen – Schluss: Zusammenfassen der wesentlichen Punkte und eigene Meinung	formal/ neutral

12.2 Wie sollte der Text strukturiert sein?

Der Grundaufbau Einleitung/Hauptteil/Schluss ist in den meisten geforderten Textarten sinnvoll und daher einzuhalten.

Hier einige Tipps zum Verfassen einer Einleitung:

- Zweck der Einleitung: Darstellen des Themas und Interesse des Lesers wecken.
  Möglichkeiten: Ein Zitat zum Einstieg angeben, eine provokative Aussage machen, eine (vermeintlich) rhetorische Frage stellen, eine persönliche Erfahrung schildern, aktuelle Statistiken nennen, eine öffentliche Meinung darstellen, ...
- Inhalt der Einleitung: Kurzer Überblick der Thematik zum jetzigen Zeitpunkt und in der Vergangenheit, kurze Vorstellung ihres Textes (was werden Sie im Folgenden tun?)

Formulierungen für die Einleitung	– It is a well-known fact that ... – In these days many people wonder about ... – Have you ever ... – Imagine this: You are .../There is ... – According to the latest statistics ...
Hinführung zum Thema	– Many people seem to think ... – Most people would agree to ... – For the majority of people ... – It has often been said that ...
Hinführung zur Ausgangslage	– The given statement claims ... – As a general statement this means ... – From this point of view ... – We like to think that ...

Struktur des Hauptteils

Unter Verwendung der gelernten Methoden sammeln und ordnen Sie ihre Gedanken/Ideen auf Konzeptpapier. Notieren und gewichten Sie ihre Argumente (entweder vom schwächsten zum stärksten Argument oder in umgekehrter Reihenfolge). Setzen Sie passende Beispiele dazu. Die Übersichtlichkeit und Darstellung des Hauptteils ist wesentlich für die Bewertung ihres Aufsatzes.

- Sammeln Sie Ideen, Argumente und Beispiele.
  Ordnen Sie mithilfe von **mind-maps**, **flow charts** etc. ihre Argumente.

- Lassen Sie zwischen Einleitung und Hauptteil eine Zeile frei und beginnen Sie im Hauptteil für jedes neue Argument einen neuen Absatz. Pro Absatz nennen Sie Argument und Beispiel(e).
- Verwenden Sie Bindewörter, um ihre Argumente in Bezug zu setzen.

Formulierungen, um Gründe anzugeben	– Regarding this fact, we can say … – The cause is that … – This is due to … – There are a couple of/various/several questions to consider when discussing … – There are many points of view to think about in this case. – The issues which should be discussed here are …
Formulierungen, um Argumente weiterzuführen	besides, still, also, too, above all, what is more, moreover, furthermore, in addition
Formulierungen, um Argumente auszulisten	– To begin with, to start with, first of all, next, then, finally … – For one thing….(and) for another (thing) … – First…secondly…thirdly…last of all … – Last but not least …
Formulierungen, um Ähnlichkeiten aufzuzeigen	likewise, equally, similarly, in the same way
Formulierungen, um Einschränkungen auszudrücken	although, even if, after all, in any case, in spite of
Formulierungen, um Bezugnahmen auszudrücken	concerning, regarding, related to, referring to, looking at
Formulierungen, um zeitliche Verbindungen herzustellen	now, then, while, as soon as, before, after, as long as, initially, previously, recently, finally, eventually, meanwhile, at the same time, in the end, at last, since, from now on, time and again, off and on, in the past, in days long gone, in the future, in present times
Formulierungen, um Gegenteile/Kontraste auszudrücken	yet, however, although, but, on the contrary, in contrast to, in spite of, despite, on the other hand
Formulierungen, um Beispiele anzuführen	– for example, for instance, in other words, such as – This can be illustrated through the story of … – It is common knowledge that … – All of us remember …

Verfassen des Schlussteils

Der Schlussteil sollte eine kurze Zusammenfassung des Wesentlichen beinhalten und mit ihrer eigenen und begründeten Meinung zur Thematik abschließen. Nennen Sie keine neuen Argumente im Schlussteil.

12.2 Wie sollte der Text strukturiert sein?

Formulierungen für den Schlussteil	– As a result ... – On the whole ... – In my opinion ... – From my point of view ... – finally, eventually, in conclusion, last of all, the final point is, there is only one point left ...
Formulierungen, um Stellung zu nehmen	– It seems to me that ... – I firmly believe that ... – It evokes the feeling of ... – I suppose ... – I (dis)approve ... – I distinguish between ... and ... – I want to point out that ... – I must concede ... – If you ask me ... – I would like to emphasize/ point out ... – First and foremost ...
Formulierung einer Schlussfolgerung	– The logical result of this is ... – In consequence ... – For that reason ... – This is why ... – This suggests ... – consequently, therefore, hence, accordingly, thus ...

Beachten Sie bei der Erarbeitung von *compositions*, dass Übung den Meister macht. Je mehr Sie sich an diesen Formulierungen versuchen, desto schneller werden Sie herausfinden, welche zu ihrem persönlichen Schreibstil passen, damit Sie Texte zunehmend flüssig und vor allem authentisch verfassen können.

> Überprüfen Sie die von Ihnen bereits verfassten Texte auf Struktur, Inhalt und Redemittel und überarbeiten Sie diese. Versuchen Sie sich an neuen Texten und überprüfen Sie Beispiellösungen, welche Sie im Unterricht besprechen. So entwickeln Sie ein sicheres Gespür für die Struktur und den Aufbau der *composition*.

Überblick

Textproduktion ist sicherlich eine anspruchsvolle Aufgabe – aber keine vor der man zurückschrecken sollte. Gut geplant vorzugehen, ist schon der halbe Weg zum Erfolg. Machen Sie sich klar, was gefordert ist (siehe 12.1), bauen Sie Ihren Text strukturiert auf (siehe 12.2).
Und haben Sie den Mut zu eigenen Einschätzungen und Stellungnahmen. Wenn Sie dann noch die Vielzahl der Redemittel berücksichtigen, die Ihnen dieses Buch vorgestellt hat, dann kann es eigentlich nicht mehr schief gehen.

Glossar

Das folgende Glossar ist in drei Bereiche aufgeteilt: Grammatik, Landeskunde und Arbeit mit Texten.

Grammatik

Adjektiv
Eine Wortart, der Wörter wie *good*, *clever* oder *necessary* angehören, die typischerweise auftreten:
- attributiv vor Substantiven in → Nominalphrasen >> **a *clever* idea**,
- prädikativ nach Verben in → Prädikaten >> **They are *clever*.**

Viele Adjektive sind außerdem:
- steigerbar >> **good – better** (Komparativ) **– best** (Superlativ),
- durch *very* modifizierbar >> ***very* clever**.

Adverb
Eine Wortart, der in der traditionellen Sprachbeschreibung Wörter recht unterschiedlicher Art zugerechnet werden, die sich schlecht in andere Wortarten einordnen lassen. Man kann drei typische Gruppen von Adverben unterscheiden:
- Bestimmte Adverben können → Adjektive oder → Verben modifizieren >> ***very* clever**, **... as we saw *clearly* ...**
- Bestimmte Adverben können die Satzkonstituente → Adverbiale realisieren und sind dabei in ihrer Position relativ frei >> **She met him *there*. *Then* they went *home*.**
- Manche Adverben haben eine textstrukturierende Funktion >> ***Furthermore*, artists who are also critics are especially likely to make vivid comments on the methods and techniques of old art.**

Adverbiale (adverbial)
Mit (das) Adverbiale wird eine → Funktion im Satz bezeichnet. Ein Adverbiale kann durch eine Adverbphrase, eine Nominalphrase >> **this morning**, Präpositionalphrase >> **up the hill** oder durch einen *clause* >> **After it had stopped raining, ...** realisiert werden.

Aktiv – Passiv
Ein Aktiv-Satz wie >> **The police arrested the suspect** und der korrespondierende Passiv-Satz >> **The suspect was arrested (by the police)** beziehen sich auf denselben Sachverhalt. Die *by*-Phrase im Passivsatz ist grammatisch nicht notwendig. Bei der Passivierung werden die Nominalphrasen verstellt. Ein Aktivsatz wie >> **He had an accident.** bietet sich also für den Fall an, wenn das Objekt neue oder wichtige Information darstellt (und das Subjekt schon bekannt ist). Im umgekehrten Fall, wie in >> **His car was buried by huge masses of snow**, bietet sich die Passivkonstruktion an, die das Neue, Interessante an den Schluss stellt, also dort, wo meist das Gewicht des Satzes liegt.

Artikel
Eine traditionelle Wortart, die eine Untergruppe der → *Determiner* bildet:
- bestimmter Artikel >> **the**
- unbestimmter Artikel >> **a, an**

Aspekt (aspect)
Die deutsche (umgangssprachliche) Konstruktion >> **Ich bin am Lesen** entspricht in etwa der Bedeutung von >> **I am reading**. Dieser Aspekt wird *progressive* genannt. Der Beispielsatz steht im *present progressive*. >> **The dog has disappeared** zeigt mit *have + past participle* den Aspekt, der als *perfective* bezeichnet wird, zusammen mit *present*

tense, also gesamt *present perfect*. In der Bedeutung ist dieser Satz vergleichbar mit „Der Hund ist weg": ein gegenwärtiger Zustand usw., aber mit Nennung eines Ereignisses, das zu dem jetzigen Zustand geführt hat. Beide Aspekte können miteinander (und mit einem Tempus) kombiniert werden >> **I've been shopping all day / I'd been shopping all day.**

clause
→ Satz

determiner
Eine Bezeichnung für die Verwendung von Wörtern, die in Nominalphrasen die Art der Referenz (Bezug auf eine bestimmte Person oder Sache, auf eine Menge / Klasse, etc.) bestimmen und vor der *premodification* des *head* der Nominalphrase stehen:
>> ***the*** books, ***these*** exercises, ***this*** country, ***all these*** stupid questions, ***their*** books
>> ***Most*** graduates move away from ***the*** town where they've been studying when they start work
Mit wenigen Ausnahmen (*a, an, every, the, no*) können *determiners* auch als
→ Pronomen verwendet werden.

Funktion
Die gängigen Funktionen im Satz (clause) sind **S**(ubjekt), **O**(bjekt), **A**(dverbiale) und der **V**(erbalkomplex), für den es unterschiedliche Definitionen und Bezeichnungen gibt. Daher die Satztypen, z. B.
SV >> **Susan is reading**
SVO >> **Susan is reading a book**
SVA >> **Susan lives over there**
Die Funktionen werden durch Phrasen (Ein-/Mehrwortphrasen), aber auch durch *clauses* realisiert >> **How you can stand all this** *(Subjekt)* **makes me really wonder.**

Hilfsverb
Eine Bezeichnung für die Verwendung der Verben *be, do* und *have* zur Bildung bestimmter Konstruktionen:
▶ The book *was* put on the table (Passiv)
▶ She *has* not been to Paris (Perfekt)
▶ *Did* you ever go to Paris? (yes-no question)

Konjunktion
ist der Oberbegriff für zwei Typen von Funktionswörtern:
▶ Koordinierende Konjunktionen verbinden zwei gleichrangige Bestandteile eines Satzes zu einem größeren Bestandteil desselben Ranges:
Angela and Gordon (zwei Nominalphrasen bilden eine größere Nominalphrase)
>> **She did her homework *and* then went to the cinema.**
▶ Subordinierende Konjunktionen leiten einen „Nebensatz" ein, der als Konstituente im übergeordneten Satz fungiert:
>> ***After*** **doing her homework, she went to the cinema.**
>> **Most graduates move away from the town where they've been studying *when* they start work.**

Modalverb
Ein Verb, das über keine Flexionsform verfügt: *can, could, may, might* etc.

Noncount
Substantive wie *water, ice, homework, advice, information*, die keine Pluralform haben, werden *noncount nouns* genannt (in Wörterbüchern oft auch als „U" bezeichnet, im Unterschied zu *count nouns*, wie *book – books*. Ein *noncount* Substantiv erscheint auch nicht zusammen mit *a/an* und zeigt Einschränkungen in der Verbindung mit dem bestimmten Artikel *the*.

Objekt
Eine Nominalphrase (oder ein *clause*) steht in der Regel nach dem Verb. >> **He didn't give me the paper** enthält zwei Objekte, **me** (indirektes Objekt), **the paper** (direktes Objekt. Beide Arten von Objekten können (im Prinzip) zum Subjekt eines entsprechenden Passivsatzes werden (**I ...; The paper ....**). Das indirekte Objekt ist dasjenige, das bei der Umstellung der Objektphrasen ein *to* (auch *for*) erhalten muss: **... the paper to me**. Das indirekte Objekt bezeichnet häufig ein Lebewesen.

Phrase
Unter *phrase* versteht man die Bausteine des Satzes (*clause*). Minimal bestehen *phrases* aus einem Wort (dem sog. *head*), wie etwa *water* in >> **Nowadays, water is expensive**. Nach der Wortart der *heads* werden die einzelnen Phrasen benannt, hier: *water* = Nominalphrase, *is* = Verbalphrase, *expensive* = Adjektivphrase, *nowadays* = Adverbphrase). Maximal können Phrasen ziemlich lang sein, z. B. in >> **More than a hundred people, who had been on a day trip to France** (bis hierher die Nominalphrase), **had to be rescued**. Wie ersichtlich, können Phrasen nach links und nach rechts vom *head* erweitert werden, z. B. >> **poor people, may have come, very silly, all cars with a catalyst**: links vom *head* steht die *premodification*, rechts davon die *postmodification*. Nominalphrasen können links, außer durch Adjektive, auch durch *determiner* erweitert werden, vgl. **several of the young children**. Weiteres siehe → Funktion.

Prädikat
Eine Bezeichnung für den Teil eines Satzes, der zusammen mit dem Subjekt das Zentrum des Satzes bildet. Das Prädikat umfasst einen Verbalkomplex, dem mehrere Hilfsverben und ein Verb angehören können:
>> She *has been reading*.
Objekte, Prädikative und nicht-weglassbare Adverbiale zählen ebenfalls zum Prädikat.
>> She *had not read the text*. >> He *gave her the book*. >> She *put the book on the table*.

Prädikativum (auch *subject complement/object complement*)
Bezeichnung für eine nach ihrer Funktion bestimmte Konstituente im Satz, die Teil des Prädikats ist und sich auf das Subjekt oder ein Objekt bezieht und dieses charakterisiert.
>> She is *a teacher/clever*.
>> They considered him *a suitable candidate*.
>> She called him *Gordon*.

Präposition
Ein Funktionswort, das nicht alleine stehen kann und mit anderen Phrasen zusammen Präpositonalphrasen bilden kann:
>> They were *in London*. She had not seen him *since then*. They agreed *on the proposal*.

Pronomen
Eine Wortart, deren Mitglieder als *head* einer Nominalphrase fungieren können:
>> *They* are clever, *What* was *that*? *She* didn't know *that herself*.
>> Most graduates move away from the town where they've been studying when *they* start work.

Relativadverb
Ein wh-Adverb, das einen Relativsatz einleitet
>> Most graduates move away from the town *where* they've been studying when they start work.

Relativpronomen
Ein Pronomen, das einen Relativsatz einleitet
>> ... she was the first person *who* made me realise that acting was more than just speaking and doing.

Relativsatz (relative clause)
Ein Relativsatz bezieht sich mithilfe eines Relativpronomens oder Relativadverbs auf die vorangehende Phrase. Man unterscheidet zwischen restriktivem oder notwendigem Relativsatz *(restrictive/defining relative clause)* einerseits und nicht-notwendigem, nicht-restriktiven Relativsatz (non-defining, non-restrictive) andererseits. Der notwendige Relativsatz hat die Form *X who/which – that* ..., der nicht-notwendige ist *X, who/which* ....
>> **Frogs, which are amphibians, lay eggs:** dieser nichtnotwendige Relativsatz nimmt an, dass *which are amphibians* ein dem Hörer bekanntes Faktum ist – „ja" „bekanntlich" – und die (mathematische) Menge der Frösche nicht verändert wird.
>> **Animals that are amphibians lay eggs:** Der notwendige Relativsatz etabliert eine Untermenge zum Vorgehenden, d.h., es handelt sich um *solche* Tiere, *diejenigen* Tiere, *die* .... Bei Übersetzungen aus dem Englischen ist zu beachten: Da der Unterschied zwischen den beiden Typen im Deutschen formal nicht gekennzeichnet werden muss, ist es sinnvoll, z. B. „ja, bekanntlich" oder „solche ... die; diejenigen ..., die" zu verwenden.

Satz (sentence, clause)
Ein *sentence* beginnt mit einem großen Buchstaben und endet in der Regel mit einem Punkt. >> **My mother was late(.)** ist ein *sentence* und gleichzeitig ein *clause*.
>> **My mother was late, because she had missed the bus(.)** ist ein *sentence* mit zwei *clauses*.

Subjekt
Eine Nominalphrase (oder ein *clause*), in der Regel am Anfang des *clause*, das denselben Numerus hat wie die Verbalphrase. Zur Identifizierung ist eine *tag question* hilfreich
>> **Most cars remained undamaged, didn't they?** (*they = most cars*, Subjekt).

Substantiv
Eine Wortklasse, der Wörter wie *person, house, university* und *democracy* angehören, die typischerweise folgende Formen haben:
- Singular *(university)* und Plural *(universities)*
- Grundform *(university)* und Genitiv *(university's)*

Substantive kommen typischerweise als Köpfe von Nominalphrasen vor:
>> **Most *graduates* move away from the town where they've been studying when they start *work*.**

Tempus (tense)
→ Zeit

Verb
Eine Wortklasse, der Wörter wie *go, laugh, put, be* angehören, die sich durch folgende Eigenschaften auszeichnen:
- Tempusformen für Präsens und Präteritum >> *go, goes – went*
- s-Form in der 3. Person Singular Präsens
- Partizipien mit *-ing* und häufig *-ed*
- können in Verbindung mit Hilfsverben Aktiv- und Passivkonstruktionen bilden.
>> **She put the book on the table – The book was put on the table.**

Zeit

Unter Zeit *(time)* wird üblicherweise all das verstanden, was man mit „wann?" erfragen kann. In der Verbalphrase werden grammatische Kategorien realisiert, die zu Vergangenheit, Gegenwart oder Zukunft, auch auf Dauer, Bezüge herstellen. Bei diesen Kategorien handelt es sich um die sog. Tempora *(tenses)*: (*present tense* wie in **I walk** und *past tense* wie in >> **I walked**). Nun kann man die Zeitbezüge der *tenses* formulieren, z. B., dass das *present tense* Zukünftigkeit ausdrücken kann, oder umgekehrt, welche Zeit-Vorstellung mit welcher *tense* ausgedrückt werden kann, z. B., dass ein vergangener abgeschlossener Vorgang mit *past tense* ausgedrückt wird. Diese Unterscheidung zwischen Zeit und Tempus ist sinnvoll, um nicht sagen zu müssen „Die Zukunft wird durch die Gegenwart ausgedrückt". Die beiden Tempora können alleine vorhanden sein *(simple)* oder mit → Aspekt kombiniert werden.

Landeskunde

American Constitution

The Constitution of the USA, which came into effect in 1788, is one of the most groundbreaking political documents ever written. It laid the foundations for democracy in the newly independent country by enabling the citizens to elect the politicians, and also established the way in which the country was to be governed. This included setting up three individual branches of government: the Legislative Branch (i. e. Congress), the Executive Branch (the President and Vice-President) and the Judicial Branch (the courts, including the Supreme Court). Each branch was given a certain amount of power over the other two—referred to as the system of checks and balances—to prevent one branch from becoming too strong. Several amendments have been made to the Constitution since it was first drawn up, the most famous being the first ten amendments, known as the Bill of Rights. These include fundamental democratic rights such as freedom of speech.

"Arab Spring" and media

In the spring of 2011, there were violent protests against the non-democratic political systems in several countries in North Africa and the Middle East. The protesters made clever use of social media to coordinate these protests and spread their message to other countries, encouraging others to join in.

Brain drain

"Brain drain" refers to the emigration of highly qualified professionals, particularly scientists, from one country to another because they can get more pay and better working conditions there. For example, many specialists have left Western Europe for jobs in the USA. Of course, this reduces the number of skilled workers in the country they have left behind, with serious consequences for the economy of that country. In order to remain competitive, each country needs people with the right kind of technical know-how. This problem is another effect of globalisation.

British Empire

Between the end of the 16th century and the mid 20th century, Britain ruled colonies throughout the world, from Africa and the Americas to the southern Pacific. Some of these colonies gained their independence long before the others (e.g. the North American colonies, which became the USA, signed their Declaration of Independence from Britain in 1776). Many other colonies, such as India or Rhodesia (now Zimbabwe), did not become independent until after the Second World War, often after many years of bitter protest. Several former British colonies belong to the British Commonwealth, an association of states that was originally formed to maintain both economic and cultural ties between these nations. The heads of the Commonwealth countries still meet today, and there are various exchange programmes and events, such as the Commonwealth Games; however, many of these states now have very little in common.

British Parliament

The British Parliament is made up of the **House of Commons** and the **House of Lords**. The politicians with seats in the Commons (the Members of Parliament, or MPs), are elected directly by the citizens of Britain and are responsible for the day-to-day running of the country, making laws and debating current issues. The members of the House of Lords, the upper chamber, are able to make changes to laws before they are passed, or even delay the passing of a law for up to 12 months, but are not involved in daily political life. There are different ways to get a seat in the House of Lords: some seats are hereditary and are passed down through the generations of an aristocratic family, others are given to senior Church of England bishops, while the rest are occupied by life peers. These are people (often former high-ranking politicians) who have the right to a seat in the Lords for their lifetime, but cannot pass it on to other members of their family.

Celtic Tiger

Between 1995 and 2007, Ireland's economy boomed as it had never done before. This period of economic growth is known as the "Celtic Tiger", when Ireland became an economic force to be reckoned with in the rest of the world.

Church of England

In Britain, church and state are not separate, as the head of state (the monarch) is also the head of the official church, the Church of England or Anglican Church. There are still close ties between the two institutions: the Prime Minister has a say in the appointment of the most senior priest, the Archbishop of Canterbury, who, along with other senior members of the Church, has a seat in the House of Lords. However, the government does not give the Church any financial support. For many English people, the Church of England is not about religion as such: church attendance is low in comparison to other religions practised in the country, but a significant percentage of the population describe themselves as Anglicans. This is often because it is a family tradition and therefore part of their cultural identity.

Civil Rights Movement

From the early 20th century, several organisations began to work towards ending segregation and discrimination against ethnic minorities in the USA. Some of them, such as the Southern Christian Leadership Conference (founded by Martin Luther King, Jr.) relied on peaceful protests, whereas others, such as the Black Panther Party, were prepared to use violence to achieve their goals. One of the most famous events connected with the movement was the March on Washington in 1963, where as many as 500,000 people demonstrated peacefully for civil rights. The movement made significant contributions towards reducing prejudice, but also cost many lives, most memorably those of Martin Luther King, Jr., and Malcolm X, both of whom were assassinated for demanding equal rights for all races.

Climate change

The temperature of our planet is rising, caused by factors such as the cutting down of forests. This has a knock-on effect on all kinds of things, such as rising sea levels caused by melting icebergs, which in turn can lead to natural disasters like flooding.

Cyberbullying

An unpleasant side-effect of social media sites and the widespread use of mobile phones: bullies now have more ways of attacking their victims. Upsetting or aggressive messages about others can be posted online and, sometimes within minutes, be read by hundreds of people, often with a devastating effect on the victims.

Fair Trade

Fair trade products allow farmers and workers in poorer countries to earn a decent wage for the food or goods they produce. Fair trade also helps to ensure sustainable farming and production methods.

Globalisation

Globalisation is an issue that affects the economy, working conditions, education, culture and environmental matters. For example, if one country suffers an economic crisis, it can also have an effect on other countries that it does business with. The world is connected in a wide variety of ways, with all the advantages and disadvantages that this brings.

Immigration

The USA has always attracted immigrants from around the world. They came for a variety of reasons: to escape religious persecution, poverty or war, to make their fortune in the gold fields, to realise their dreams in the land of opportunity. Often, the reality was very different, with immigrants being forced to live in slums, work long hours for little pay, and suffer prejudice and discrimination, especially if their ethnic background meant they did not fit comfortably into American society. Assimilation was easier for some groups than for others, e.g. the white Protestant northern Europeans who arrived in the 19th century had far fewer problems than the Asian or Latin American immigrants who came later. Throughout the 20th century, immigration laws became stricter, greatly limiting the number of visas available to prospective immigrants each year. Today the government is trying to find ways to reduce the number of illegal immigrants, although some politicians would like to pass laws to give long-term illegal immigrants and their families the right to stay.

National Curriculum

In 1989 the government introduced a standardized programme of study for all state schools. It set out which subjects were to be studied in each school year, and when the pupils were to be tested. The subjects range from English and maths to modern languages, science, and subjects dealing with life skills, such as social education. Independent and private schools do not have to follow the National Curriculum, although the national exams (e.g. GCSEs and A-levels) are the same for all pupils, no matter what type of school they attend.

National Health Service

Founded in 1948, the National Health Service (NHS) was set up to provide free healthcare for all British citizens, regardless of their income. It was funded by national insurance contributions, which all workers had to pay, and by the government. It was the first scheme of its kind in the world. The basic system remains unchanged in that all employees pay national insurance and that all Britons can receive free treatment from a local general practitioner. However, NHS costs have risen dramatically over the last 60 years, which means, for example, that dental or eye treatment is no longer free. Further problems include waiting times of several months for patients requiring routine operations, and the low quality of care available in some NHS-run hospitals. Due to this, many people have additional private health insurance.

Religion and science in the US

One of the controversies regarding education that has arisen in recent years concerns the teaching of evolution. In some states, pressure groups campaign to prevent schools from teaching evolution as scientific fact. Instead, pupils are to be taught creationism, a literal interpretation of the Bible in which God created the world in 7 days, approximately 10,000 years ago. Alternatively, they may be taught the concept of intelligent design, which states that all creatures on earth have evolved for a reason, not by chance, and that the world as it exists today was "designed" by God. Those who support these theories say that evolution cannot be proved, and that it does not explain everything adequately. Critics feel that not teaching evolution as scientific fact means taking a backward step in the field of science.

Social Media
Nowadays it is difficult to imagine life without social media. It is used by young and old alike to share information, photos, jokes, or simply to keep in touch.

War on terrorism
Following the terrorist attacks on the World Trade Center and the Pentagon on 11 September 2001, President George W. Bush announced his intention to fight terrorism throughout the world, specifically targeting Al-Qaeda. The US army, with help from other nations such as Britain, fought wars in Afghanistan and Iraq, overthrowing the dictator Saddam Hussein in the process; despite this, it has not been possible as yet to establish peace in Iraq. Furthermore, many US citizens have become concerned about the negative effects of the war on terrorism, such as a reduction in civil liberties. Even greater controversy surrounds the Guantánamo Bay prison, where several suspected terrorists have been held for some years without trial and often without any real evidence that they have any connection to a terrorist group.

Working conditions
Working conditions in developed countries are, in most cases, vastly different from those in the developing world. Many companies now prefer to have their goods manufactured in countries in which the wages are lower; however, the workers may have very few rights and be vulnerable to exploitation.

Arbeit mit Texten

Act
A major division in a play, usually subdivided into → scenes.

Action
Action is what happens in a fictional text. There may be → internal action and → external action.

Advertisement
(advert (BE), short form "ad") – It tries to sell a product, a service, an idea or a candidate. The purpose is to persuade people to do something.

Aestheticism
Period in the history of English art (1880–1900). Following the honesty of → Realism, aestheticist artists focused on beauty, trying to celebrate the power of art to create a sensual, pleasant experience. Oscar Wilde is a major representative.

Allegory
Stylistic device that uses personified ideas in order to present an abstract concept, i.e. when Death, Time, or Friendship appear as figures in a play. The late medieval drama *Everyman* provides good examples.

Alliteration
Alliteration is when neighboring words begin with the same letter in order to produce a rhythmic effect.

Alternate rhyme
Type of → rhyme that consists of alternating rhymes: >> **abab cdcd.**

American Revolution
Period in the Anglo-American history (1775–1783) that established the independence of the United States from Britain. The declaration of independence (4th July 1776) is celebrated every year.

Amphibrach
Lyrical → foot consisting of one unstressed, one stressed and one unstressed syllable.

Anapaest
Lyrical → foot consisting of two unstressed and one stressed syllable.

Anaphora
Lyrical device, the repetition of a word at the beginning of a line or a sentence.

Antagonist
The enemy or counterpart to the protagonist.

Argumentative text
Argumentative text is used to convince the reader of the author's opinion (e.g. speeches, essays, editorials, …).

Aside
Presentational device in dramatic texts, when a character says something that, by convention, is inaudible to others present. It not only provides insight into a character's thoughts and feelings, it also gives the audience an advantage in knowledge, leading to → dramatic irony.

Assonance
Type of → rhyme that consists of identical vowel sounds only.

Authorial narrative situation
Type of narrative in which the narrator is not part of the events narrated, has insight into the thoughts and feelings of the characters, knows about the past and the future, and comments on the narrative from an external, authorial position; → first person narrative situation, and → figural narrative situation

Ballad
Narrative poem that tells a heroic, romantic, tragic, or comic story; intended to be sung.

Beiseitesprechen
→ aside

Bildungsroman
Subgenre of the novel sometimes also called "novel of development;" presenting a protagonist who rises from simple beginnings to a position of respectability. Examples are: **Charlotte Brontë's** *Jane Eyre* (1847), **Charles Dickens's** *David Copperfield* (1849–1850), and **James Joyce's** *A Portrait of the Artist as a Young Man* (1916).

Blank verse
Type of language, often in dramatic texts, that is structured by → metre, but not rhymed.

Botenbericht
→ messenger report

Briefroman
→ epistolary novel

Bürgerkrieg, amerikanischer
→ Civil War

Caesura
Break in the middle of a poetic line.

Caption
Words underneath a picture or cartoon.

Chain rhyme
Type of → rhyme that consists of three lines, the first and last rhyming, the middle line forming the embracing rhyme for the next group of three lines >> **aba bcb cdc.**

Character
The people in a fictional text are the characters.

Characterization
The way in which the characters are presented to the reader/audience.

Chiasmus
Syntactical aspect that reverses the sequence of sentence elements, for instance subject, verb/verb, subject; often found in poetry.

Civil War
Period in American history (1860 – 1865) that began with the secession from the Union of Southern states and later lead to a bloody military conflict (over 4 million dead and wounded) between the North and the South, ending with the victory of the Northern states.

Climax
The part of the plot in which suspense reaches its peak/highest point.

Closet drama
Drama written for private reading, not for performance on the stage.

Column
An article that appears on a regular base in a magazine or a newspaper. It can be humorous or serious. It always expresses the opinion of the writer, not the magazine or newspaper it is published in.

Comedy
A subgenre of drama written often in low style that features common people who are exposed to ridicule, often ending happily.

Comic relief
Feature of literary texts, often in tragic drama, where a character creates a moment of laughter in order to counterbalance the overall serious tone.

Commonwealth
Period in English history (1649–1660). Following the English Civil War and the execution of Charles I, England saw the regime of Oliver Cromwell (succeeded later by his son), experienced religious tolerance but also the closing of its theatres by the Puritans.

Commonwealth of Nations
Association of around 50 nations that once were or still are dominated by Britain.

Consonance
Type of → rhyme that consists of identical consonant sounds only.

Dactyl
Lyrical → foot consisting of one stressed and two unstressed syllables.

Dark Age
→ Middle Ages

Descriptive Text
Describes the characteristics of living things or objects, focusing on the physical side of things.

Dialogue
Form of speech in dramatic texts, when different characters are on the stage, more than one of them contributing to the conversation.

Direct characterization
→ explicit characterization

Discourse
The way a narrative is organised, presented, put in order, in short: narrated.

Discourse time
The time that it takes to read (or tell) a narrative; rarely the same as → story time.

Drama
A → play, usually fictional but sometimes based on actual events (e.g. historical drama). Is written to be performed and usually divided into → acts which are subdivided into → scenes.

Dramatic irony
Feature of literary texts that involves different levels of knowledge, in particular a moment where a character is not aware of the consequences of a word or deed, other characters (or the audience), however, already foresee or know the future consequences.

Embracing rhyme
Type of → rhyme that consists of a → rhyming couplet embraced by two rhyming lines >> **abba cddc.**

Enjambment
Continuation of a syntactical unit beyond the end of a poetic line into the next line.

Enlightenment
Period in the history of English and European thought (17th–18th century) that emphasised the power of the intellect. Influential British representatives are **Francis Bacon, Thomas Hobbes, David Hume,** and **John Locke.**

Epanalepsis
Lyrical device, repetition of a word, interrupted by at the most two words.

Epic
Long narrative poem that celebrates the heroic deeds of its protagonist in a sublime style.

Epigram
A short and witty saying that makes a strong, critical statement.

Epipher
→ Epistrophe

Epistolary novel
Subgenre of the novel in which the plot is conveyed through a series of letters. **Samuel Richardson's** *Pamela* (1740) is an early example.

Epistrophe
Lyrical device, the repetition of a word at the end of a line or sentence.

Erlebte Rede
→ free indirect discourse

Erzählte Zeit
→ story time

Erzählzeit
→ discourse time

Essay
Type of prose text that discusses a particular topic from a highly subjective point of view, offering personal insight without claiming to be a scientific discussion. **Francis Bacon, Jonathan Swift,** and **Henry David Thoreau** are key practitioners of the form.

Euphemism
Using gentle words instead of regular expression to soften a maybe harsh circumstance or situation.

Exaggeration
A strong overstatement

Experiencing I
An aspect of the narrator in a → first person narrative situation; refers to a narrator who is currently experiencing the events, not yet knowing what the outcome will be. Often the narrator will be speaking from a privileged position later in time, thinking back about his or her own past experiences; → narrating I.

Explicit characterization
The reader/audience is being told by the narrator, another character or the character himself/herself what sort of person the character is.

Expository text
The author analyses a complex matter in an objective way.

External action
Description of what characters do and of the events taking place.

Falling action
The part of the plot where suspense is reduced.

Feature story
Deals with one or more individual cases in order to make a general point on something.

Figura etymologica
Lyrical device, use of two words derived from the same etymological root, for instance "to *do* great *deeds*".

Figural narrative situation
Type of narrative in which there is no perceptible narrator; the events are told in a passive way, through the eyes of often changing characters, also called → focalisers; → authorial narrative situation and → first person narrative situation.

First person narrative situation
Type of narrative in which the narrator (who is often also the protagonist) is part of the events, does not have insight into the thoughts and feelings of the other characters; → narrating I and → experiencing I; → authorial narrative situation and → figural narrative situation.

First person narrator
The first person narrator is part of the story and refers to himself/herself as "I".

Flashback
Is the description of an important scene that took place in the past but is important for the plot.

Flat character
A flat character has only one or two significant traits and thus represents a single quality and is a minor character.

Focaliser
A character in a narrative that uses a →figural narrative situation whose perspective is presented for at least part of the narrative; often used in conjunction with →interior monologue or →free indirect discourse.

Foot
Smallest unit of recurrent grouping of syllable stress in a poem, for instance →iamb.

Foreshadowing
Also known as anticipation; is when the narrator hints at later events.

Formal language
Register which is used in texts that are official.

Free indirect discourse
Literary technique for presenting the inner mind of a character. A free indirect discourse presents the thoughts and feelings of a character using the present tense and first person pronouns but keeping the conventions of literary language; →psycho narration and →interior monologue.

Free verse
Type of language, often in dramatic texts, that is not structured by →rhyme or →metre.

Gattung
→Genre

Gedankenbericht
→psycho narration

Genre
Description of a type of literary text that shares a number of characteristics with other texts; a textual strategy agreed upon by writers and readers. Basic genres are **poetry**, **drama**, and **prose narratives.**

Gothic fiction
Subgenre of the →novel or →romance, popular during →Romanticism. The gothic novel uses a medieval or often European setting, featuring supernatural events, haunted castles, ruins, or monasteries; places its characters in threatening scenes evoking horror or terror; and emphasises emotions over rationality. **Horace Walpole's** *The Castle of Otranto* (1764) started the tradition in Britain; **Mary Shelley's** *Frankenstein* is a popular example.

Heroic couplet
Two rhymed lines of text written in an iambic pentametre.

Iamb
Lyrical →foot consisting of one unstressed and one stressed syllable.

Imagery
When language is used beyond its normal meaning, e.g. dictionary definition.

Implicit characterization
The reader/audience has to find out what sort of person the character is, based on what he/she says and does.

Indirect characterization
→implicit charaterization

Industrial Revolution
Period in English history, beginning around 1830, during which the technological advancements (steam engine, railways, factories etc) lead to a major change in the lifestyles of the population, leading also to a sizeable migration from rural into urban areas, creating a huge working class.

Informal language
Register employing the conventions of spoken language – may make use of slang and colloquialisms.

Innerer Monolog
→ interior monologue

Intensive reading
Den Text gründlich und detailliert lesen, um Gesamtaufbau, Struktur, Stilmittel und Inhalt vollständig zu erkennen und zu verstehen.

Interior monologue
Literary technique for presenting the inner mind of a character. An interior monologue is not part of the narrative situation but rather a switching into the actual thought processes of a character, using the present tense, first person pronouns, and the often disconnected sentence fragments that are typical for thoughts that have not yet been transformed into written language; → free indirect discourse and → psycho narration.

Internal action
What is going on in the minds of the characters.

Intertextuality
Literary device in → postmodern texts that connects two texts, for instance through direct quotation, through the adoption of plot devices or through the insertion of already existing characters, for instance in **Tom Stoppard's** *Rosencrantz and Guildenstern Are Dead* (1966).

Irony
Uses words in a meaning opposite to their literal meaning.

Jambus
→ iamb

Kernel
A part of a narrative that provides crucial information for the → plot; → satellite.

Kurzgeschichte
→ short story

Lesedrama
→ closet drama

Limited point of view
Is found with the first-person narrator. The reader's view is limited by what the character "I" in the story experiences and shares with the reader. Can also be found with a third-person narrator, when he/she keeps to the experiences of one or two characters.

Literal
Meaning of something is the common sense of the words, not figurative.

Lyrical I
The "voice" in a poem, the person speaking, the subjective centre of experience; not to be confused with the author. Called explicit lyrical I if stated directly; otherwise: implicit lyrical I.

Major character
Central character; he/she plays an important part, but is not the main character/protagonist.

Mauerschau
→ teichoscopy

Messenger report
Presentational device in dramatic texts, when a messenger comes onto the stage to narrate events that happened off-stage, often in order to avoid the portrayal of excessive violence or scenes involving too many people, for instance a battle; → teichoscopy.

Metafiction
Type of literary discourse in which a piece of art makes obvious its own constructedness, i.e. a novel that discusses the novel as an art form or has an intrusive narrator who questions the very idea of novel writing, as in **John Fowles's** *The French Lieutenant's Woman* (1969).

Metaphor
Rhetorical device that compares two ideas, putting one word for another and transferring part of the meaning, for instance "she is an angel".

Metonymy
Rhetorical device that compares two ideas, putting one word for another to which it is closely related, for instance "to read Shakespeare", putting the author for his work.

Metre
Description for a type of line in poetry, stating the number of times a particular → foot is repeated; example iambic pentametre.

Middle Ages (Mittelalter)
Period in English history between the departure of the Romans and the beginning of the Renaissance.

Middle English
Variety of English spoken between 1066 and the Renaissance (beginning around 1500). As a result of the Norman invasion, English changed dramatically, getting rid of most of the verb conjugations and noun declensions. Also, the influence of French is highly obvious in the vocabulary, with numerous loan words adopted into English. **Geoffrey Chaucer's** *Canterbury Tales* (ca. 1386) is an example.

Modernism
Period in the history of English art (ca. 1890–1945). Modernism was marked by a sense of disorientation, influenced by political developments (World War I) and the realisation that the traditional art forms are not longer adequate for addressing the reality of „modern" life. Often, modernist artworks are marked by a significant break with artistic traditions and they present life as a chaotic, fragmentary, and isolating experience. **Virginia Woolf, T. S. Eliot, John Dos Passos,** and **James Joyce** are key practitioners.

Monologue
Form of speech in a dramatic text, when one character gives a longer speech, addressing other characters on the stage.

Narrating I
An aspect of the narrator in a → first person narrative situation; refers to a narrator who is telling the story at a later point in time, giving the narrator the benefit of hindsight, making it possible to comment on earlier moments while knowing the outcome. The narrating I will often talk about him or herself at an earlier stage, also called → experiencing I.

Narrative Prose
Short stories, novels, etc

Narrator
The person who tells the story.

Neoclassicism
Period in the history of English art (17th–18th century) that draws its formal and stylistic inspiration from Greek and Roman antiquity. **John Dryden's** work is an example.

Neutral language (register)
The style you can find in most novels, articles, letters, etc

News story
Also news items, news reports; it never expresses an opinion but presents facts on recent events.

Non-fictional text
Refers to the real world and can be used as form of information, persuasion.

Novel
Type of narrative dominant since the early 18th century, marked by its social realism, its focus on characters and events that could in fact exist; in opposition to → romance. **Daniel Defoe's** *Robinson Crusoe* (1719) starts the realist novel in England.

Old English
Variety of English spoken until 1066. As a Germanic language, Old English has a fully developed case system, complex endings, and verb conjugations similar to modern German. For modern readers, Old English is only comprehensible after special study. **Beowulf** is the best known Old English text.

Omniscient narrator
A third-person narrator who has an unlimited point of view.

Parallelism
Syntactical aspect that repeats the sequence of sentence elements, for instance subject, verb / subject, verb; often found in poetry.

Play
→ Drama

Plot
The structure of action. A set of events which are connected and are usually centered on a main problem or differing conflicts.

Poem
Fictional text structured by lines and rhythm. The lines are often grouped in → stanzas.

Poetic justice
Feature of literary texts that demands that good deeds be rewarded and that the villain be punished.

Point of view
The perspective the story is told from.

Polyptoton
Lyrical device, repetition of a word in different forms, for instance "called" (simple past) and "calls" (third person singular, present tense).

Postcolonial literature
Description for the works by authors who write from a formerly colonized country, often dealing with the history of colonialism, the struggle for independence, the cultural domination of the West, or in celebration of indigenous artistic traditions. Examples are **Chinua Achebe's** *Things Fall Apart* (1958), **Salman Rushdie's** *Midnight's Children* (1981), **Nadine Gordimer,** and **J. M. Coetzee.**

Postmodernism
Period in the history of English art (1945 —). Following Modernism, Postmodernism has been described as a continuation or a break with Modernism. In postmodern art, the history of a particular art form is ironically quoted and playfully redefined. Artists are highly interested in the process of production, making their art a comment about art (→ Metafiction). Works by **Peter Shaffer, A. S. Byatt,** or **John Barth** are examples.

Poststructuralism
Method of literary analysis (also called deconstruction) that supersedes → structuralism and, in contrast to the earlier movement, does not believe in the existence of underlying ordering principles. Poststructuralists focus on a text's contradictions, logical breaks, and the overall instability of words, which they believe do not have stable meanings.

Protagonist
The main character, hero (male) or heroine (female).

Psycho narration
Literary technique for presenting the inner mind of a character.
A psycho narration is part of the narrative situation, uses the same narrative past and third-person pronouns when referring to the character; the language and style is that of "normal" literary prose; → free indirect discourse and → interior monologue.

Pun
Wordplay. Words with different meanings or sounding the same can be deliberately used.

Realism
Period in the history of English art (1840–1880). Following the radical changes that the → Industrial Revolution caused in England, artists started to get interested in the lives of average people, portraying in plain style simple people and their worries, for example in **George Eliot's** *Middlemarch* (1871—1872).

Register
Level of language used in a text: formal, neutral, informal, slang.

Renaissance
Period in English (and European) history after the end of the Middle Ages, marked by a rebirth of classical learning and the arts of antiquity as well as by technological advances (book printing, gun powder etc.).

Restoration
Period in English history after the → Commonwealth. With the crowning of King Charles II in 1660, the monarchy was restored in England and the theatres reopened.

Rhyme
The similarity of the sound of two or more words or parts of words.

Rhyme scheme
Grouping of → rhymes in a → stanza creating a recurring pattern, for instance >> **abba abba.**

Rhyming couplets
Type of → rhyme that consists of two subsequent lines >> **aa bb cc.**

Rhythm
The arrangement of stressed and unstressed syllables in a line.

Rising action
The part of the plot where suspense is build up.

Romance
Type of narrative dominant in the middle ages and still popular today, marked by fantastic features such as ghosts or dragons; in opposition to → novel.

Romanticism
Period in the history of English art (1780–1830) that emphasised the role of artists, the power of the imagination to represent the deeper significance of a sublime nature. It started as a countermovement to the rationalism of the → Enlightenment. Important artists are **William Wordsworth** and **Samuel Taylor Coleridge.**

Satellite
A part of a narrative that does not provide crucial information for the → plot; → kernel.

Scanning
Suche nach Schlüsselwörtern, den *key words*, im Text durch Überfliegen, anschließendes Lesen des Abschnitts, in dem das Schlüsselwort steht, um gezielt und schnell grundlegende Informationen zu gewinnen.

Scene
A subdivision of an → act in a → play. It can also be a smaller part of action without a change of place or time.

Setting
Place, time and atmosphere of the → plot.

Short story
Type of short narrative that typically presents a single plot with a moment of crisis, has few characters who are flat and hardly developed, and spends little to no time on setting, description etc. The writings of **Edgar Allan Poe** are popular examples.

Simile
A comparison between two things which are different by using the words "like" and "as".

Skimming
Schnelles Überfliegen eines Textes, um die Kernthemen zu erkennen.

Slang
Very informal language and can indicate that a character is part of a social group, a background, an age group.

Soliloquy
Form of speech in a dramatic text, when only one character is on the stage, giving voice to his thoughts and feelings.

Sonnet
Lyrical subgenre, traditionally a love poem, written in 14 lines. Established by the Italian poet Petrarca, who divided a sonnet into two groups of eight lines (octave) and six lines (sestet); the English or Shakespearean sonnet often has three quatrains and a heroic couplet.

Speech
Spoken text delivered to an audience.

Speech bubble
Used in cartoons in order to visualize direct speech of one or more.

Spondee
Lyrical → foot consisting of two stressed syllables.

Stanza
Groups into which lines have been arranged.

Story
1) The content (or "what") of a narrative; → discourse. 2) The chronological sequence of elements in a narrative; → plot.

Story time
How long it take for the events in a narrative to "really" take place; can cover many years, even centuries; rarely the same as → discourse time.Structuralism
Method of literary analysis derived from linguistics that believes that texts are the realisations of underlying ordering principles, i.e. that all fairy tales draw from a basic group of plot elements that they realise into concrete narratives.

Symbol
An object that stands for another matter, event or thing.

Synecdoche
Rhetorical device that compares two ideas. A part is taken for the whole, or a general term for a subordinate word. Example >> **To take up the sword,** meaning **to go to war.**

Tail rhyme
Type of → rhyme that consists of changing → rhyming couplets followed by a line ending in a repeated sound patter >> **aab ccb ddb.**

Teichoscopy
Presentational device in dramatic texts, when a character directly comments upon events that are happening off stage, invisible to the audience, often in order to avoid the portrayal of excessive violence or scenes involving too many people, for instance a battle; → messenger report.

Thesis
An idea or opinion/ view which is being discussed in a formal way usually by an author of an argumentative text.

Third-person narrator
A third-person narrator is not a person in the story and refers to the characters as "he", "she" or "they" or uses their names.

Three Unities
Dramatic convention, derived in parts from Aristotle, that demands that a play have one plot, one setting, and takes place within 24 hours.

Tragedy
A subgenre of drama written in high style that features a high hero who commits a mistake and is punished for it at the end of the play.

Trochee
Lyrical → foot consisting of one stressed and one unstressed syllable.

Unlimited point of view
Found with the omniscient narrator entering into character's minds and moving around, not following any one character.

Utopian novel
Subgenre of the novel that presents an ideal, often future, society as a means to criticise the present; negative utopias (also called dystopias) present a future in which the ills of the present have deteriorated into catastrophe. Famous utopias are **Edward Bellamy's** *Looking Backward: 2000–1887* (1888) and **William Morris's** *News from Nowhere* (1890); dystopias are **Aldous Huxley's** *Brave New World* (1932) or **George Orwell's** *Nineteen Eighty-Four* (1949).

Vergleich
→ simile

Word scenery
Feature of dramatic texts, involving the creation of a sense of location exclusively through words, not through an actual stage set.

Zäsur
→ caesura

Stichwortverzeichnis

A

Abenteuerroman 226
About a Boy 185
Acceptable Behaviour Contracts
   (ABCs) 60
ACT (American College Testing) 84
Afghanistan 111
Africa 71
African Methodist
   Episcopal Church 108
Ageing population 55
Age of invention 87
A-Levels 45, 48
Monika Ali 152
All for Love 145
Altenglisch 143
alternate rhyme 162
American Dream 87, 92
A Midsummer Night's Dream 144
amphibrach 160
Amphibrach 160
Analyse 8, 205
Anapäst 160
anapest 160
Anapher 167
Anglicans 65
Anglo-Catholics 65
Anti-Semitism 68, 94
Anti-social Behaviour Orders
   (ASBOs) 60
"AS" (advanced subsidiary) exam ... 48
Assembly line 87
Ästhetizismus 150
Asylum seekers 61
Atomic bomb 110
W. H. Auden 156
auktoriale Erzählsituation 186
Jane Austen 149, 187
Australia 71
authorial narrative situation 186
Autobiography 148, 195

B

BA (Bachelor of Arts) 84
Baccalaureate 48
Bachelor's degree 51, 84
Back-benchers 39
Baptists 67, 106
Aphra Behn 145, 147
Beiseitesprechen 177
Beowulf 140
Beveridge Report 57
Bildanalyse 203, 206, 212
Bildbeschreibung 201
Bill of Rights 79
Biography 196
Black Muslims 96
Black Panther Party 96
Blair, Tony 41
William Blake 148, 157, 164, 173,
   174, 176, 178, 187, 188
blogger 117
Boston Tea Party 70
Botenbericht 177
Brainstorming 22
Breadbasket of the world 88
British Empire 69
British Parliament 38
British settlers 98
British society 55
BSc (Bachelor of Science) 84
BTECs and OCR Nationals 48
Buchdruck 144
Bullying 119
George W. Bush 78, 104

C

caesura	160
Cambridge	50
Canada	69
Canterbury Tales	140
Captain Cook	71
caption	204
Caribbean	61
cartoon	209
Cartoon	212, 213
Catholic Church in Britain	68
William Caxton	144
Celtic Tiger	124
chain rhyme	162
checks and balances	79
Child benefit	58
Chinese Exclusion Act	94
Church in Wales	67
Church of England	64
Church of Scotland (the "Kirk")	66
city academies	47
Civil Rights Movement	95
climate change	131
J. M. Coetzee	193
Cold War	110
Samuel Coleridge	148
colonies	69
comic relief	177
comic strip	210
Common Sense	148
Commonwealth Games	72
Commonwealth of Nations	72
– Principles of the	73
Communism	110
community colleges	84
comprehensive schools	45
conditional sentences	31
Congress of Racial Equality (CORE)	96
Conservative Party	40
Constitution, American	79
Courts	59, 78
Creationism	85
crime	59, 101
Crime prevention	60
Oliver Cromwell	145
Crown colonies	71
Cuba	109
Cuban Missile Crisis	110
cultural Christianity	64
currency	74

D

dactyl	160
Daktylus	160
Dark Age	144
Das kommunistische Manifest	149
Death of a Salesman	181
Death penalty	102
Death row	102
Daniel Defoe	147, 184
Democrats	80
discourse time	189
discrimination	62
Discrimination	95
Dominions	71
Drake, Sir Francis	69
Drama	153, 172
dramatische Ironie	177
drugs	101
John Dryden	145

E

economy	120
Editorial	195
editorial cartoon	210
Einleitung	223
Electoral College	82
electoral system	40, 81
elementary schools	83
George Eliot	149
Elisabeth I	144
Elizabeth I	69

embracing rhyme 162
Emergency Quota Act 94
employment 52, 87
Friedrich Engels 149
Enjambement 160
enjambment 160
environment 129
Epanalepse 167
Epipher 167
E pluribus unum 93
Louise Erdrich 152
Erzähltext 153
Erzählungen 185
Erzählzeit 189
Essay 196
George Etherege 145
ethnic background 56, 91
ethnic minorities 62, 97
etymologie 14
Euphemismus 166
European Community (EC) 74
euro-sceptics 74
evangelicals 65
evolution 85
exaggeration 209
Executive Branch 77
Exposition 173, 174
expression 202

F

facial expression 202
fair trade 123
Falkland Islands 72
families 56
feature Story 195
federalism 79
Margaret Ferguson 155
fictional text 12
figura etymologica 167
figural narrative situation 187
figurative language 199

Fin-de-Siècle 150
first-person narrative situation 187
First World War 109
F. Scott Fitzgerald 188
flow chart 21
Foe 193
Henry Ford 87
Frankenstein 191
Benjamin Franklin 148
Free Churches 67
Freedom Rides 97
future forms 28

G

Gandhi 71
Gedichtanalyse 165
General Certificate of Secondary
    Education (GCSE) 47
gerund 32
geschweifter Reim 162
Gestalten 9
gestures 202
Gibraltar 69
globalisation 113, 115, 120, 129
global warming 132
grammar schools 46
Great Awakening 106
Great Depression 88
grids 20
Großgattungen 153
Guantánamo Bay 112
Guckkastenbühne................ 145

H

Haltung des Autors 200
Hamartia 172
Hamlet 144
Harare Declaration 73
Harry Potter 185
Hauptteils 223
Elizabeth Haywood 147

heading	198, 204
headline	198
Head of State	38
healthcare	57, 100
health insurance	57, 89, 100
Hendiadyoin	166
Henry VIII	68
Hexameter	160
High Church	65
higher education	50
high schools	83
Oscar Hijuelos	152
Hilfsmittel	9
hire and fire	88
höfische Dichtung	146
Homeland Security	104, 111
homeschool	83
homicide rate	101
homosexual priests	66
Maxine Hong Kingston	152
Nick Hornby	185
House of Commons	38
House of Lords	39
House of Representatives	76
Hyperbel	166

I

iamb	159
Ich-Erzählsituation	187
Idiom	214
"I have a dream" speech	97
Immigration	61, 87, 91
– illegal	94
– Immigration Reform and Control Act	94
– quota system	94
Immigration Act	94
immigration policies	93
immigration tests	94
imperialism	70
income support	58
India	61, 69, 70
Indians	98
Industrial Revolution	52, 114
integration	63
intelligent guessing	13
intensive reading	12
Intention	205
interkulturelle Kompetenz	6
internet	115
Interpretation	205
IRA	43
Iron Curtain	110
Ironie	209
irony	199, 209
Kazuo Ishiguro	152
Ivy League	84

J

Jesse Jackson	97
Jambus	159
Jane Eyre	141
Jehovah's Witnesses	108
jews	68, 92, 106
Jim Crow Laws	95
Jobseeker's Allowance	54, 58
B. S. Johnson	189
James Joyce	151
judicial branch	78
Julius Caesar	144
juries	59

K

Karikatur	209, 210, 212, 213
Karl I	145
Karl II	145
Katharsis	172
Katrina, Hurricane	97, 104
John F. Kennedy	107
Kettenreim	162
King, Martin Luther	96
Kolloquium	11

kommunikative Kompetenz	6
Kontext	139
Korean War	110
Kreuzreim	162
Ku Klux Klan	96
Hanif Kureishi	152
Kyoto Protocol	81

L

labor unions	88
Labour Party	41
language skills	54
Leader of the Opposition	39
legal drinking age	101
legislative branch	76
Lesetechnik	12
Letters from an American Farmer	148
Liberal Democratic Party (Lib Dems)	41
linguistic turn	150
literacy rate (US)	86
Literaturgeschichte	139
Local education authority (LEA)	45
Love in Excess	147
Low Church	65
Martin Luther	144
lyrical ballads	148
Lyrik	153, 154
Lyrische Formen	154

M

Maastricht Treaty	74
Macbeth	144
Magistrate	59
"Magnet" schools	84
John Major	74
Malcolm X	96
March on Washington	97
Christopher Marlowe	167
Marshall Plan	110
Karl Marx	149
mass production	87

masters degrees	51
maternity leave	53, 89
Mauerschau	177
Mayflower	105
Medicaid	100
Medicare	100
melting pot	93
Members of Parliament (MPs)	39
Mennonites	106
Metapher	150
Methodenkompetenz	12
Methodists	67, 106
Metonymie	165
metonymy	165
Metrum	159
Mexico	94
middle class	90
Migration	126
Arthur Miller	181
John Milton	146
Mimesis	185
mind map	21
minimum wage	53, 89
Mitschrift	19
Mittelenglisch	143
Moby Dick	141
Moderne	151
monarchy	38
Monolog	177
Monroe Doctrine	109
Mormons	108
Toni Morrison	152
Mrs Dalloway	188
Muslims	62, 68, 108
My Fair Lady	175

N

Nachkriegsroman	151
National Association for the Advancement of Colored People (NAACP)	96

National Curriculum 45, 49
National Health Service 43, 57
National Insurance Act 57
Native Americans 98
naturalismus 149
Neighbourhood Watch 60
New Labour 41
NHS Foundation Trusts 58
Friedrich Nietzsche 150
"nine-to-five" job 53
"No Child Left Behind" Act 86
non-fictional text 12
North American colonies 70
North Atlantic Treaty Organisation
    (NATO) 110
Northern Ireland 44, 67
NVQs (National Vocational
    Qualifications) 48

O

Oliver Twist 141
online community 116
Orlando 184
Oroonoko 145, 147
Othello 144
Thomas Otway 145
Oxford 50
oxymoron 166

P

Paarreim 162
paid holiday 89
Thomas Paine 148
Pakistan 61
Panama Canal 109
Paradise Lost 146
Paradoxon 166
Parks, Rosa 96
parliamentary democracy 38
passive voice 30
past perfect progressive 27

past perfect simple 27
past progressive 24
paternity leave 53
Patient's Charter 58
Pearl Harbor 110
Pentameter 160
personale Erzählsituation 187
PhDs (doctorates) 51
Phrasal verbs 34
Pilgrim Fathers 105
Harold Pinter 175
Plaid Cymru (Party of Wales) 42
Plymouth Colony 105
poem 12
poiesis 185
political parties (GB) 40
polyptoton 167
population facts (US) 90
postkoloniale Literatur 151
Postmoderne 151
Powell, Colin 97
Präsentation 11
Präsentationsprüfung 11
preparatory ("prep") schools 50
Presbyterians 67, 106
present perfect 26
present perfect progressive 26
present perfect simple 25, 26
present progressive 24
Presidential candidates 82
President of the United States 77
Pride and Prejudice 149, 187
primary schools 45
Prime Minister's Question Time ... 39
Principles of the 73
private education 49
private schools 84
prohibition 101
pronoun 199
Prosa 153, 184
protestants 93

Prüfungsgespräch 11
Prüfungsstress 6
public education 83
public schools 50
public services 57
Puerto Rico 109
pun 199, 209
punishment 60, 101
Punkteverteilung 9
Puritans 92, 105, 106
Pygmalion 175

Q
Quakers 67, 106

R
race relations 61
Race Relations Act 62
Rachetragödie 172
railway system 87
Walter Raleigh 69
Realismus 149
Redbrick Universites 51
Religion 64–67, 105–107
religious education 49, 85
Renaissance 144
Reorganisation 8
repetition 199
Reproduktion 7
Republicans 81
"Respect" campaign 60
Restaurationskomödie 173
retirement 100
rhetorical question 199
Rhythmus 160
Condoleezza Rice 97
Robinson Crusoe 147, 184
Roman 147, 149
Romantik 148
Romeo and Juliet 144, 178
Roosevelt Corollary 109

Rosencrantz and Guildenstern Are Dead 179
ryming couplet 162

S
Sachtext 195
Salvation Army 67
SATs (Scholastic Assessment Tests) . 84
sayings 214
scannen 20
Scannen 20
Scanning 12
Schauerroman 149
Schlussteil 224
Science-Fiction 185
Scotland 44
Scottish National Party (SNP) 42
secondary schools 45
Second Empire 70
Second World War 110
segregation 95
Senate 76
separation of church and state 106
September 11 2001 (9/11) ... 108, 111
sex education 49, 85
Shadow Cabinet 39
Peter Shaffer 173
William Shakespeare 144, 164, 174, 176, 178, 187, 188
George Bernhard Shaw 175
Mary Shelley 191
simile 209
simple past 24, 26
simple present 23
Upton Sinclair 139
Singapore Declaration 73
single-panel cartoon 210
Sinn Féin 40, 43
sixth-form college 46
"SKI", ("Spend the Kids' Inheritance") 55

skimmen 20
Skimming 12
Slavery 70, 95
– National Anti-Slavery Society 95
social media 118
social security 58
social security taxes 100
social services 59
social welfare 99
Sonett 144
Southern Christian Leadership
     Conference 96
Spätromantik 149
specialist schools 47
speech 195
spondee 159
Spondeus 159
Stamp Act 70
stanza 161
State Courts 78
state education 45
state pensions 58
statutory holiday 53
J. Hector St Jean de Crèvecœur 148
Tom Stoppard 179
story time 189
Strophe 161
Subjektivität 156
summary 197
Supreme Court 78
symbol 209
Symbol 209
Symbolcharakter 150
synecdoche 165
Syntax 159

T

tables 20
tail rhyme 162
Temporary Assistance for Needy
     Families programme 100
tenses 23, 25
Terrorism 111
Tetrameter 160
Textbaustein 186
Textfunktion 198
Textgattung 12
Texttypen 195
Textverstehen 7
Thatcherism 40
Margaret Thatcher 40
Theatertradition 146
The Compleat Angler 146
The Country-Wife 145
The Great Gatsby 188
The Jungle 139
The Lord of the Rings 185
The Man of Mode 145
The Picture of Dorian Grey 141
The Rover 145
The Tempest 144
Dylan Thomas 169
Tories 41
Trading companies 69
Trimeter 160
Trochäus 159
trochee 159
tuition fees 84
Tuition fees 51

U

Übertreibung 209
umarmender Reim 162
unemployment 52, 53, 89
unemployment insurance 57, 100
Unionists 67
United Kingdom Independence Party
     (UKIP) 43
United Reform Church 67
Universities 50, 84
upper house 39
US Patriot Act 111

Utopia 140

V
Venice Preserved 145
Vergleich 209
Versfuß 159
Vice President of the United States .. 77
Vietnam War 110
visual 209
vocational qualifications 48
voluntary aided schools 46
Voting Rights Act 97

W
Wales 44
Alice Walker 152
Izaak Walton 146
War of Independence 70
WASPs (White Anglo-Saxon Protestants) 107

welfare state 56
West Indies 69
white-collar workers 53
Oscar Wilde 150
Roger Williams 106
women priests 66
Virginia Woolf 151, 184, 188
William Wordsworth 148, 163
Workers Registration Scheme 62
workers rights 88
working conditions 88
Working conditions 53
Wörterbuch 13
Worterschließungstechnik 13
William Wycherly 145

Z
Zäsur 160

Bildnachweis:
S. 203: © akg-Images GmbH, Erich Lessing;
S. 206: Gordon Fraser;
S. 212: toonpool.com, Riemann

fit fürs abi

Jetzt fürs Smartphone! Die kostenlose Fit-fürs-Abi-App

Abi-Wissen in Bestform

- Die umfassende Vorbereitung auf das Abitur
- Hilft zuverlässig, Abiturthemen erfolgreich zu trainieren
- Mit vielen Tipps und Hinweisen für die Prüfung

Zwei starke Begleiter

Oberstufenwissen für die Fächer:
- Biologie
- Chemie
- Deutsch
- Englisch
- Erdkunde
- Geschichte
- Mathematik
- Physik
- Referat und Facharbeit

Klausur-Training für die Fächer:
- Biologie
- Chemie
- Mathematik
- Physik

www.schroedel.de

Schroedel. Gut gemacht.